# Shattered Dreams

## By

## Pamela Hayes

This book is a work of fiction. Places, events, and situations in this story are purely fictional. Any resemblance to actual persons, living or dead, is coincidental.

ISBN: 1-4033-6772-8 (e-book)
ISBN: 1-4033-6773-6 (Paperback)

Library of Congress Control Number: 2002111791

This book is printed on acid free paper.

Printed in the United States of America
Bloomington, IN

Photo: Getty Images

1stBooks - rev. 02/12/03

# Chapter One

After making everything in the Master bedroom dust-free and gleaming, Felicia took her paper towels, Windex, can of Pledge, and preoccupied expression to the living room, where she got on her haunches, and squirted glass cleaner on the coffee table.

When she spread the mist around with her dust rag, she realized what she had done.

"Damn," she muttered, quickly wiping up the Windex with a paper towel. She was relieved to see that it didn't harm the coffee table's finish. Just left it looking a little dull, but a few shots of Pledge gave it the radiance she wanted.

She stood, sighed. She knew why she was so lost in thought, mistaking her coffee table for a mirror.

This morning she learned the awful truth.

Her dreams had been dashed.

Pulverized.

Shattered.

For the past few days, she had thought she was pregnant. But about ninety minutes ago, her period arrived, telling her that she had been wrong, giving her proof of her mistake in red letters, so to speak.

She moaned unhappily. What a huge disappointment; she had so desperately wanted to be pregnant.

And her husband Warren wanted to be a father just as much as she wanted to be a mother. And when she told him that they weren't going to be parents, after all, he'd be as let down as she was.

But he had warned her that it could be a false alarm.

And she had become annoyed with him for not sharing her optimism. "Thanks, Warren," she had said flatly. "You really know how to look on the bright side of things."

"Felicia, I want you to be pregnant. You know that," he had said. "But you have to consider that you could simply be late."

She had shaken her head vigorously. "I'm never late." She placed her hand on her stomach. "I'm going to have a baby." Her tone was resolute.

"But you have to consider the possibility that you aren't," he continued to argue. "So, don't get all excited until you get it confirmed."

But she had just known. A woman always knew something like that. And later that morning, she was going to dash to the drug store and buy a pregnancy test, which would have provided substantiation.

But then her period arrived, making the trip to the pharmacy unnecessary.

Of course, she had sighed unhappily and her eyes filled with tears, and she tried banishing the disappointment from her mind by engaging in housecleaning.

*You and Warren have to see a doctor,* counseled her inner voice.

That was true. They had to find out why she had not become pregnant. It had been over a year since she stopped using her diaphragm.

And they had been making love four/five times a week, so by now, she should be taking prenatal vitamins, lumbering around with a protruding abdomen, experiencing cravings.

But alas, that was not the case.

And there was a reason.

And she had to find out what it was.

The doorbell rang, bringing Felicia out of her thoughts. She glanced at the wall clock. It was morning, just a few minutes after eleven. *Who could that be?*

UPS. But she wasn't expecting a package. Maybe, it was an itinerant salesperson, hawking magazine subscriptions, or wanting to know if she had cable.

Or perhaps it was a neighbor, wanting coffee and conversation, something she was in no mood for.

She decided to ignore the door. But her automobile was in the driveway, which wouldn't mean anything to a salesperson. They didn't know the make of her vehicle. But the car would tip off a neighbor that she was home.

But then too, she could have been on the commode, in the shower. Or out with a friend.

But giving people the brush off made her feel guilty, so she went to the door, glanced through the peephole, and pulled open the door.

"Hey, girl," Angie greeted effervescently from the porch. Angie was Felicia's hair dresser/manicurist and friend. And Felicia liked the way Angie beautified her, and usually, she enjoyed the hairstylist's company, but right now, she didn't want to be bothered with her.

"Hi, Angie," Felicia said, pushing open the storm door. "Come on in."

Angie entered, bringing in the smell of Poison, her favorite fragrance, and perfectly coifed hair. She was about 5'7, slender, with skin the color of peanut butter, and shoulder-length hair that was a weave.

If she hadn't told Felicia that the hair wasn't authentic, Felicia would not have guessed.

"This was in the box," Angie said, handing Felicia envelopes, and a few catalogs. "When I drove up, the mail lady had just put it in."

2

"Thanks," Felicia said, accepting the day's delivery. And she had an idea what was inside the manila envelope. She flipped it over, and glanced at the return address, and sure enough, it was a typewritten label she had prepared.

She moaned unhappily. "They didn't want it," she shrieked, and tossed the mail across the room, sending the dreaded manila envelope, and bills from the phone and credit card companies, and catalogs for shoes, clothes, and citrus fruit hurtling to the carpeted floor. "I just can't take much more of this," she wailed.

Sighing, she covered her face with trembling hands.

"Felicia, what's wrong?" Angie asked, with solicitude in her voice. "Why did you toss the mail aside like that?"

Felicia removed her hands from her face, and regarded Angie's perfectly made up face, which was twisted with confusion. "That," Felicia spat, pointing to the manila envelope on the floor, "was a story I mailed to *Good Housekeeping*." Felicia wrote short stories and articles for profit. "I really worked hard on it, making sure my sentences were varied, using colorful verbs. For all the good it did."

"They weren't interested," Angie stated unnecessarily.

"Obviously!" Felicia snapped. "They sent it back."

"Okay, since you're upset, I'm going to let you get away with biting my head off," Angie joked. "But girl, you've been writing and submitting for quite a while now…So, this isn't the first time, you've received a thumbs down. It's just something authors have to put up with."

Felicia took a deep breath. "I know, I know. I'm just having a bad day."

"I can tell," Angie said.

"And another disappointment didn't help matters." She paused. "What are you doing here, anyway?" Felicia asked, scooping the envelopes off the floor.

"We had plans," Angie revealed. "Remember?"

Standing, Felicia said, "What plans?" She placed the mail on the coffee table.

"Today is my day off. And we made a date to go to the mall and then grab lunch. Remember, we said we'd split a turkey sub at Danny's Sub and Pub?"

"Yeah," Felicia said, recalling.

"But evidently, it slipped your mind."

"Sorry."

"Felicia, what's going on? Did you and Warren have a big quarrel about something? Was that the other disappointment?"

She shook her head. "No, nothing like that."

"Then what?" Angie placed her hand on Felicia's shoulder. "I'm your friend. You can talk to me." Her tone was sweet and caring. And the kindness made Felicia erupt into sobs.

Angie hugged Felicia. "Shhh, shhh," she whispered like a loving mother, patting Felicia's back.

Felicia wept like she was at a loved one's funeral. When she was composed, she lifted her head from Angie's chest and looked away, ashamed.

"You okay?" Angie said.

Felicia nodded. "Just a little embarrassed for breaking down and crying like that." She went to the sofa.

"Oh, don't worry about it. No one's here, but you and me," Angie said. "Now, what's put you in this state? But hey, I don't want to go dipping in your business, so if you don't want to discuss it."

From the sofa, Felicia said, "This morning I had my period."

Angie shifted her eyes from left to right. "Okay. But why would that upset you? I mean, we chickadees have to go through that."

Felicia sighed. "I've never discussed this with you. But over a year ago, I stopped using my diaphragm." Her tone sounded like she was making a confession.

Angie nodded. "You want to become pregnant?" It was a statement.

"Yes, and all this time, Warren and I have been trying and well, it hasn't happened. Until this morning, I thought finally, I had become pregnant, but it turned out, I was late."

Angie sat next to Felicia on the couch. "Well, okay, it didn't happen this time," she said encouragingly. "But it will happen."

Felicia sighed. "I'm beginning to wonder. Warren and I have been trying all this time."

"A year is quite a spell. Have you spoken to a doctor?"

"No, but I intend to. This very morning, I'm going to make an appointment."

"Girl, it may be as simple as taking some hormones to agitate those reproductive organs."

"You think so?" Felicia said, desperately wanting to hear some positive news.

Angie nodded. "But only a doctor can tell you for sure. But you know, Annie Ruth, the heavy girl at the salon where I work?"

Felicia nodded.

"Well, she and her husband had been trying for over eight years to have a child."

Felicia rolled her eyes. She really didn't need to hear that.

4

"Well, they said, 'screw it,' and decided to adopt. Steven, their first born is adopted. And when he was just a few months old, Annie Ruth discovered she was pregnant. And now they have six children. But who would want a half a dozen kids?"

Felicia thought a house full of children would be wonderful.

Angie shook her head. "But they have them…For some women, it's just more difficult to become pregnant." She shrugged. "I don't know."

"Well, as I said, Warren and I are going to see a doctor," Felicia said. "I'm sure it's no big deal." But in truth, she wasn't so sure. But she had to think positively.

"It'll happen," Angie pep-talked. She switched subjects. "So, do you still want to hit the stores? Girl, I got my income tax check a few days ago, and I'm itching to spend some of this cash." Her tone was excited. "Lunch is on me."

Felicia had no desire to traipse from store to store, eyeballing shoes, and purses, and dresses, and earrings, and sniffing fragrances and listening to clerks ask, 'Can I help you?'

"It'll do you good to get out," Angie added. "Help take your mind off things."

Angie was dolled up and she wanted to put it to good use, Felicia realized. She wanted to go to the mall, wiggle her ass, and have men gawk at her. Felicia could not be bothered. Wrinkling her nose, she said, "Girl, I'm going to pass. I just want to hang around here."

Angie stood. "Well, that's your call. But I'll see you for your hair appointment day after tomorrow. And don't worry, everything will turn out fine."

# Chapter 2

Immediately after Angie left, Felicia went to the wall phone in the kitchen, and called Warren's office. Clarice, his friendly receptionist answered. "Hi, Clarice," Felicia said pleasantly. "Is Warren there?"

"He sure is. I'll buzz him."

"Thanks."

Less than a minute later, Warren was on the line.

"Fefe," he greeted cordially. Fefe was his nickname for her. "If you're calling to ask if we can get together for lunch, well, I'm sorry, I can't," he said apologetically after they had gone through the 'Hi, how are you?' drill.

Sometimes if Warren's schedule permitted, she'd prepare a picnic lunch and they'd eat in his office. Or they'd grab something from one of the eateries in the business park where his office was located. "You know, I'd love to spend a romantic afternoon with my gorgeous wife," he said, "but things are kind of hectic around here today. And I have to be in court at two." He was a lawyer, running his own firm.

"Actually, I didn't call about lunch," she said.

"Well, you do sound kind of down. Something wrong?"

"I had my period this morning."

He took a deep breath. "Felicia, I'm sorry. I know how much you wanted to be pregnant."

"Yeah, it hurts." She was on the verge of tears.

"Hey, I feel your pain. I wanted it too." His disappointment only reinforced her depressed state.

"I'm sorry, Warren," she said.

"About what?"

"For letting you down."

"Hey, look, we can try again," he said brightly. "And think of all the fun we'll have doing it." His voice was low and seductive.

She smiled sadly. "I'm going to call my gynecologist. She also deals with fertility issues. I think we should see her. We've been trying all this time to have a child, with no luck. Something's wrong. We have to find out what it is."

"I agree," he said.

"So, I'm going to make an appointment for as soon as possible. What's good for you, morning or afternoon?" she inquired, thinking that she sounded like a doctor's receptionist. "I know you have to see clients and make court appearances."

"Doesn't matter," he said. "I can juggle my appointments. Get a continuance, if necessary."

She sighed. "Okay...Well, I better let you get back to work."

"And baby, listen," he said, "don't worry. I love you."

"Love you too." She clicked the phone and dialed 411.

James Earl Jones', rich, authoritative voice welcomed her to Verizon, then an automated voice asked, "What city and state?"

"Willow Oaks, Virginia," Felicia answered.

"What listing?"

Felicia revealed the name of her doctor.

And when she pressed the fourth number to the doctor's office, her call waiting beeped.

Whoever it was would just have to wait. She was anxious to make this appointment.

"What is the nature of your visit?" the doctor's receptionist asked when Felicia said she needed to see the doctor.

*I'm trying to get knocked up, and it ain't happening,* Felicia thought sarcastically. "I'm having trouble conceiving," she said.

She heard a clacking sound. The girl was no doubt checking the doctor's availability on a computer. "Well, I have something next Tuesday at 10:15," she said. "How's that?"

"Well, that's a week away," Felicia complained. She wanted to see the doctor ASAP. "Don't you have something sooner?"

"I'm sorry, Mrs. Wainwright. I've given you the earliest appointment avail—"

"Well, I guess next Tuesday, it is," Felicia said irritably, and put down the phone.

*Next Tuesday was like two lifetimes away,* she thought, sighing. But even if she saw the doctor tomorrow, she knew that she wouldn't find out what was wrong immediately.

There would no doubt be testing, and waiting for lab results.

She had heard about the nightmares that infertile couples went through. Men having to make certain that their underwear wasn't too tight...and the woman having to take her temperature, and the couple having to make love when the woman was her most fertile.

She didn't know anybody, who had actually endured it. She had obtained her information from movies she had seen on Lifetime and articles, and novels that she had read. And the whole process certainly didn't sound like a day at the amusement park. Imagine telling Warren, *Baby, I'm fertile. Bring out the hard-on.*

She rolled her eyes.

7

Curious as to who had phoned earlier, she clicked star 69, and ascertained that her baby sister Sandra had called.

*What did she want?* To borrow money, or maybe she needed a baby sitter. She only called when she wanted something.

And Felicia was in no mood for her. But her little niece, Laquita might need her. So, she dialed the number.

"Hey, Felicia," Sandra caroled. Evidently, she looked at her caller ID and recognized Felicia's number.

"You rang," Felicia said flatly ala Lurch from *The Addams Family.* "What's up?"

"Can you drop by the apartment today, around 2:30?" Sandra's tone was as sweet as bowl of sugar cubes. "As you know, I don't have a set of wheels, and I can't find a ride, and I don't have money for a cab."

*I have no car. I can't get a ride. I don't have money for a cab. Can you come to me? Everything was about Sandra,* Felicia thought. *And what about a bus?* But Sandra probably didn't feel up to taking a bus. "What is this about?"

"I'll tell you when I see you."

"Stop being mysterious."

"I don't want to get into it on the phone," Sandra said.

Felicia rolled her eyes. "Later today, huh?"

"Yeah," Sandra replied.

"Well, is it life and death?" Felicia asked.

"Sort of."

*Yeah, I bet. If it were, she would have said so right off the bat.* Well, Felicia had no desire to accommodate Sandra. Sometimes, like now, Sandra's self-centered crap pissed her off. "Look, unless somebody is in the hospital, it'll have to wait," Felicia said, scarcely concealing her annoyance. "I feel like hell today, and I'm going to lie down, and watch a movie."

"All right, fine," Sandra said petulantly.

*Get over it.* "How's tomorrow morning around eleven?"

"Cool. See you then," Sandra chirped like an unhappy bird.

Click.

Sandra just hung up in Felicia's ear. Didn't bother to say goodbye, kiss my fanny, nothing.

Felicia put down the phone, got a pouch of popcorn from the cabinet, and placed it in the microwave.

And while the grease sizzled, and the kernels exploded, and the bag bulged, and the kitchen began to smell like the concession stand at a movie theater, she thought about Sandra.

Felicia loved her baby sister, but the girl (the woman, actually. Sandra was twenty-four) was so self-absorbed and only interested in what put a smile on her face.

Sandra had no direction in her life, zero missions; zero goals.

Unless trying to becoming the most popular stripper at some dive was a goal.

Felicia was disgusted by the fact that Sandra doffed her clothes at some watering hole. She claimed she was earning oodles of money. But if that was the case, why was she constantly strapped for cash and asking Felicia for assistance?

*What went wrong with Sandra?* Felicia wondered, now sitting on her king-size bed, with a bowl of popcorn in her lap, and a glass of Pepsi on the nightstand. She grew up in the same house as Felicia and their older sister, Denise, and Felicia and Denise turned out okay, putting themselves through college, earning degrees.

Denise was living in Vermont, teaching at a community college, while working on a Masters.

When Sandra was seventeen, and a junior in high school, she became pregnant by a thirty-three year old married loser, named Juice.

She had the baby, Laquita, and chucked high school. Felicia and Denise tried to tell her to stay in, that education was important. "I don't need the shit," Sandra had replied.

And that damn Juice should have been arrested for statutory rape, but Felicia's alcoholic mother, Maggie, didn't care enough to press charges. "Sandra laid down with that man," Maggie had slurred. "She spread her thighs, so she got to deal with what she did."

Felicia would wager that Maggie's ignorance and weak character had plenty to do with how Sandra turned out.

Some people thought it was unfair to blame parents for the shortcomings of adult children. Well, in Felicia's opinion, if a parent is a lousy role model, and doesn't teach their child anything worth knowing, it will affect how a child turns out.

Some children, more than others, need role models, parental advice, and guidance. Felicia and Denise got that from teachers and certain neighborhood women. Sadly, Sandra never found someone to look up to.

Felicia loved her mother, but deep down, she knew the woman loved her husband, Roosevelt, more than her three daughters.

And what was so great about daddy? He was a serial adulterer, but regardless, Maggie looked the other way. Women called the house bragging to Maggie that they were involved with Roosevelt, and one was so lowdown that she said in Felicia's ear—" I fucked your daddy. Why don't you tell your Mama 'bout it?"

Felicia took her advice. Maggie slapped her face. "Don't you be up in here telling no damn lies," she spat, her breath reeking of vodka.

"I'm not lying," Felicia said, holding her stinging cheek.

"Yes, you is, and I don't want to hear no more of it," Maggie hurled, categorically refusing to believe that her husband slept around.

Eventually, one Saturday night, Roosevelt walked out on Maggie. She begged him not to go. "I'll be better, Rosie," she pleaded. "Just tell me what I havta do. Baby, don't leave me. I can't live without you." She dropped to her knees.

Felicia vividly recalled the scenario, her mother's tear-stained face, and shrieking voice. Roosevelt seemed amused by the entire scenario.

Felicia shook her head in disgust. No damn way would she beg some clown to stay with her. If he wanted to exit, let him go. She'd help him pack.

Being in the company of Maggie was never a day at the circus. The woman was constantly scowling, belittling everything and everybody. Felicia figured that she was bitter because her husband didn't treat her the way she wanted to be treated.

But when daddy-oh left, Maggie became nastier, perpetually snapping at her daughters, calling them "little whores" and "bitches," crabbing about how difficult it was to make ends meet on her salary as a chambermaid at a fleabag. They lived in a run-down house that Maggie inherited from her father.

When Maggie became overwhelmed by life, her brother, Tyrone signed her into Central State, a state-supported mental institution.

During those periods, Felicia and her siblings stayed with Tyrone and his wife, Lillie Mae and their two children. Lillie Mae was as sweet as the cakes she was famous for making.

She kept an immaculate house and every Saturday night, she baked a cake for Sunday's dessert, and she'd leave extra batter in the bowl and give each of the children a spoon to enjoy the creamy concoction.

Felicia had fond memories of her time with Tyrone and Lillie Mae. God, how she wished they had been her parents. And when she was a little girl, she promised herself that one day she'd have a family life like Lillie Mae and Tyrone.

Shortly after Felicia and Warren had married, one night, Maggie phoned Felicia. "Hey," Maggie said, sounding even more low and miserable than usual.

"Hey, ma," Felicia replied.

"I was sitting in here thanking."

"'Bout what?" Felicia asked.

"Thangs."

"Such as?"

"Life…and dying."

The thought of her depressed, unhappy mother pondering weighty issues like death and dying made Felicia uneasy.

"You know, they say if you kill yourself, you going to hell," Maggie said. "Ever heard that?"

"I most certainly have, and I believe it's true," Felicia said emphatically, wanting to terrify Maggie.

"What difference do it make if you go to hell, if you already living in hell when you alive, here on the earth? Now, tell me, ain't that a good point?"

"No it's not a good point," Felicia said rapidly. "Only God can decide when it's time for any of us to go." She took a deep breath. "Ma, you okay?"

"Child, I'm fine."

"You don't sound fine, talking about suicide."

"Well, I am," she repeated. "And I want you to know that I love you and your sisters. Now, I may not have always shown it, but I love y'all."

They said good bye, but Felicia wasn't so sure that her mother was "fine."

So she and Warren drove over to Maggie's run-down house, and banged and banged on the door. Eventually, Warren broke the kitchen window, and unlocked the door.

And to their horror, they found Maggie in the den, on the floor, dead. Blood was splattered everywhere, The coroner said the bullet wound in the head was self-inflicted. She left a note saying that she just couldn't go on.

For months, Felicia was broken hearted. She had known that Maggie had emotional problems. And she had berated herself for not demanding that her mother see a counselor and get a prescription for antidepressants.

Sighing, Felicia came out of her reverie, and tears were in her eyes.

She had no desire to reflect on that gloomy period in her life. *That stuff was in the past.*

She put a tape of *Pretty Woman* in the VCR.

*Pretty Woman* was one of her favorite flicks. She had seen it at least five times. It was amusing, romantic, and unrealistic.

Affluent, successful, handsome men just didn't sweep prostitutes off their feet.

It was all fantasy, Felicia thought, half-ass paying attention to Julia Roberts on the big screen TV; her mind was on her own fantasy.

She wanted to create a beautiful home for her husband and children.

11

Some of her girlfriends found that amusing. *Girl, you need to get with the program,* they said.

They wanted to be entrepreneurs, and CEO's, and bank presidents, and to them, any woman who wanted to take care of her house was an oddball, an anomaly; a dinosaur from another era.

Well, that was their opinion. Felicia wanted to keep her house spotless, clip coupons, go food shopping, watch the soaps, take care of the kids, wipe runny noses, bake cookies, take the kids to swimming lessons, dental appointments, assist them with homework, and prepare them health-building meals.

But she wasn't a naïve babe.

She realized that men could drop dead, become incapacitated, or like dear old dad, take a walk.

And so, she'd be able to take care of herself and her children, she obtained a college degree.

Being a wife and mom meant the world to Felicia, but she also enjoyed writing. In addition to being a homemaker, she penned articles and short stories, which kept her at home, where she wanted to be.

And like her, Warren wanted a conventional family life. His father abandoned his mother when he was just four, so he yearned for a traditional family arrangement as well.

When they wed, he had just graduated from law school, and she was a senior in college, in her last semester, working on an English degree, with a concentration in journalism.

After graduating, she had planned on seeking employment on a newspaper. But because she had tied the knot, she forgot about becoming a black Lois Lane. It really wasn't important to her, anyway. Homemaking had a stronger appeal to her.

Warren had received decent offers from law firms requesting his services, but because he wanted to be his own man, call the shots himself, he declined them. So, he maxed out his credit cards, and rented a cramped office next to a mom and pop hotdog joint.

Felicia worked as his unpaid secretary. In the beginning, nothing was happening. They'd spend the day, sitting in his office, flirting, or reading *Essence, Ebony, Emerge, Good Housekeeping.*

But slowly, business trickled in, giving Felicia a reason to use her appointment book and pencil.

A transsexual wanted a name change…a man wanted to adopt his stepson. A few people wanted to have wills drawn up. There were a handful of DUI's, and a couple of divorces.

Warren handled anything and everything, save drug dealers or people charged with possession.

He was anti drugs and he refused to handle such cases.

Eventually business grew and Warren gained a reputation for getting the job done. He took on a partner, hired a paralegal and two secretaries. The growth necessitated relocating to a roomier office in a high rent business-park amid banks, upscale eateries, and trendy beauty salons and gyms.

Felicia ceased working at the office, and became a full-time homemaker. And after five years of marriage, wonderful getaways, and togetherness, she and Warren agreed to start a family.

They wanted four kids.

Gender didn't matter. They simply wanted to be the parents of a quarter dozen healthy, smiling children.

And for over a year, they had been trying to have one. Felicia was beginning to wonder if there were some physical reason her dreams of a family life would not become a reality.

"We don't know what's going on," Warren told her several hours later when he had returned home from work.

He had showered, and changed into leisurely clothes. They were on the patio, discussing the situation over tall frosty glasses of iced tea.

"Well, something is wrong," she said, putting down her tumbler. "I mean, we've been trying for over a year. By now, I should be pregnant."

"Well, we won't know anything until we've talked to the doctor," he said.

"And that appointment isn't until next Tuesday…So, I have to wait for over a week." She blew out frustrated air.

"Well, brooding about it isn't going to do you any good. Hey, I have an idea," he said brightly.

"What?"

"Let's go out to dinner?"

"Tonight?"

"Yeah."

"Well, Friday is usually the night we eat out," Felicia said, making excuses. She was wearing jogging attire and she didn't feel up to getting all dolled up to go out.

Warren shrugged. "So, we'll eat out twice this week. Tonight, and Friday."

She moved her lips to object.

Anticipating her response, Warren said, "It'll do you good."

He was trying to lift her spirits, and she loved him for it. "Okay, but let's do something casual like Apple bees."

Usually, on Friday night, they patronized the King's Palace, which was very upscale, with a fireplace, and foods like chicken cordon bleu and filet mignon on the menu.

Felicia loved the cuisine, and the service, but this evening, she didn't have the stamina to deal with their dress code.

But she was so grateful to have a loving husband like Warren, who wanted to lift her spirits when she was down, and try to make her happy.

# Chapter 3

Felicia pulled her Volvo into a space, and under the clear sky, she walked down the cement path, leading to her destination.

It was a bright, gloriously warm afternoon, and rambunctious, unkempt children played on the monkey bars. One child was eating a sandwich, with a piece of bologna dangling from two slices of white bread. Another messy little boy avidly licked an orange Popsicle, dripping juice onto his white tee shirt.

They all were eyeing Felicia curiously. She'd bet they were wondering what was this well-dressed, Volvo driving woman doing in their neighborhood.

A little black girl with plaits and itty-bitty pieces of lint in her hair, skipped up to Felicia. "Miss, you got a doll-lah?" she asked. "I wanna buy me a bag of 'tatoe chips."

Three other children were in her company. "I'm sorry, sweetheart, I don't have it," Felicia lied to the miniature panhandler.

If it were just that one child, she would have fished a dollar from her purse. But she was in no mood to play Santa Claus to a virtual playground of kids.

Continuing her journey, Felicia heard one of the girls say, "She lyin.' I bet she got a whole lotta dollars. Stingy bitch."

Now, you know that doesn't make any kind of sense, *Felicia thought.* Children talking like that within hearing distance of an adult. That little thing needs some home training.

Two women, sitting in lounge chairs were keeping vigil over the children. Bottles of Pepsi were on the grass next to them. They greeted Felicia. "How you doing?" one asked; the other nodded.

"Just fine," Felicia said. "How y'all doing?"

Entering the vestibule, she heard one of them say—" She probably somebody's caseworker."

"But caseworkers don't drive no car like that," the other said.

"Then on know who she is."

Felicia climbed the stairs to apartment G, kicking a stray McDonald's cheeseburger wrapper out of the way.

She detested coming to this section of town, where groups of men could be found huddled in the corner of a nearby convenience store, smoking cigarettes, and probably engaging in illegal activity, like selling narcotics.

15

Via the newspaper, she knew that drug dealing and sex for money took place in this area.

And a woman was busted for turning her apartment into a tavern…Selling liquor without a license.

Felicia reached apartment G, and tapped on the door.

It swung open, and a young woman dressed in a lace burgundy bra and matching panties appeared in the doorway. "Hey," she greeted. "Come on in."

Felicia could not believe her eyes. God, did this woman have any couth, any class? "Why don't you put some clothes on?" Felicia snapped. "Prancing around here like that."

Shutting the door, and smiling, Sandra said, "This is my house, and I'm comfortable dressed this way. Besides, I'm not outside."

"Well, what if somebody had seen you?" Felicia said. "Like a canvasser, or anybody." She shrugged.

Sandra giggled. "Well, they would have gotten an eyeful. Besides, I looked through the peephole. If somebody had been out there, I would have put on a robe."

The junky one bedroom apartment had a Murphy bed in the living room, a stereo, and a towering stack of CD's. Magazines and clothes were strewn everywhere. On the 13 inch TV, *The Price Is Right* was on. A heavy black woman was playing Plinko.

Sandra slept on the Murphy bed, and her daughter used the bedroom. She told Felicia if somebody broke in the apartment, they'd have to go through her to get to her daughter. And they'd better be ready to do battle.

Felicia was tempted to tell Sandra she needed to spruce the place up, that keeping a messy house was not setting a good example for her daughter.

But she kept mum. She wouldn't like it if someone told her that she needed to tidy up her house.

"Where's Laquita?" Felicia asked, looking around for her seven-year old niece, a niece whom she adored, and Laquita felt likewise about her. And if the child was there, by now, she would have dashed out with her lips puckered for a kiss, and her arms opened for an embrace.

"Girl, that thang went to the store with Debra Ann," Sandra revealed.

*That thang.* Felicia knew that Sandra meant no harm, but she hated when she referred to the child that way. After all, she had a name…a name Felicia loathed.

Felicia liked traditional names like Joyce, Carolyn, or Elizabeth, etc. Nowadays, black folks were naming their children Keisha, Moesha, and Tatanesha. And people had a right to name their kids anything they damn well pleased, but Felicia was a champion of the tried-and-true. "Who is

Debra Ann?" she asked, wondering if Laquita was in the company of a trustworthy individual.

"A neighbor," Sandra revealed, sashaying into the kitchen.

From behind her, Felicia asked, "Well, can you provide a little more info? Like, what do you know about this neighbor? I mean, you shouldn't let your child run around with just anybody."

"Girl, chill," Sandra ordered. "I trust Debra Ann. The woman spends more time in church than a preacher."

Sandra and Felicia were sisters, but they were as different as pickles and oranges. Felicia enjoyed books, museums, and art galleries. 'That old shit' bored Sandra.

Sandra's idea of a blast was guzzling beer, listening to loud music, playing cards, and the lottery.

"I'm making a lil lunch," Sandra said, at the stove. "Oodles of noodles. I'll happily share them with you. Want some?" she offered.

"No, thanks," Felicia said.

"What, you think you too good for oodles of noodles?" Sandra teased. "Only steak and lobsta for you?" Using a fork, she fished long strands of pasta from the beat-up aluminum pot and plopped them into a chipped bowl.

"I'm simply not hungry," Felicia said graciously, in no mood for Sandra's gibberish about her being a snob. Felicia's husband was a successful lawyer, and she lived in a roomy, four-bedroom house. She had been to college and sold a few articles, and she didn't lose sleep about paying her bills.

Sandra was envious. When they had conversations, discussing mundane topics, and Felicia mentioned that she enjoyed Haagen-Dazs ice cream, or Baskin Robbins hand-packed, Sandra would say, *Too rich for my blood. I have to buy the store brand. But you got a wealthy husband.*

Or when they mentioned what the other was having for dinner, Sandra would make comments like—*I'ma make some Hamburger Helper. What you havin', steak?"*

She unnerved Felicia with her annoying mess.

If Sandra was so unhappy with her life, then she should put away her G-string, get a GED, and work on improving her existence.

And truthfully, Felicia hadn't had a crumb that day. And a bowl of those piping hot oodles-of-noodles would quiet the hunger growls in her stomach. But she had no desire to eat food prepared by a chef strutting around in her underwear.

They left the kitchen and went to a cheap dinette table.

"Why did you ask me to drop by?" Felicia asked, watching Sandra attack her pasta with gusto.

"Do I need a motive to see my sistah?" Sandra teased.

"You never call unless you want something. So, what's up?" Felicia asked bluntly, watching Sandra twirl a second helping of steaming pasta around the fork, making Felicia's mouth damp. After she vacated these premises, she was going to stop at Wendy's and grab a burger. "You want money?"

Sandra nodded. "A little?" She sipped Coke from a mug emblazoned with a colorful Christmas scenario. Reindeer pulled two people sitting in a coach in the direction of a snow-covered house. Sandra got those mugs from Hardees. Last Christmas, with the purchase of an eight piece bucket of chicken, the mugs were going for 99 cents each.

"Thought so," Felicia said snippily.

Sandra frowned. "Why you being so bitchy?"

Because for over twelve months, I've been trying to get pregnant, and it isn't happening. So, I'm going to see a doctor, and I'm worried sick, *Felicia thought.*

But Sandra would be the last person Felicia would open up to.

All Sandra cared about was Sandra, and…her daughter.

Sandra knew that Felicia was trying to become pregnant, but Sandra was not the kind of person with whom one had heart-to-hearts. Now, if you wanted an update on Mary J Blige's latest song, or what was happening on *One Life To Live,* or any of the other stories, Sandra was the lady to ask.

But she didn't read books or the newspaper. She wouldn't even know that George Bush was the president if his face wasn't plastered everywhere.

"So why do you need money?" Felicia asked.

"Rent." She popped another servings of noodles into her mouth.

"Rent," Felicia said.

Sandra nodded. "They threatening to kick me and Laquita out on the street. They already done posted a pay or vacate notice on the door."

Felicia exhaled. "How much, Sandra?"

"Seven hundred."

"Your rent is only four eighty," Felicia said.

"Well, my light bill is two months behind, and the electric company has sent a turn off notice. I have till tomorrow to pay it."

"I don't know, Sandra," Felicia said, shaking her head.

Sandra jumped out of the chair and sashayed to the table were the TV was perched. *Price is Right* was now doing the showcase showdown. She grabbed pieces of paper off the table, and extended them to Felicia. "Here is the shut off notice from the Power Company, and a pay or get the hell out notice from McPherson realtor, the owners of this hellhole."

18

Felicia examined the notices, though she didn't doubt that Sandra was telling the truth. When she said, I don't know, she was thinking that she shouldn't help Sandra out of this jam. Sandra already owed her quite a bit of money. "I shouldn't do this, but—"

Sandra smiled. "When people say, 'I shouldn't do this, but...' Usually, they're going to do it."

Sandra's arrogance annoyed Felicia. "For a beggar, you have some attitude," she said tartly.

"I ain't no beggar," Sandra replied defiantly.

"Well, what do you call, asking me for money? Something you've done many times before, I might add...And it's always the same excuse. You're about to be evicted. The refrigerator and the cabinets are empty. Laquita needs shoes...Laquita needs school clothes. You've got to take Laquita to the doctor."

"I don't need you to remind me of how hard it is to make ends meet," Sandra said, irked.

"Your daughter is the only reason I help you. If it weren't for that little girl, I wouldn't give a damn if your behind ended up on the street, carrying a cardboard sign that said, '*Homeless, Will work for food.*'"

"Well, uh, ain't that something to say to your baby sistah," Sandra spluttered, astonished.

*Yeah, it was pretty dreadful,* Felicia thought. She took a deep breath. "Look, I'm sorry. Of course, I don't want to see you homeless. But why do you let your bills go into arrears?"

Sandra made a face. "Listen at you, talking 'bout some arrears. Always trying to be so proper. And I might not read books like you do, but I know what arrears means?"

"I'm sure you do," Felicia said sarcastically. "Probably seen it countless times on your pay or vacate notices."

Sandra's expression looked as if she had smelled a fart. "Money gets tight sometimes. It ain't easy for a single woman to make it out here, you know."

"To hear you say it, you're making a bundle at that dive where you work."

"Frankie's isn't a dive. It's a gentleman's club."

"A euphemism for a strip joint! There's nothing gentlemanly about men watching some ho peel off her clothes."

Sandra was outraged. "Let me tell you something, Miss Felicia, I ain't no ho. And I enjoy my job. The only negative is working for tips. My salary fluctuates, and sometimes, I have trouble paying my bills. And I'm trying to get into section eight housing, but there's a two year waiting list."

Yes, Sandra was trying to move into a better area of town. "Well, while you're waiting for affordable housing, you could go into another line of work, something where you could wear more dignified clothing, and receive a steady salary…Something that would make it so you can pay your bills and not have to ask for handouts."

"Hey, I don't need a lecture," Sandra said, sounding fed-up.

"Look, you're a smart, attractive woman." Sandra was not well read, by any means. But the girl was not stupid. "But I don't think you realize that. You could do so much better." Felicia had said it all before, and things never got any better. But maybe if she repeated it often enough, it would sink in.

"I like what I'm doing," Sandra said in a bored tone.

*Yeah, stripping fulfills that exhibitionist part of your personality.* "Well, that's good and fine, but it's not taking care of your needs. Laquita's needs."

She scrunched her face and said irritably, "Felicia, from time-to-time, I get in a bind. I mean, I could be the assistant manager at Kroger and that could happen!"

"If you were an assistant manager at Kroger, you would have a more stable income, and you could afford a better place to stay. And your *binds* probably wouldn't be as frequent."

Sandra rolled her eyes. "My point is that I could get in a tight spot even if I had a better paying job."

"Oh, girl, puh-leeze," Felicia spat, reaching her breaking point. "You're just making excuses. And I don't see how you can be happy parading around half-naked in front of a bunch of horny men."

"Well, I *like* it," Sandra said in defense of her profession. Her expression became faraway, distant. "When I'm on stage, dancing, all eyes are on me," she said. "And I can tell by the expression on those guys faces what's going on in their minds. They're thinking, "I wonder what she's like in bed? Man, I'd love to fuck her.'"

Felicia looked horrified. "Sandra, must you be so vulgar?"

"Oh, lighten up! I believe we exotic dancers do a service for marriages, relationships."

Felicia frowned. "Now, that comment intrigues me. How the heck do you figure that *strippers*—" Felicia refused to give the profession the more dignified term exotic dancer—"do marriages a service…I mean, counseling, vacations, children, church, a high paying job can help a marriage, but *strippers*? Now, that's a good one."

"Sexually, couples can get in a rut," Sandra said. "They become familiar with each other's bodies. They know each other's movements," she spoke with authority, like she was some relationship expert. "So men come to the club, and get all h and b."

Felicia looked confused. "H and B?"

"Hot and bothered, girl," she sang in a you-don't know-anything tone. "And then they go home and tear their wives and girlfriends to pieces."

"Well, I doubt if most women would look at your line of work as doing them a favor."

Sandra sipped from her mug of Coke. "Humph! Some women ought to send exotic dancers thank-you notes, give us recommendations. Because of us, they get a good banging."

"Some logic," Felicia said.

"Child, men come to those clubs to get aroused…worked up. To them, a dancer is like a picture out of *Playboy,* or a dirty movie, something that gets them stimulated." She chuckled. "Hell, one night, this man told me that when he jerked off, I was in his thoughts." She said it as if she had been complimented.

Felicia's eyes widened. "You say that with such pride."

"Well, I like having that effect on people." She wiggled her shoulders.

Felicia rolled her eyes. Sandra was sad. She actually thought all she had going for her was her body.

"And I love being the only negress in the club," Sandra said.

"Negress?" Felicia repeated, disapprovingly. *Now, she's using degrading language in reference to herself.* "Sandra, you're a black woman. I can't believe that you'd call yourself a negress."

"Just joking! Girl, I wouldn't let no white person call me that, but I can say it about myself. That's like we can call each other niggers, but we'd get royally pissed off if a white person did it."

"True," Felicia conceded. But still, she didn't like the idea of a black woman referring to herself as a negress.

Sandra said, "And I told Seth, the owner of the club, that if he hired another black woman, I'm handing in my thong."

*I wish he'd put three other black women to work,* Felicia thought. *And let you make good on your threat. But then too, you'd probably find another dump to shake your fanny.*

Sandra was saying, "Because, I'm the only black chick in the place, I stand out. White ass is all over the joint, and so the lone black bootie is more eye-catching. When I'm dancin', I can hear those white guys in the audience saying, 'She looks good. I ain't never had no chocolate puddin'."

*God, this woman was so crass,* Felicia thought. Her potty mouth could use a few generous squirts of toilet bowl cleaner. "Doesn't that bother you?" she asked, making a face.

"What?"

"Being referred to as chocolate pudding?"

Sandra shrugged. "Ain't nothing but talk."

"Well, such statements should offend you," Felicia said. *And they would if you had any self-esteem.* Felicia had to get out of there. She had had enough of this visit. She felt like she was in the audience of *The Jerry Springer Show*.

She unzipped her purse and pulled out a wad of money, counting out seven one hundred-dollar bills, which she handed to Sandra. She had a hunch that Sandra's summons was money-related.

So before going to Sandra's apartment, she had stopped at First Union and cashed a personal check.

"Thanks, Felicia," Sandra said, smiling at the sight of the money. "I'm going to pay you back."

Felicia smiled wryly. *Yeah, right, Sandra. Just like you reimbursed all the other money you 'borrowed' from me in the past.* "Well, I'm sorry, I missed my cute little niece," Felicia said, getting to her feet. "But give her some sugar for me."

"You know, I will," Sandra said.

"I'll talk to you later."

# Chapter 4

When Felicia exited the apartment, Sandra took the bowl she had used to the double sink, and rinsed it out. The only other dirty dishes were a pot and her favorite mug, not enough to make a sink of water.

She threw some ice cubes in her mug, poured Coke over them, and took it to the living room sofa.

She glanced at the TV in front of her, and saw the noon news. *Who wanted to hear that depressing shit?* The news was nothing but endless reports of death and misery. She got the remote off the coffee table, and pressed the mute button.

She'd restore the sound when *The Young and The Restless* came on. *Young and Restless* was her favorite story. For years, she had been following the trials and tribulations of Jill and Miss Chancellor. She liked that first Jill—the one with the gigantic breasts.

With them tits, if girlfriend had wanted to be an exotic dancer, she would have been a hot ticket at the club.

Taking a swig of her soda, Sandra thought about Miss Felicia's negative reaction to her profession. And she didn't give a damn what her sister thought. Sandra enjoyed taking off her clothes for a crowd. It was fun with a capital f.

She wiggled her shoulders. Sure, it was more fun to dance for guys who looked like Denzel Washington or the yummy Shemar Moore, who used to play Malcolm on *Young and Restless*.

Putting on a show for gross, fat, out of shape guys wasn't exactly a fun thing to do.

It would be nice if the club had a sign that said, *We only allow nice looking men. No ug-mos permitted.*

A lot of people thought dancers were whores, and they can think what they wanted, because Sandra knew that she was not a whore.

Men had offered her money to go home with them, and she told them, n-o. "Girl, you are fine," this man told her one Saturday night. "You really turn me on when you're up there, making those moves." He shoved a hand in his pocket and pulled out some money. "This is yours, if you come home with me," he said, showing her three one hundred-dollar bills.

She shook her head. "Sorry. Sandra don't do that."

"What if I gave you five?" he asked. "We can swing by the ATM and I'll get two hundred more."

She still said no, and her phone, electric and cable were due. And she'd let those services be cut off before she had sex for money.

That dude pissed her off thinking she could be bought like merchandise from a supermarket shelf.

Dancing filled Sandra with pride.

And as far as she was concerned, she deserved every bit of attention she was receiving from dancing.

At one time, she looked scarier than a nightmare.

Her skin was/is the color of the outside of an Oreo cookie, and she had a whopper of a nose, and her hair was short and nappy.

She had suspicious about why her hair was knotty.

Oh, yeah, she had a good idea.

Her sisters, Felicia and Denise, had soft hair. Mama's hair was soft, and so was daddy's.

So, why was Sandra's crowning glory tangled and unruly?

She believed Mama had fucked around on daddy. Sure, Mama had acted like a natural fool over daddy, but that didn't mean she couldn't have done a little creeping with some other man, and became pregnant with Sandra.

She damn sure could have, and that could very well explain Sandra's knotty hair.

Sandra knew that the man she called daddy really wasn't her daddy, but it really didn't matter.

Screw it.

Her thoughts returned to her appearance—the early years.

In school, the kids teased her. *Ooh, they were nasty,* she thought, remembering. "Your nose is biiig," they taunted.

Or, "Your nose is all over your face."

Or, "You big-nose bitch."

At the time, she lacked the courage to fight back. And the harassment went on in elementary and high school.

God, she hated going to school.

And when the bullies had been exceptionally ruthless, she'd come home from school, crying her eyes out.

"Why do I have to be so ugly?" she had wailed to Felicia.

"You're not ugly. You're beautiful," Felicia said, wiping away her tears.

"You're just saying that because you're my sistah," Sandra whimpered.

"No, I mean it," Felicia countered.

"No, you don't. I'm ugly. Ugly, ugly."

"Sandra, stop," Felicia ordered. "It's not true. Not a word."

"Is too. Why can't I look like a Miss Black America?" she sniveled. "I hate being dark."

"There's nothing wrong with dark skin," Felicia had said. "Look at some of the girls in *Essence* and *Ebony*. They have dark skin. And Diahann Carroll and Phylicia Rashad are chocolate sisters."

"But they're pretty," Sandra spat. "I wish I looked like you, Felicia. I wish I was pretty like you."

"Sandra, there's nothing wrong with your appearance. You look fine."

Sandra knew that Felicia was just being kind and she loved her sister for trying to make her feel better.

When Sandra was 17, she met Juice. But his mama named him Melvin.

He was 34, married, and fit pipe at the shipyard.

He told Sandra that he was having problems with his wife, Lorraine, and one day, when the time was right, he was going to leave 'that evil ass thang.'

Sandra opened up to Juice about her insecurities regarding her appearance.

"Baby girl, ain't nothing wrong with your looks. You a knockout," he sweet-talked.

"You think so, Juice?" she asked, smiling. No male had every told her that she was attractive.

"Yeah, I mean it. Now, I wouldn't even be talking to you if you weren't a fine looking girl. Juice likes pretty women."

So, she and Juice became involved. He was her first lover.

And when she became pregnant, he spat, "Get an abortion."

"I'm not doing that," Sandra replied desperately, appalled that he'd even suggest it. "I couldn't live with myself if I did something like that."

"Well, I don't want nothing else to do with you. I already have three kids and I don't want no mo. So, you figure this one out by yourself."

And that was the last she had heard of Juice. When he dumped her, she realized that he ain't care nothing about.her from jump street.

Felicia had warned her that Juice was up to no good, but she hadn't listened. He just told her that mess about her being a knockout, so he could get in her panties.

And when she became pregnant, mama was zero help.

Mama didn't seem to care that her teenage daughter was unmarried and pregnant. Sandra knew that it wasn't her mama's problem, but still, she was her daughter, and she was a teenager, and she was pregnant and scared. A hug, and a "everything will be okay, baby" would have helped.

But Mama didn't say jack about the situation. "Don't worry," Felicia told Sandra. "I'll be here for you."

At the time, Felicia was twenty-one, a junior in college, and checking groceries full-time at Food Lion. Felicia made sure that Sandra received prenatal care. She even paid for her doctor's appointments. And when Sandra was in labor, experiencing agonizing pain, Felicia was in the hospital room, holding her hand, assuring her that everything was going to be okay.

And when the baby came into the world and Sandra took her home, she didn't know what to do with a baby...how to take care of a child. And Laquita was a cranky one, always crying, and screaming her head off, and Sandra just didn't know how to handle it.

But Felicia came to the rescue, helping her take care of the infant. Felicia knew how to shush the child. Once, Laquita was in Felicia's arms, she quieted down.

Felicia took Laquita to the park, to the grocery store. She even bought a stroller for the outings.

Later, Sandra met Richard, another man in his thirties. Richard was okay, but there was no chemistry. He did nothing for Sandra. He didn't make her nipples hard or her pussy wet. Richard was round and wore glasses and had a receding hairline. But he was crazy about her and good to her child, taking them to all-you-can-eat-buffets, and to movies.

"I have family and friends in Maryland," he had said. "I'd like to move back up that way. I'd like for you to come with me."

Why not? Sandra thought. She was fed-up with Willow Oaks. A change of scene would be nice. "Sandra, you can't do this," Felicia said, sounding frantic. "You can't just pick up and leave."

"Felicia, I'm nineteen. I can do what I want."

"Well, leave the baby with me."

"Girl, have you lost some of your brain cells?" Sandra exclaimed. "I'm not leaving my baby behind."

"You know, I'll take good care of her."

"Yeah, I know. But Laquita is my daughter, and wherever I go, she goes with me. We're a team."

So, Sandra relocated to Maryland and the move was difficult on the baby. At the time of the move, the child was two, and attached to her Aunt Felicia and being separated from her was difficult. Laquita cried nonstop. "I want Aunt Fe...le. . sa," she wailed. "Aunt Fe...le...sa."

For weeks, the poor thing was miserable. Usually, she had a healthy appetite, but after the move, she nibbled at her food. She slept fitfully, tossing and turning and waking up during the night, crying for her Aunt Felicia.

For the sake of the child, Sandra seriously considered returning to Virginia. After all, a parent should do whatever was necessary to make their child happy.

"Give her time," Richard said when Sandra expressed grief over Laquita's unhappiness. "She'll adjust."

And he was good with the girl, taking her on strolls, and trips to the amusement park. Buying her toys and candy, treating her like she was his flesh and blood.

And he was right. Eventually, Laquita grew accustomed to her new surroundings.

Sandra found employment at a Dairy Queen, making barbecues and blizzards. The job didn't pay much, but she really liked working there.

One afternoon, she was sprucing up the apartment, and while dusting, she found some old albums of Richard's.

One was of Labelle. Sandra adored Patti Labelle, and the song, Lady Marmalade. She didn't understand the French in it, but the tune made her snap her fingers and tap her toes.

She put on the album and danced around the room. After the song ended, she breathlessly studied the album, admiring the wild costumes that the singers wore. She loved Patti Labelle's flamboyancy. Sandra had seen her perform in concerts on TV and girlfriend knew how to work a crowd into frenzy.

Looking at the album, Sandra became fixated on Patti's nose.

It was quite prominent, but in recent pictures she had seen in magazines, the songbird's nose didn't appear as large. Hmmm. She wondered if Miss Patti had a nose job.

Now Patti Labelle could blow, no doubt about it. And she had scads of adoring fans, so who cared about the size of her nose? But Sandra had to admit that Miss Labelle's renovated nose was an improvement.

If she and Patti was on friendly terms, she would have asked, *Girl, did you get your nose done? Tell me all about it.*

For days, Sandra was consumed with Patti Labelle's nose.

When she ate a meal, brushed her teeth, assisted her daughter with her bath, she thought about Patti's nose, how it went from wide and mashed down to attractive.

One morning, Sandra grabbed the phone book, and made a consultation appointment with a plastic surgeon to discuss the possibility of having her nose reduced.

He told her that it could be done, that the procedure was as commonplace as a tonsillectomy.

She took the subject to Richard. "There's nothing wrong with your nose, baby," he said.

"Well, I hate it. I've hated it since I was a little girl," she pouted.

"Well, if it'll make you happy to buy a new nose, then go for it," he said.

*Buy a new nose,* Sandra thought. Richard made it sound like she could go to Nose-R-Us, and pick out one to her liking. And shit, she was talking about surgery, going under the knife, slicing and blood and bandages. The thought made her physically ill. God, something could go wrong.

Lord. What if she lost her ability to smell? She wouldn't be able to whiff perfume, shampoo, or inhale the wonderful aroma of freshly ground coffee or just baked bread.

There were some odors that she could live without—a fart, shit, or a landfill. But there were pleasant fragrances. And what if she lost the ability to enjoy them.

She shook her head, thinking, *No, uh-uh.* She couldn't let herself engage in negative thinking. Now, she despised her nose, and something could be done to make it prettier, and she was willing to take the risk.

*It'll be okay,* she pep-talked herself. The doctor said the procedure was as commonplace as a tonsillectomy.

Richard got a loan from his credit union to pay for the service. She was hoping that would be his reaction. She didn't give a damn about Richard. All she wanted him for was to pay the bills.

On a sunny Thursday morning, she had the operation performed, and for *weeks*, her nose was swathed in bandages.

Around her eyes, she looked as though a mugger had beaten the hell out of her. Her face was puffy, and the skin under her eyes took on more colors that a box of crayons. Purple mixed in with her jet-black skin. A few days later, the swelling subsided and the skin around the surgical area took on a yellowish hue.

This had better be worth it. Going through all this painful shit, *Sandra thought, looking at herself in the mirror.*

When the swelling had completely vanished, and the bandages were removed, and her normal coloring had returned, Sandra could not believe her eyes. *My goodness,* she thought. *Lord have mercy.*

My nose.

There was less of it. Gone was that bulb-shape. Her new nose was smaller, and it brought out her eyes, and emphasized her cheekbones.

She shook her head in amazement. "You look nice," Richard said. "But that was the case even before the surgery."

He could say such sweet things. Too bad she didn't give a damn about him.

Even Laquita could see that Sandra felt better about herself. "Mama happy. Mama happy," the child said, displaying her snaggled teeth.

Her coworkers at Dairy Queen told her she looked different.

One of the girls always wore perfectly applied makeup. "Girl, give me some tips," Sandra requested of her.

The girl happily answered Sandra's questions.

Sandra had always wanted to try makeup, but steered clear of it because cosmetics would have only brought attention to her face, and she didn't want to do anything to accentuate her previously oversized nose.

But after getting a new nose, she experimented with foundation, rouge, eye shadow, and lip color.

In the beginning, she was heavy-handed, so she took it down just a few notches. And she loved the reaction wearing the stuff brought from the opposite sex. Men began to notice her.

In the grocery store, the drug store, at work, they checked her out, even flirted. And she loved it. Never before had men given her a second glance.

"Sandra, why don't you do something about your hair?" suggested Erica, a coworker.

That statement rubbed Sandra the wrong way. She didn't appreciate Erica implying that something was wrong with her hair, although she knew the nappy mop was nothing to brag about.

And keeping the mess styled was a pain in the ass. This faggot beautician, Furious, who wore long braids down to his ass, and snug leather pants, permed and rolled it with small rollers.

And every morning, Sandra was in the bathroom, bending her hair with a sizzling curling iron. Her hair wasn't long enough to twine around the entire rod.

Furious made her hair look okay, but it damn sure won't all that.

When she had grown weary of getting a perm every eight weeks, and having a roller set once a week, and twisting it with the curling iron every morning, she tried a curly perm.

That way, she wouldn't have to go to the hairdresser once a week, and bend her hair every morning. But shit, the perm didn't hold.

Then, she tried a wrap.

Every night before hitting the sack, she swathed her head in a silk scarf so that she'd have a hairstyle in the morning.

She got sick of all the hair changes, and decided to just let the shit go natural.

She wasn't happy with the boy's look hairstyle, but it was nice not having to worry about perms, and rolling it.

And after she went the natural route, she noticed that men weren't paying as much attention to her. *I guess men like more feminine hairstyles.*

She always yearned for thick, shoulder-length hair. She didn't give a damn about having hair like a white woman. She'd be content with a head full of knots that she could perm, and curl with decent size rollers, and twine completely around a curling iron.

Her sisters had hair galore. And she'd have loved having a head of hair too.

She complained about her hair to Furious. "Why don't you try a weave," he said. "Girl, you would look fierce with a weave." He explained that a full weave would cost her five hundred and fifteen dollars.

"Furious, I know you done lost your mind," she exclaimed. "Five hundred and fifteen dollars. Boy, you talking about electric, cable, phone bill and two weeks worth of groceries. And how often would I have to have it done?"

"Well, to put the hair in would be five fifteen. And every two or three months, you'll have to have it tightened, and that would be less."

"How much is less?"

"One sixty," he said.

"One sixty," she repeated, thinking that didn't sound bad. Richard paid the bills, so she could come up with one sixty every two months.

"And you can use the same hair over, but Miss Furious ain't going to lie to you," he said. "From time-to-time, you might have to add a new track or two. And it's fifty dollars a track. And twice a year, you'll have to put in new hair."

Furious showed her a gigantic album of before and after weave pictures. Prior to getting a weave, many of the models had boys-length hair. And some had thin hair.

But man, did they look striking with the weaves. It was amazing.

God knows, those weaves helped their appearances.

"And look at what a weave did for Janet Jackson," Furious said.

"How do you know Janet wears a weave?" Sandra asked, frowning. Sandra loved Janet's music and dancing.

"Miss Thang, please. You have cablevision. Remember when Janet played Penny on *Good Times*?"

Sandra had forgotten that Janet had been on *Good Times,* and to think of it, she played Sharlene, Willis's girlfriend on *Different Strokes* too.

Furious said, "Penny's head was nappy. But now, look at Janet's hair. Girl, you know, Miss Janet is wearing some tracks. And she wearing the good stuff too."

And it looked good. Boy, Sandra wished her head looked as nice as Janet Jackson's did.

One night after sex, Sandra told Richard that she wanted to get a weave, and that the process would cost five hundred dollars. "That's a lot of money to spend on your hair," he said, sounding surprised.

"I know. But baby, don't you want me to look nice for you?" she said in the dark room, sounding sweet and encouraging.

"You look nice now."

"Yeah, but I think I'd look better with a weave," she cajoled.

So, Richard gave her his Visa card.

And a few days later, Furious permed and braided her hair, and then sewed tracks of authentic looking fake hair onto the braids.

The procedure took over two hours, and Sandra was getting antsy sitting in that damn swivel chair, listening to other patrons drone on about what was happening on the soaps, or how somebody's child was getting unbelievably sassy.

But when she saw herself in the mirror, she realized the procedure was worth the wait. Her face broke into a super-size smile. She was astounded by how the hair had enhanced her appearance.

She happily handed Furious, Richard's credit card, and tipped the effeminate hair stylist ten-dollars.

She bounced out of the salon, and going to the car, her hair bounced right along with her.

People stared at her long, thick hair.

Men smiled.

Women eyed her covetously.

At the stoplight, she saw two black women in a car, and one said something to the other, who looked over at Sandra. "That's a wig," the girl said. Sandra had read her lips.

*Ho, I don't give a damn what you think,* Sandra thought.

She just loved having long, bouncing hair, which brought her attention aplenty.

When she bumped into men at the grocery store, or the Laundromat, they frequently asked, "How you doing?" wearing a she's-nice-looking smile.

Until the nose job, and the weave, men seldom gave her the time of day.

One Friday afternoon, Drucilla, a twenty something year old woman, who lived in her apartment complex, asked Sandra to go bar hopping that night.

Sandra agreed. She had never been in a bar. When she was involved with Juice, they'd rent a room at the Thrift Inn, and eat food from Taco Bell, and screw.

Sometimes, he'd grab a pint of vodka, some orange juice and plastic glasses, and they'd drink and fuck.

Juice explained that because he was married, they couldn't be seen in public together, and he didn't want people gossiping.

Richard was a homebody type. His idea of an outing was trips to the movies and to the mall. Give Richard a bowl of Pop-Secret and a movie from Blockbuster's and he was happy.

So, the only time Sandra heard loud music was when she blasted the stereo in the apartment.

On the night of the outing, Sandra and Drucilla dolled up and hit the jam-packed club.

Guys bought Sandra drinks, and took a spin with her on the dance floor.

She snapped her fingers and twirled around. *Fabulous,* she thought.

The loud music and the booze had put her in a par-tay mood. "Girl, I like that song," Drucilla said, dancing in her seat, and bobbing her head to *Men in Black.* Looking around the club, she said, "I wish one of these motherfuckers would ask me to dance."

"Why don't you ask somebody?" Sandra suggested.

"Nah, girl. I like men to do the asking. Hey, why don't we dance? Shit," Drucilla said.

"You and me?" Sandra exclaimed.

"Sure, why not?"

"Girl, I don't want people thinking I'ma dyke," Sandra objected.

Drucilla broke into a grin. "Girl, you crazy." She jumped to her feet. "Come on, let's throw down."

They joined the throng on the platform, twirling and spinning, and attracting attention. A few men bobbed their heads approvingly, which spurred Sandra to dance more seductively.

She stretched her arms to the ceiling, and thrust one hip sideways and then the other, acting like a dancer on *Soul Train.* She remembered how enthusiastically Tina Turner had danced on stage during some of her televised concerts, and she aped a few of Tina's moves.

She was receiving more attention. Egged on by the spectators and the vodka/grapefruit concoctions, Sandra pushed her breast together and jiggled them.

The exhibition was just too much for Drucilla, so shaking her head, she walked off the dance floor, leaving Sandra to do a solo. And Sandra didn't mind one bit. Why share the spotlight?

She continued to dance, skipping around the stage, causing people to move out of the way and let her have the floor. The onlookers formed a circle and clapped. "You go girl," they cheered.

Oh, Sandra loved every minute of being in the limelight, of having people clap for her—admire her.

And she knew it was because of her new nose, makeup, hair and dancing abilities.

She wondered what all her critics at Booker T. Washington Elementary School would say if they saw her now. She'd bet those punks who ignored her in middle and high school would want to date her now.

Huffing and sweating, and feeling like a superstar who just did a concert, she exited the dance floor, guys bought her drinks, and told her what a great dancer she was. "Hey," a man greeted when she was sipping a glass of water.

"Hey yourself," she said flirtatiously. Her self-esteem was higher because of her new look.

"I saw you up there and, lady, I havta tell ya, you can boogie. You had the crowd in a frenzy."

Sandra smiled at the compliment. "Think so, huh?"

"Know so. By the way, I'm Tyrell. People call me Ty." He offered his hand.

"Please to meet you, Ty," she said and shook his hand.

"Well, I own this joint, and on Monday, Tuesday and Wednesday nights, business is kind of sluggish. People are working. Being a few days before payday, their cash is low. But things pick up on Thursdays. People get paid and they want to relax and have a few drinks."

*And why the hell are you telling me all this?* Sandra wondered.

"On the slow nights, we feature dancers to drum up business. And after seeing the show you put on tonight, I was wondering if you'd like to work here a few nights a week, dancing?"

He didn't have to ask twice.

So three nights a week, Sandra began jitterbugging topless at Ty's Place, earning pretty good tips.

She ditched her job at the Dairy Queen. She was making a little more dancing and her hours were shorter.

Richard strongly disapproved of her new gig. "I want you to quit that damn job," he ordered.

She frowned. "What?"

"You heard me."

"Yeah, I did hear you. In fact, everybody in this apartment complex probably heard you. But I can't believe you barked an order at me. Just who the hell do you think you are, telling me what to do? I'm not giving up that job. I happen to like it." She reveled in the attention, the tips, and the free drinks.

"I don't care if you like it or not. I refuse to have my girlfriend up on some stage, shaking her hind-parts for a bunch of men," he bellowed.

"You ain't got no say in it, Richard," Sandra spat. She loved stripping, and she wasn't about to give it up, for some chubby couch potato.

"Well, if you want to stay in this apartment, you will quit that damn job," he snapped.

"Fuck you, Richard," she yelled.

She was not that crazy about Richard from the get-go, and his disapproval of her job was just the excuse she needed to boot him out of her life.

Sure, he paid the bills, but if she danced a few extra nights, she could pay her own rent. Fuck that nerd.

She didn't need Richard's tired ass.

But little Laquita admired him, and he had been good to the child, and her daughter would be hurt if she and Richard went their separate ways.

But in time, she'd get over it, Sandra figured.

Eventually, Sandra returned to Willow Oaks dancing topless at Frankie's. Felicia strongly disapproved, but it didn't matter, Sandra liked being an exotic dancing. And she wasn't giving it up for anybody or anything.

# Chapter 5

For dinner, Felicia whipped up a homemade pizza and a salad. She loved making pizza from scratch, kneading the dough, simmering the sauce, and grating the mozzarella.

Actually, she enjoyed cooking everything from scratch. "Since you went to all the trouble of making a pizza," Warren said after they had eaten, looking happy and satisfied from having had a first-rate dinner. "I'll wash the dishes." They had dined at the kitchen table.

"Well, you know how much I enjoy cooking," she said, gathering up the plates, silverware and glasses and taking it to the sink. "So, making the pizza wasn't a chore. I loved doing it."

"Maybe, that's why it tasted so great," he said, collecting what she could not tote. "Because you did it with love." At the sink, he eyed her for a moment. "What, you aren't going to say, gag me?" he asked. Usually when he said something corny, that was her response. But she just wasn't herself since she had gotten her period yesterday.

"Well, I'm going to take you up on your offer to do the dishes," she said. "I'm going to go upstairs and lie down." She left him in the kitchen, squirting Palmolive into the sink, while she climbed the few steps to the bedroom. She got comfortable on the bed, grabbed the phone off the night table, and dialed eleven numbers.

"Hello," a woman said in her ear.

"Hey, girl," Felicia said, feigning cheer.

"Felicia!" Denise exclaimed. "It's so good to hear your voice. But who died?"

Felicia chuckled. "Nobody. Why would you say that?"

"Well, usually, we gab on Sunday. And today isn't Sunday." Felicia and her sister took turns buzzing each other every Sunday.

Felicia said, "Well, I'm feeling kind of down, and I—"

"I can tell by your voice."

"I just wanted to talk to my sister," Felicia said.

"Well, what's wrong, sweetie pie?" Denise asked.

In Felicia's mind's eye, she saw her plump sister, wearing a concerned expression. Denise was the color of a graham cracker, fat and happy. She never missed a meal, and always had dessert and went back for seconds and thirds. She wore fashionable clothes from *Sixteen Plus* and *Added Dimensions.*

Denise was a graduate student, teaching History at a community college. When she was at work, dealing with her colleagues, lecturing, advising students, she was articulate, displaying her vast vocabulary. But among family and friends, she left that "mess" at the door, and was just herself.

"Well, you know that Warren and I have been trying to have a child?" Felicia said.

"Yeah, you told me."

"And until yesterday, I thought I was pregnant. But I got my period—"

"Oh, Felicia, I'm so sorry to hear that…Well, you'll just have to keep trying," Denise said, encouragingly. "And think of all the fun you'll have."

"That's what Warren said." Felicia sighed. "Denise, we've been trying for over a year. I made an appointment to see a doctor."

"Well, if you've gone all this time without success, talking to a specialist might be a good idea."

She sighed. "And the appointment isn't until next week. I'm so worried what the doctor will tell us."

"Felicia, it may not be anything serious," Denise said.

"I hope not." And dwelling on it was not going to improve her disposition, so she abruptly changed the subject. "I saw Sandra today."

"Oh, and how is the little lap dancer?" Denise said snidely. She did not approve of Sandra's career any more than Felicia did. "Still taking it off for an adoring crowd?"

"Girl, you know it. And she claims to be making a fortune."

Denise raspberried. "Yeah, right."

"I don't believe it either. Supposedly, she makes a killing, but she has trouble making ends meet. She recently hit me up for a wad of cash to pay her rent and electric bill."

"And I'm sure, you gave it to her," Denise said.

"Well, yes."

"Felicia, you ought to stop being a fool," Denise said bluntly.

"Denise, what the hell was I suppose to do, refuse to help her?"

"That's what I would have done." In the past, Sandra had gotten "loans" from Denise, but after not being repaid, Denise categorically refused to give Sandra another penny. So, when Sandra got in a jam, she knew not to phone Denise.

Felicia said, "Yeah, but had I turned her down, she would have been evicted…all of her possessions would have been put out on the street."

"That's what happens when you don't pay your rent," Denise said.

"Girl, have a heart. Sandra is your sister. Our sister."

"I care about her," Denise said.

"Sure doesn't sound like it."

"Well, I love her. And I know raising a child by herself can't be easy. In the beginning, I helped her out, gave her money that she never paid back. Never made an effort to pay back, I might add. I have bills to pay. I just can't help her anymore."

"But girl, there's Laquita," Felicia said. "I can't let the little girl end up on the streets or go hungry."

"I understand that. But Felicia, you would be doing Sandra a favor if you refused to bail her out when she gets into these scrapes."

Felicia frowned. "Doing her a favor? Now, how do you figure that?"

"Sandra, is just like you, me and everybody else. She loves creature comforts…She wants food in her icebox and in her cabinets. She wants a place to lay her weary head when she's exhausted. And also, she cares about her daughter…And she'd never do anything to harm that kid." She took a deep breath. "So, if you refuse to assist her when she gets in her little jams, that'll be her wake up call. And when she gets it together, she'll think twice about how she handles her money, or maybe, she'll find a better paying job." She paused. "Girlfriend, you make things too easy on Sandra. She knows if things get tight, she can always rely on you to bail her out. And if you stopped doing it, she'd start doing a better job of handling her business. She'd be forced to."

Felicia had to concede that Denise made a good point. But she just couldn't see jeopardizing Laquita's well being because of Sandra's irresponsibility.

Laquita meant the world to Felicia. When the girl was born, Felicia had practically been a mother to her, teaching her to walk, and toilet training her, taking her to the park. "So, you're saying I should practice tough love with Sandra?"

"You'd be doing her a favor."

Maybe Denise was right. "So, what's being going on with you?"

"As you know, I had the flu for two weeks."

Oh, yes. The last time they talked, Denise complained of feeling miserable and cut their chit-chat short.

"Are you all better now?" Felicia asked, concerned.

"Oh, yeah. Thank Jesus. But girl, it was pretty rough in the beginning. I had a fever, chills. My head hurt so bad I thought I had a brain tumor. But the doctor gave me some pills and a shot, and I'm all better."

"That's good."

"But you know, something wonderful came out of my bout with the flu," Denise said.

Felicia frowned. "Some good came out of you being sick?" she asked curiously.

"Yes, ma'am. Felicia, you know I'm a blimp." Denise did not believe in euphemisms. She just told it like it was. "And I'm not going to say that I've been battling the bulge because that would be a lie. Food is important to me. I love me some Haagen-Dazs macadamia brittle, and Kentucky Fried Chicken, and at least twice a week, I eat a medium pizza all by myself."

Felicia was getting queasy just listening to Denise say she ingested all that fat and grease.

"But when I was cooped up in that bed, I had no appetite. I was drinking ginger ale and eating a little broth and a few saltines. And..." she sang.

"What?"

"My stomach went down. It isn't as poked out. And my thighs don't jiggle as much. And I like it, Felicia. So, I'm going to lose me some weight. But I have a long road to travel before I'm as skinny as Tyra Banks. Not that I have any interest in being the size of a supermodel. Some of those babes could use a milkshake and some cheeseburgers."

Felicia chuckled. "So illness made you trim down?"

"Just a wee bit. Tomorrow, I'm going to Wal-Mart and buy a scale, and I'm going to start walking."

"They say walking is good for weight loss," Felicia stated.

"Uh-huh."

"Have you told Eugene your plans?" Felicia asked. Eugene was Denise's live-in boyfriend, and he was super-size too. About the size of the father on *The Fresh Prince of Bel Air,* in fact, and he bought his clothes from a store for big and tall men.

And Eugene's appetite was as big as Henry VIII.

He and Denise had been together for a little over three years, and last summer, they visited Felicia and Warren.

And Felicia threw a backyard barbecue. Not that Felicia was counting, but Eugene ate about seven hot dogs, four or five hamburgers, slabs and slabs of ribs, bowls and bowls of potato salad, an entire bag of Fritoes and washed it all down with can after can of Dr. Pepper.

Felicia took them to the mall, and they stopped in the food court for lunch. From Wendy's, he devoured two triples and two orders of fries and a Thick and Frosty. Denise ate two doubles. And after eating all that, they stopped at a Chinese place and got bourbon chicken.

Watching them put it away was like being a spectator at an eating contest.

Felicia didn't believe for a minute that they actually craved all that food. They were just piggish. Bottom line.

"Eugene doesn't believe I'm going to shed pounds," Denise said. "He said, 'Girl, you live for vittles. You're addicted to food like an alcoholic is addicted to gin.' But I'm going to show his ass."

"I know you will," Felicia said, believing it. When Denise made up her mind about something, she got the job done. Felicia always admired that about sister girl.

"But I know, it's not going to be easy," Denise said wearily. "You know, everything revolves around food. All the holidays are about eating. In February, people give their sweethearts chocolates, and then March is Easter and out comes the hams, leg of lambs, chocolate bunnies, jelly beans, rolls, and bunny-shaped cakes." She exhaled. "The summer is picnic and backyard barbecue time, and there are the high calorie sodas and chips and burgers. Halloween is candy. Thanksgiving and Christmas is about food. The last day of the year is about food—drinking high calorie liquor and champagne, and eating wonderfully salty deli meats and dips and cheeses…Every significant event in our lives revolves around food, glorious food."

Felicia giggled. "And listening to you is making my mouth water, and not too long ago, I had eaten."

"So, considering the important role food plays in our lives, it's not easy to avoid it if you have a weakness for the stuff. Losing weight requires self-control and discipline. And I'm going to put in extra hours at doing something about my weight. As much as I love a yummy meal, I'd enjoy a smaller stomach and firmer thighs."

"Well, you know I'm in your cheering section, wishing you much success in your efforts," Felicia said.

"I know it. And everything is going to be all right. You will become pregnant." Denise said emphatically, looking on the bright side of things.

"Thanks for the encouraging words," Felicia said.

Hanging up the phone, she thought, *I hope Denise is right.*

Felicia wanted children. She couldn't imagine a life without them.

# Chapter 6

Felicia entered *Carolee's House of Beauty. Carolee's* was a popular salon, but it was a Wednesday, a slow day. The place hopped on Friday and Saturday when women came in and got prettied up for the weekend. She had a standing appointment every Wednesday morning at 10:30. She loved the way Angie styled her shoulder length dark brown hair, but she didn't fully appreciate the look until around Saturday when the curls loosened a bit. Felicia's thick hair held a curl the way a tightwad clutched a five-dollar bill.

She was grateful to see that there were only a few customers scattered here and there, having their nails and hair done. She was in no mood to put up with beauty parlor chitchat, listening to inane gossip about other customers, or what somebody read in the *National Inquirer* about this or that celebrity.

*Who cared what Whitney Houston and Bobby Brown were up to? Felicia Wainwright had her own difficulties.*

On the walls were pictures of beautiful black women, with perfect makeup, and exquisite hairdos. Most of the clientele at *Carolee's* were black, but a few white women came in for weaves.

"Hey, Felicia," Angie said flatly, doing the finishing touches to a regular's hair.

*Who licked the cream out of your Oreo?* Felicia thought, noticing that Angie was not in a joking mood. She took a seat in a chair across from Angie's station. On the coffee table in front of her was a stack of magazines, *Essence, Ebony, Jet, Glamour, True Confessions.*

"Close your eyes now, Miss Anderson," Angie said to her patron, an older woman whom Felicia had seen in the shop a few times. After squirting the woman's thinning salt and pepper hair with a holding mist, Angie and the woman went up to a glass case, where people paid their bill and scheduled services. The case was filled with brushes, shampoo, conditioners and curling irons. "Okay, Miss Anderson, I'll see you in two weeks," Angie said, accepting the woman's tip and shoving it in the pocket of her smock.

"You ready?" she said to Felicia, still sporting that unhappy expression.

Felicia followed Angie to the shampoo bowls. Sitting in a chair, in front of a sink, she asked, "Who ruffled your feathers?"

She craned her neck to the front of the salon. "The shop's namesake."

"What'd Carolee do?" Felicia asked.

"This morning, she had a taste for some Dunkin Doughnuts. She loves those things. Eats them a few times a week with chocolate milk." She rolled her eyes. "Maybe her wide ass would decrease in size if she'd stop doing that."

Felicia chuckled perfunctorily. She felt hypocritical putting down a heavy person, since her sister was not a twig. Besides, it just wasn't right to criticize people.

Angie said, "So, she asked me if I'd go and get the doughnuts for her, like I'm some errand girl or something ... I'm a hair stylist in this salon, and I pay booth rent. But I want to be a team player, so I agreed to do it."

Nodding, Felicia still wondered what was the big deal.

"And girl, Miss Thing bit down on one and said, 'Shit! I don't know what this doughnut is, but it ain't lemon filled. Lemon filled is the only kind of doughnut that I eat.' And her tone was real nasty. She threw the doughnut down and started breaking all the filled ones in two. And said, 'Ain't this some shit? I told you to get a dozen, and make sure four of them were lemon filled and not one of these damn doughnuts have lemon filling. You can't do a damn thing right." Angie blew out frustrated air. "I distinctly recalled asking the girl at Dunkin for four lemon filled. Is it my fault that the girl didn't put them in the box?"

"Angie, don't worry about it," Felicia said, trying to make her friend feel better. "Maybe Carolee is just having a bad day, and taking it out on you."

"I don't care about her bad day. I didn't appreciate that bitch speaking to me like that. And doing it in front of customers, and coworkers. And that's not the first time that she's embarrassed me like that. It really made me hot."

"I can see," Felicia said.

"I thought about giving her a piece of my mind." Sighing, she said, "But that would have made things worst. After all, this is her shop. And if I pissed her off, she could have told me to leave. And I need this job."

As Angie washed Felicia's hair, she thought about how she wished she were in Felicia's position.

The girl lived in a nice home, wore beautiful clothes, had a successful, handsome husband, picking up the tab. She didn't have to worry about punching a time card. And taking shit off bitchy doughnut freaks.

If Angie had Felicia's life, she'd happily toss her hair styling equipment into the Dumpster behind the salon.

She'd tell all her whining customers to go to hell. *Ugh, these customers make me sick,* she thought, rinsing Felicia's hair.

They come in with pictures from *Essence* or some hair magazine, asking for a particular look. And more often than not, creating the look wasn't possible.

Their hair texture or length didn't make it feasible. But hey, 'the customer is always right,' so she tried creating the look, and when it didn't happen, their facial expression showed that they were unhappy with her work. The nasty ones came right out and let her know that they didn't like it. "I don't know how you even got a license," one woman snapped.

Then there were those who showed up for appointments forty-five minutes late, and became pissed when they found her working with another client. If they had brought their butts in at the scheduled time, they would have gotten their service performed.

And some discussed their tribulations with her?

She had heard stories about annoying in-laws; a woman who was sexually abused as a child; children who stole from their parents. Women who had breast implants or tummy tucks. A boyfriend who wanted to get his dick sucked, but refused to eat his girlfriend's pussy.

Angie didn't want to hear the shit. She was a hair stylist, not *Dear Abby.*

So, hell, yeah, she'd love to chuck it all.

In all honesty, Mrs. Warren Wainwright wasn't Angie's cup of tea. Felicia was okay. But Angie found her on the boring side.

Felicia went to church, and contributed canned vegetables and fruits, and cereal to the church's food drive.

The only reason Angie even gave her the time of day was because she hoped to meet a successful man through Felicia.

She figured that Warren had some single friends. And more than likely, they were professionals. And she had gone to Felicia and Warren's backyard barbecues and met a couple of guys, but nothing came of it.

She'd have to keep trying. Once she found someone, she'd cut all ties with Felicia.

And now Felicia was worried that she may not be able to have a child. Angie wiggled her nose as if she smelled something rank.

Who'd want to be bothered? Changing stinky diapers, waking up at two o'clock in the morning to feed some brat.

Felicia could keep that mess. Angie was not into kids, at all. She had had two abortions.

If she were in Felicia's position, she'd travel, take cruises; dine in nice restaurants.

Screw, that mother shit.

# Chapter 7

Felicia and Warren sat in the waiting area of Dr. Claire Fallmont, a revered OB/GYN and fertility specialist. In their company were mothers-to-be and their doting husbands.

One of the women told another—" I was so worried about it. I called the doctor."

"What'd she say?"

"That it was the Braxton-Hicks thing."

"I've heard about that. Exactly, what is it?"

"A fake contraction."

They jabbered about prenatal vitamins, stockpiling disposable diapers, and cures for a.m. queasiness. "With my first two children, I had no problem with morning sickness," said a plump redhead with zillions of pimples. "But this time around. Man oh man, it's been rough."

"Well, the old standbys are ginger ale and crackers. I've been eating so many crackers, my husband says we should buy stock in Nabisco."

Hearing them flapping their gums nonstop drove Felicia mad with jealousy and insecurity. She jumped up from her seat and scurried outside. It was a beautiful April morning, with temperatures in the low seventies. The air was cool and the sun was radiant.

Felicia would love it if this were the climate all year round. Next month, that sticky, oppressive humidity would make its presence known. She hated sweltering weather.

When she was taking a deep breath, she heard Warren say, "You okay, Fefe?"

"I'm scared," she admitted, in a scarcely audible tone. "I don't know what's wrong...why I can't get pregnant. Hearing those women made me so sad. I felt like crying. I didn't want to do that in front of all those people."

He touched her shoulder sympathetically. "Fefe, it may not be your fault. Have you considered that I may be shooting blanks? I visited Dr. Fallmont's website and read about infertility. I could have a low sperm count, you know. So, hey, I'm scared too."

She turned to face him. "Warren, I'm so sorry," she said compassionately. "I've been so preoccupied wondering if something is wrong with me that I didn't stop and consider what you might be feeling." She silently scolded herself for not giving any thought as to what her husband might be going through. She hugged him, and he let her. He was a loving man, but usually he didn't go for public displays of affection.

43

After the embrace, he glanced at his wristwatch. "I think we better go back in. It's almost time for our appointment."

They returned to the waiting room, and she reclaimed her seat.

Warren resumed reading *Time* magazine.

After a seemingly interminable wait, Dr. Fallmont appeared. "Mr. and Mrs. Wainwright," she greeted with a smile, acting like she was encountering Felicia for the first time, when she had been her gynecologist for a few years.

The good doctor was a petite, attractive woman in her late forties, with long brown hair that hung to her derrière. She favored mini skirts, which put her eye-catching legs on display. Felicia had never seen her in anything else,

To Felicia, she looked like a soap opera actress playing a doctor. And because of her sexiness, Felicia kind of distrusted her.

She'd preferred a doctor who looked like Rosie O'Donnell, or Sally Jessy Raphael. She knew she was being prejudiced and stupid, that the doctor's appearance had nothing to do with her qualifications.

Besides, Dr. Fallmont had always given her first-rate treatment.

The medico ushered Warren and Felicia to her office.

They took seats in the lavish room, which contained a three-tier bookcase, a big oak desk and diplomas on the wall. From the looks of the place, Dr. Claire Fallmont was doing okay.

Dr. Fallmont offered them water, coffee, or juice, but they declined.

"How long have you been trying to have a child?" the doctor inquired, looking at Warren and Felicia.

"Over a year," Felicia said.

Dr. Fallmont lifted an eyebrow. "I see. Well, I'll need to ask you some questions." Holding a clipboard, she rose from her desk and grabbed a nearby chair with wheels, which she positioned in front of Felicia and Warren. She sat, and crossed her shapely legs.

Out of the corner of her eye, Felicia saw Warren checking out the doctor's gams. She didn't mind Warren viewing other women. Hell, she looked at great looking men all the time. And everything was fine as long as it was kept at looking.

"Now, I have a *bunch* of questions," the physician warned. "So, be patient."

She wanted to know if Felicia had irregular periods?

Severe menstrual cramps?

Pelvic pain?

Abnormal vaginal bleeding?

She wanted to know if Felicia had ever had an abortion.

It went on and on. Felicia felt like she was giving a deposition. The doctor scratched check marks in the yes or no boxes on a questionnaire attached to her clipboard.

And then she interrogated Warren, asking if he ever experienced genital injury. "Have you ever, for example, been playing a sport, or got in a fight which led to you getting hit in the testicles?"

Suppressing a smile, he replied, "No."

She wanted to know if he ever had a vasectomy.

"No," he answered.

*And what a dumb question,* Felicia thought. *If the man had had a vasectomy, he would realize that that was the reason I can't get pregnant.*

The doctor asked Warren if he had ever impregnated another woman.

"Not to my knowledge," he replied, jokingly.

Looking at them both, Dr. Fallmont inquired, "Are either of you using prescription medications?"

They shook their heads no.

"Lubricants, K-Y or Vaseline?" she inquired.

They indicated no by shaking their heads. *I juice up marvelously,* Felicia thought.

The doctor asked, "How often do you have sex?"

Feeling a little embarrassed; Felicia let Warren take that one. "About five times a week," he replied easily, clearly proud of his prowess.

Looking at Felicia, Dr. Fallmont said, "With that kind of activity, you should have gotten pregnant by now."

Felicia felt like an accusation had been tossed at her. But recalling what Warren had said outside, this might be his problem.

The doctor told them that they would have to come back at a later date for thorough examinations.

At the appointment desk, they requested an appointment for complete physicals.

Looking at her computer's screen, the receptionist said, "I have something in two weeks. Would you like to come in the morning or the afternoon?"

"Two weeks?" Felicia spluttered. She couldn't believe that she was going down this road again. "I'm anxious to get this over with. Can't you make it sooner?"

"I'm sorry. Two weeks is the earliest I can fit you in."

Sighing, Felicia accepted a late morning appointment for half a month away.

"I don't believe this," Felicia complained when she and Warren were in his car, on the highway.

"What?" he asked, keeping an eye on the traffic ahead of them. It was lunchtime and cars were piled on top of each other. They inched by a Wendy's, a Taco Bell, a Kentucky Fried, a bank, a supermarket and a car dealership.

"That she wants us to come back in two weeks. I wish I could have gotten something sooner."

"Hey, since I'm off the rest of the day, why don't we enjoy it?" Warren said brightly. "We can stop at Uno's and grab a bite. I could go for one of their steak subs. And afterwards, we can hit the mall, and run up our credit cards."

Felicia made a disapproving face. "Warren, how can you think of food and a shopping spree at a time like this?"

"Well, for starters, I'm hungry, and I'm off today, and I wanted to do something."

She sighed. "Well, I'm in no mood for food. But if you want to stop, fine. I'll have a soda while you eat...But there are plenty of cold cuts and cheese at home, so you could make a sandwich. And I really want to go home. But if you *must* stop, we can," she said, knowing that she was being wishy-washy, and hating herself for it.

"We'll go home," Warren acquiesced.

"Now, I feel guilty," she said.

"About what?"

She blew out frustrated air. "I feel like I'm raining on your parade. You have the day off, and you want to turn it into a special occasion. But I'm not in a good mood. I just wanna go home. But if you want to go out," she said, wanting to please him.

He chuckled. "Just forget it." His tone was patient. "And you shouldn't do this to yourself."

She frowned. "What?"

"Torture yourself about the unknown. I mean, last night, you tossed and turned, waking me up a few times."

"I was worried about this morning's doctor's appointment."

"I know. But Felicia, you don't know anything, and you aren't going to know anything until we've been examined and X-rayed. So, if there's anything to lose sleep over, well, just do it after you know something for certain."

"Good advice," she conceded. "But you know me, Miss Worrywart. When I've got something to do...see a doctor, take a test at DMV, I fret about it until it's over and done with." She wished she were the type who didn't let anything faze her. But hey, that wasn't who she was.

***

The days inched by. Felicia cleaned the house…dropped Wisk tablets in the washing machine…shopped for food, took clothes to the dry cleaners; drove the car in to be inspected.

Her routine was the same, but her mind was constantly on why she hadn't become pregnant.

And as was the case every Sunday afternoon, she and Warren visited his mother, Miss Shirley.

She had unlined skin the color of just brewed coffee, thinning salt and pepper hair. She was seventy-four but looked a decade younger.

Warren was thirty-one and Miss Shirley was forty-three when she became pregnant with him. He definitely was not planned.

It just happened.

When he was four, his father deserted the family, leaving Miss Shirley with a mortgage to pay and three teenagers and a new baby to support. But she rolled up her sleeves and handled it admirably, going to work as a custodian for the school system. But now she was retired.

Miss Shirley helped out at the food bank. And every Sunday, she baked a cake, always giving Felicia and Warren thick slices to take home.

Shortly after they arrived, Warren's mother told him that the upstairs faucet was dripping. So, he got the tools from the garage and went to take care of it. When he was out of sight, Miss Shirley asked, "Felicia, what's wrong?"

"Who said anything was wrong?" Felicia replied from the couch.

"Child, I know you," Miss Shirley said in her no nonsense tone. "And your eyes look sad."

Almost from the day, Felicia and Warren tied the knot, Miss Shirley had been asking them, 'When are y'all going to give me some grandbabies?' 'I'd like for y'all to have a child before I die. At the time, she was approaching seventy.'

Felicia explained to her mother-in-law what had been going on for the past year. "Warren and I have seen a doctor, and in a few weeks we're going to be tested."

"Well, let's just hope that it ain't nothing serious," Miss Shirley said, frowning. "You've been feeling okay, haven't you?"

Felicia nodded.

"Can Warren say the same thing?"

"He hasn't complained to me," Felicia said. "And when your son isn't feeling well, he becomes a big baby, wanting round-the-clock attention. So, if he wasn't feeling well, I'd have known it."

"Well, maybe the doctor can give you some hormone shots and that'll take care of it. Maybe the doctor needs to give Warren something to make his sperm stronger." Miss Shirley shrugged. "I don't know what to say to you, baby. I just hate to see you looking all sad."

Felicia smiled warmly and said, "Thank you for caring, Miss Shirley."

Whatever the problem was, Felicia hoped it could be taken care of with an Rx as simple as taking two tablets a day for a few weeks, and voila, problem solved.

# Chapter 8

Felicia and Warren went back to see Dr. Fallmont. And over several appointments, Felicia's uterus, cervix, vagina, reproductive system were checked.

Warren saw a urologist.

And then the verdict arrived. Dr. Fallmont was sitting behind her desk with the Wainwrights perched across from her. Felicia's heart was beating frantically. If Warren were the problem, she would be supportive and understanding.

Dr. Fallmont said, "Mrs. Wainwright, the reason you haven't been able to conceive is because your fallopian tubes are damaged."

Felicia swallowed the lump in her throat. "Damaged?"

The doctor nodded. Warren took Felicia's hand.

"Well, uh…this can be corrected, can't it?" Felicia spluttered, hopefully. "I mean, you can perform surgery?" The idea of surgery terrified her, but in order to have children, she was willing to be wheeled into the operating room.

Dr. Fallmont shook her head. "Surgery won't help."

"Well, um, how do you know?" Felicia demanded.

"Because your fallopian tubes are damaged beyond repair. I've seen patients with your problem before. I'm sorry." But she didn't sound remotely sorry.

"I don't want your damn sympathy," Felicia spat.

"Felicia, calm down," Warren said, looking embarrassed by her outburst.

But Dr. Fallmont's facial expression appeared as though she had asked one of her office workers to pick her up a pint of Chop Suey for lunch. And her professional detachment fueled Felicia's anger.

Felicia pulled her hand from Warren's and stretched across the desk, looking the doctor directly in the eye. She banged the desk with her fist. "Now, you listen to me, my husband and I want four children…and we are damn well going to have them."

"Well, you have other options, of course."

God, this woman's calm, patient tone was really pissing Felicia off.

The bitch calmly sat there and told Felicia that she could not have children. And on her desk, in a silver frame were two teenagers, Dr. Fallmont's precious son and daughter. It was so easy for her not to care, when she had a family, when she had known motherhood.

The doctor said, "You can adopt. And the other alternative is a surrogate, who can be inseminated with your husband's semen and after the child is born, she—"

"I know how the surrogate thing works," Felicia snapped. "And I'm not interested in using one. I want to have my own child."

"Well, that won't be possible," Dr. Fallmont said.

"We'll just see." Felicia grabbed her purse and jumped up from the seat. "You know, just because you have those medical degrees," she railed, pointing to the certificates on the walls, "doesn't mean you know everything. There are other doctors. I can get another opinion."

"I'll be more than happy to recommend someone," Dr. Fallmont said calmly.

Felicia made a face. "Lady, take your recommendation and cram it up your ass. And stop coming to work in mini skirts. It looks unprofessional! And you're too old to be wearing them." She stormed out of the office with Warren behind her.

\*\*\*

"I can't believe the way you carried on," Warren snapped when he was behind the steering wheel and Felicia was in the passenger's seat of his Volvo. Felicia also drove a Volvo. "You carried on like a two year old who couldn't have her way, telling the doctor to cram it."

"Well, I was…I am upset," Felicia said, her voice still shaky.

"But Felicia, for quite a few weeks now, you've been worried about what the doctor might tell us. So, surely, you considered that you'd hear something like what the doctor told us." He took a deep breath. "You're going to feel mighty self-conscious when you go there again."

"I have no intention of going there again," she replied. "I'm going to find another gynecologist. I don't need that quack."

Turning the key in the ignition, he said, "You know, you need to take a deep breath, and chill out. You really aren't thinking rationally."

Watching him back out of the parking space, she said, "So, what are you saying, Warren, that I'm insane?"

"No. But you're acting like the doctor is your enemy."

"She is. She told me that I can't have children."

He shook his head in disbelief. "Man, I can't believe how unreasonable you're sounding. This is not like you at all. Usually, you're so together. I mean, Dr. Fallmont examined you and reported the facts. End of story. She didn't slice you open and damaged your fallopian tubes, you know."

Felicia looked appalled. "Why are you taking her side in this?"

"I'm not taking anybody's side. I'm just giving you a reality check. All Dr. Fallmont did was present you with the facts."

"Well, I don't accept her *facts,*" Felicia retorted. "And besides, a mistake could have been made. Did you stop to consider that? The lab could have goofed." She blew out frustrated air. "It happens, you know. I've read stories about doctors misdiagnosing patients, telling perfectly healthy people they have cancer ... or some other dreadful disease ... performing unnecessary operations."

"Felicia, the doctor said they ran the test twice."

"I don't care if they ran them fifteen times," she exploded. "Doctors and labs are not infallible. Now, I'm going to get pregnant, Warren."

\*\*\*

At home, she bathed, put on a robe, unplugged the phone, and sipped white wine while sitting on the patio, aware of the birds tweeting, and thinking about what happened in Dr. Fallmont's office.

Now that she had calmed down...a bit, she considered that perhaps she had behaved a little irrationally towards the doctor.

*A little?* said the voice in her head. *You behaved like a damn fool.*

And maybe she had, but for weeks, she had been worrying and wondering about the outcome of those tests. And when she was told that she couldn't have a child, well, all her pent-up anxiety erupted.

And she still didn't accept the doctor's findings.

She was wrong to have gone off on Dr. Fallmont; her rage had been misdirected.

But as she told Warren in the car, she'd bet that the lab had blundered.

She simply refused to believe that she could not become pregnant.

So, yeah, the lab goofed.

There could be another woman, a patient of Dr. Fallmont's, whose fallopian tubes were damaged beyond repair. And the lab could have inadvertently put Felicia's name on that other woman's test results.

"Felicia, come on," Warren said in a fatigued, fed-up tone when she told him her theory. They were in bed. The lamp on the bedside table was on. Felicia had been reflecting while Warren read a John Grisham page-turner. He gobbled those books up the minute they hit the bookstores. "You don't really believe that," he said.

"It's possible."

"Felicia, stuff like that only happens on soap operas."

"Oh, it happens in real life," she hurled, annoyed that he was rejecting her theory. "I've read articles about labs making mistakes. Now, it's rare, yes, but it does happen…So, I'm going to get another opinion."

"Get another opinion? So, you're going to see another doctor?"

"That's right."

He sighed. "Felicia, you need to accept this. Now, the doctor told us that there are other methods for us to have a child. We could get a host mother, or we could adopt—"

She shook her head. "Look, I don't want to hear about any of that. Warren, you're an attorney, and let's say, uh, you had a client on trial for murder and the jury found him or her guilty. Now, you wouldn't just leave it at that. Now, would you?"

"No, I wouldn't."

"Of course, you wouldn't. You'd file an appeal, and try to unearth new evidence…or use a new legal strategy. You'd try to gain your client his or her freedom."

"You know, I would," Warren said.

"So, can't you see I just can't accept what I've been told. Seeing another doctor is my way of double-checking it."

"Felicia, Dr. Fallmont said the test was run twice. So, it's already been *double-checked*."

"Well, I'll triple check it, damn it," she spat. "I have to see another doctor."

Later that night, Warren was snoring, and Felicia lay in the pitch-blackness, wide-awake.

Sighing, she went downstairs and poured a glass of white wine. She knew it was too late to be drinking wine, but she figured it would help her to sleep. She also took two Aleve, so she wouldn't wake up with a savage headache.

# Chapter 9

First thing, the following morning, she whipped up waffles, sausages, and scrambled eggs. "You aren't eating anything?" Warren asked, pouring Mrs. Butterworth on two waffles and noticing that the only thing in front of Felicia was a glass of white cranberry juice.

She shook her head. "I have no appetite."

When Warren kissed her goodbye, and went off to work, she took a refill of juice up to their bed, turned on the TV. Some consumer expert on *Good morning America* was droning on about the pitfalls of balance transfers.

She didn't care. The TV was on for background noise. Anything was preferable to total silence. She glanced at the bedside clock. 8:23.

Last night, from the yellow pages, she had gotten the name Dr. Gabrielle Arboleda, a fertility specialist.

And figuring that the doctor had an answering machine, she called the office, and a recorded message told her that the physician started doing business at nine. And the minute the bell struck nine, she was going to call and make an appointment.

She hoped she wouldn't have to wait a hundred years for a meeting.

\*\*\*

Four days later, she was in Dr. Arboleda's office. The fertility specialist was an affable Hispanic woman, who explained that she had gotten Felicia and Warren's files from Dr. Fallmont and reviewed them. "It won't be necessary for me to see your husband since he's already been examined, and checks out fine."

"So, how are we going to handle this?" Felicia asked.

"Well, since I have all the information I need on you, I'll simply re-run the test," the doctor explained.

"I'm confident the lab made a mistake," Felicia said.

"That happens sometimes," the doctor said softly.

Felicia was grateful that Dr. Arboleda at least considered that possibility. To hear Warren and Dr. Fallmont tell it, laboratories were incapable of erring.

"I'd like for you to take care of all my gynecological needs," Felicia said, like she was rewarding the woman for considering that the lab could have been wrong, giving her hope.

\*\*\*

Less than a week later, Dr. Arboleda compassionately told Felicia that the lab did not make a mistake. "I'm sorry, Mrs. Wainwright. Your fallopian tubes are damaged beyond repair." She paused. "Now, because you had no faith in the initial laboratory, I had another lab handle your recent tests."

"Damaged beyond repair?" Felicia repeated, in a distraught, faraway tone. "And there's nothing that can be done to fix it? There's no pill I can take, or surgery that would repair the problem?" She had already posed these questions to the other doctor, but she needed to ask again.

Dr. Arboleda shook her head. "I'm sorry."

Well, at least she offered a sympathetic expression, Felicia thought, which was an indication that she seemed to grasp the depth of Felicia's pain, unlike that ice-cold fish Dr. Fallmont.

Felicia's hopes for a baby had been crushed. She took a deep breath, and like an automaton, rose from the chair, and slowly found her way to the door. When her hand was on the knob, Dr. Arboleda said, "Mrs. Wainwright." Her voice was soft and caring.

"Yes," Felicia said, not bothering to turn around.

"You are clearly upset."

*No kidding. Well, there's nothing wrong with your eyesight, is there, doc?*

"I don't think that you should be driving home in your condition."

"My *condition*? You make it sound like I've had too many rum and Cokes," Felicia joked, smiling wryly.

The doctor chuckled. "Is there someone I can call to pick you up? Or maybe I can order you a cab. And you can collect your car later, when you're more composed. I just don't think you should be behind the wheel of an automobile right now."

Felicia turned to look at the doctor. "Thank you for your concern," she said sincerely. "But I'll be okay." *A few years ago, I found my mother dead in the den, and the walls had been painted crimson with her blood. I survived that. I'll get through this.*

She left the office, and while driving down the boulevard, she saw Wendy, with her red pigtails, smiling at her, suggesting that she come in and have a burger.

Felicia made a sudden left and joined a few cars at the drive-thru, and eventually yelled for a double cheese with lettuce, tomato and extra pickle, a medium Coke and French fries. "Ma'am, you want me to super-size that?" the girl asked in a tinny voice. She sounded Hispanic.

"I'm fine with what I ordered," Felicia replied politely.

In the auto ahead of her, on the backseat were two black kids of preschool age, waving. No doubt they were eagerly anticipating a kid's meal, she thought, acknowledging them with a reciprocal wave.

Leaving the fast-food joint, she hoped the burger was, as she requested. Sometimes they got her order wrong, putting mayonnaise and onions and ketchup on it.

Ugh!

At a stoplight, she inspected it. *They got it, right.* If they hadn't, she would have turned right around and told them to fix it. She wanted to take a bite right there at the stoplight, but she thought eating while driving was tacky.

At her kitchen table, she ate the meal, without really tasting it. When she picked up another room temperature French fry, the phone rang.

"Hello," she said into the wall phone.

Dr. Arboleda's receptionist wanted to know if she was okay. "I'm, um, fine, thank you," Felicia spluttered, thinking that it was so dear of them to call and ask about her. They certainly knew how to generate repeat business.

After saying goodbye, she went back to her meal. But the sight of the partially eaten food disgusted her. So, she tossed it in the trash container. And poured herself a goblet of icy Chardonnay. Girl, it's a quarter till one in the afternoon, said her inner voice. Too early to be drinking wine.

*People have wine with lunch,* Felicia thought, *so just shut the hell up. I need this damn wine to calm myself down.*

She sipped and frowned. She hated the smell and taste of alcoholic beverages. But she loved the effect.

About twenty minutes later, she was buzzing and when her wineglass was on e, she poured a refill and took it to the patio. *Your fallopian tubes are damaged beyond repair.*

Your fallopian tubes are damaged beyond repair.

She closed her eyes and took a deep breath.

There will be no pregnancy...Or cravings, or baby shower, or water breaking or going to the hospital and giving birth.

Her girlfriends won't hover around her hospital bed, and ooh and ah over the new baby she'd be cradling.

They wouldn't snap pictures, and tell her that the baby had Warren's eyes, or her coloring.

"Oh, God, this isn't fair," she muttered. "This just isn't fair."

With tears rolling down her cheeks, she went upstairs, and brushed her teeth, making certain to scrub her tongue.

She hated waking up with the taste of stale alcohol on her tongue. Yuck.

When her breath was fresh, she climbed into bed, and drifted off.

And when she awoke, she felt herself being nudged. Through bleary eyes, she saw Warren, hovering above her, looking concerned.

"Felicia, Felicia," he said.

"What?" she asked. "Is the house on fire?" But she didn't see any flames, or smell any smoke.

"No, no. Are you okay?"

"I'm fine. But you don't seem that way. What's the matter?"

"It's five thirty in the evening," he said.

He was wearing the same suit and tie he had on that morning, only it was rumpled. So evidently, he just came in from work. Sighing, she sat up and glanced at the clock on the nightstand. He was right. It was 5:30.

"Why are you in bed this time of day? You sick or some—"

"I'm okay."

Sitting on the edge of the bed, he said, "Well, why are you sleeping at this hour?"

"Ever heard of a siesta?" she joshed.

"It's not like you to snooze in the daytime. Finding you sleeping threw a scare in me."

"Sorry. I didn't mean to upset you." She told him about her adventure at the doctor's office.

"Felicia, I'm so sorry." He sounded warm and compassionate.

"So, sitting before you is a barren woman," she said, feeling bitterness, sadness and injustice.

"Don't talk about yourself like that." he admonished and lay down across the bed.

"Just calling it like it is. I'm barren. I can't get knocked up." She took a deep breath. "This is so messed up. I want to be a mother. I want a child. I want children. But because of my defective fallopian tubes, it ain't going to happen." She angrily shook her head. "I think about all the horror stories."

Warren sat up. "What are you talking about?"

"Stuff I've heard on the news. Women dropping their kids off at daycare and not returning to pick them up…And what about that sweetheart who deserted her four children at the public library? And from time-to-time, there's always a news story about a baby being found in a trash can, discarded by some teenager or coed who feared what mommy and daddy might do if they found out they were pregnant." Taking a deep breath, she climbed off the bed, and went to the window.

She separated the drapes and parted the blinds. Mr. Kelly, a friendly septuagenarian, was trimming his hedges.

Felicia liked Mr. Kelly. When she and Warren went away for two weeks in the summer, the Kelly's kept an eye on the house, and even collected them from the airport. ('Oh, Mr. Kelly, you don't have to do that. We can use a taxi,' Felicia said the first time the offer was made. 'Oh, forget that,' the old man replied. Cabdrivers are like armed robbers. 'They'll take you for every dime in your pocket.')

Occasionally, Felicia and Warren took them to dinner, and on their birthdays and Christmas, Felicia baked them cakes, and cookies, respectively.

"And who could forget Susan Smith?" she stated, shaking her head in disgust. "Driving those two beautiful children to their watery graves. Sick bitch."

"It's not just women," Warren said. "Men do shit too. Some won't pay their child support, or find some bimbo to support them, so they can avoid paying. Or working under the table is another way they get around paying…They're lucky to have those kids and they should watch out for them."

"Life isn't fair, and I don't care if I'm whining and sounding like a cry baby," she said.

He went to the window and wrapped his arms around her waist. And laid his head on her back. "You have a right. And I feel your pain, baby."

"How?" she pouted. "You're not the one with the problem."

"But I can't make the woman I love pregnant. That hurts, you know."

"Warren, if you want a divorce, I understand," Felicia said.

"Ha ha," he said.

"I mean it."

He turned her to face him. Regarding her solemnly, he said, "Felicia, are you for real? You can't think I'd want to divorce you because you can't have children."

"I know how much you want them. When we were dating, I remember our late night talks about the future, about our goals and desires. And one of yours was to have four kids by the time you were forty."

"I know," he said.

"I can't give you kids." Feeling like a failure in his eyes, she couldn't face him, so she turned away from him, and resumed looking out the window.

"Well, I don't want to divorce you because you can't have kids." He took her hand. "Look, at me…please."

She turned and gazed into his eyes.

"I married you for you…for the great person that you are. And you're a good person, Felicia…" He cupped her chin. "You're drop-dead gorgeous."

She blushed.

"You can write. You have a sense of humor. You have faith in God. My family adores you. And you've been wonderful to my mother, and you know how to rattle the Revere Ware." He touched her hair. "I want to be with you when every strand of this turns white." His eyes dropped to her breasts. "And when those sag."

She couldn't help but chuckle.

"We can adopt, you know," he said. "The firm is doing well. We have a nice home, money in the bank…We're educated. We go to church. And most of all, we want to be parents…So, we should have no trouble adopting. And, also, we could use a surrogate."

"I know about the options," she said wearily, remembering the brochures they had gotten from the first doctor.

"We'll be okay," Warren said, encouragingly.

But Felicia looked uncertain.

\*\*\*

"Oh, Warren's words were warm and wonderful," Felicia said to Denise. It was Sunday and they were on the phone.

"But you don't think he meant what he said?" Denise inquired.

"Well, yeah, at that particular moment, I'm sure he was being sincere about loving me, and it being okay that I can't become pregnant." She sighed. "But I wonder if at some point, he'll feel cheated."

"Girl, I'm in the dark. Flip up the light switch," Denise said. "Just what are you getting at?"

Felicia got her goblet of white wine from the nightstand. Since the doctor told her the heartbreaking news, she had been using wine to anesthetize the pain. Usually, in the afternoon, she drank a bottle. And in the evening, she had another. "Well, Warren wants a child, and right now, he's young, but at some point, he's bound to start thinking about the future and mortality. He's going to wonder who'll watch out for him when he's old and gray."

"Well, I'd think you'd do that," Denise said.

"I'll be old and gray too," Felicia said. "I'll need somebody to watch out for me." She sighed and took another sip of wine. "Warren could grow to resent me. He'll see his buddies having children, and he'll want them too. And he just may grow to resent his *defective* wife. Who knows, he may trade me in for a model that works?"

"Now, you stop talking like that," Denise said like a stern mother. "Warren loves you."

"But I can't have a child," she countered.

"And he accepts that. Warren is an educated, intelligent man. He's not going to resent you because your body won't let you get pregnant. That would be asinine. And besides, you and Warren aren't the only people in the universe dealing with infertility. Now, you don't have to make a life without children. You have alternatives, damn it all."

"I know, I know," Felicia said. "We can adopt."

"Or use a surrogate," Denise said. "A woman can get artificially inseminated with Warren's come."

Felicia erupted into laughter. "Girl, you're a mess."

"Well, you're sounding so depressed, I thought I'd say something to make you giggle."

"Well, you did," Felicia said. "Thanks. But Niecy, I don't know about that surrogate mother thing."

"What about it?"

Felicia made a disgusted face. "It just sounds weird."

"What's so strange about it?" Denise challenged. "It's a way for a couple to have a child when nature won't cooperate. And you and Warren can certainly afford it."

"I just don't like stuff like that. It's abnormal."

"Girl, stop being so narrow-minded and get with the times. Be grateful that you're living in an advanced era," Denise said.

Screw technology. Felicia didn't like the idea of another woman having her husband's child.

Imagine. Some woman pregnant with Warren's child, her belly swollen with his seed. The very thought made Felicia uneasy.

# Chapter 10

Since being told that she'd never give birth, babies were in Felicia's brain nonstop.

It seemed that everywhere she went, she saw them, in shopping carts at the supermarket, strapped to car seats, on some woman's hip, in some man's arm, smiling and drooling, and staring off into their own world.

In television, and magazine ads, she saw chubby, plump-cheeked, adorable infants hawking Pull-ups and Pampers, strained peaches, balm for diaper rash. *Just be patient,* she said inwardly, giving herself a pep talk. *This is driving me crazy right now, but eventually, I'll come to terms with it. And this helps.*

She poured herself a second glass of wine. And when her lips was on the rim, there was banging on the front door. Frowning, she pulled it open and found her sister, Sandra on the porch. "Girl, why are you pounding on the door like that?" Felicia demanded.

"I'm just in a good mood," Sandra sang, and sashayed into the house.

Shutting the door, Felicia said, "Lord, with all that ruckus, you'd think some lunatic was chasing after you or something."

Sandra was dressed in shorts that barely concealed her ass cheeks and a sports bra. Her strappy sandals displayed toenails painted cranberry red. The sight of Sandra made Felicia think of an HBO special on prostitution. Or the taxi cab series. She could easily see Sandra sprawled in the backseat, in a throaty, lazy voice, talking about her life as a stripper, using four-letter words every other sentence.

"Where's Laquita?" Felicia asked.

"In school," Sandra replied. "And you need to check the clock. It ain't but a few minutes after one."

"So, what brings you here?" Felicia asked, going to the kitchen to get the glass of wine she had left on the countertop. She knew Sandra wanted something. That was the only time she called or came around. And if her woe was money-related, Felicia wasn't giving her a damn dime. Sandra did not pay her debts so Felicia National Bank was going to reject her application for a "loan." She sipped her wine.

"Little early to be wining it up, don't you think?" Sandra inquired.

Felicia shrugged. "I was in the mood. Shoot me."

"You don't have to get all testy," Sandra said. "I just made an innocent comment. What's up with you, anyway?"

"What do you mean?"

"You don't seem yourself," Sandra explained. "And…" She nodded to Felicia's unmade up face, rumpled jogging clothes, and hair that looked like she just emerged from a twister.

Felicia only did the full makeup thing, foundation, rouge, mascara, eye shadow, and lipstick on special occasions.

But she always kept her hair styled, and an hour before Warren came in from work, she bathed, put on a little mascara and lipstick, some Coco Mademoiselle, her favorite scent, although her mademoiselle days were behind her.

"Problems, sister dear," Felicia said flatly.

"Well, let me tell you *what* happened at the club," Sandra chirped, yanking open the refrigerator. Looking inside, she said, "Let me see what you got. You always keep a fridge full of goodies. This is so nice," she complimented, taking in the bowls of strawberries and fried chicken covered with Saran wrap, cups of rice pudding, deli meats and cheeses, cans of Coke, Sprite, and cartons and bottles of juices, etc.

*What a piece of work,* Felicia thought. *The self-centered thing didn't say nary a word about what was wrong with me.*

And she irked Felicia snooping in her icebox. The contents were none of Sandra's damn business. And Felicia damn sure did not appreciate Sandra putting her hands on her food.

Who knew where her paws had been? She could have been digging up her nose, or scratching her butt. And being a stripper, she could have given some dude a hand job.

Sandra plucked a few strawberries from a bowl. "I met this fine looking dude," she warbled and bit off a gigantic berry. "Tall, and I like 'em tall…muscular, built like *The Rock.*"

Felicia was not a wrestling fan, but when channel cruising, she had run across *The Rock,* shirtless, and strutting in a ring, looking all tasty. And she didn't believe for a millisecond that any man who looked like that would be interested in Sandra.

Ol' girl was distorting things. Or maybe she needed to see an eye specialist.

Sandra said, "And his skin's the color of a Hershey with almonds. And he's just as sweet."

"Well, good for you," Felicia said dryly, and exited the kitchen. Going to the living room, she said, "You know, the other week, I found out I can't have children. Messed up fallopian tubes."

"Oh, well, you'll be all right," Sandra said.

*What the hell does that mean?* "Well, the way I've been feeling lately, I'm not too sure."

61

"Anyway, Jason, that's the guy I met," Sandra chattered on, "He told me that he liked the way I danced, and he wants to take me to a Mary J Blige concert in Philly this coming Saturday night. We gonna drive up Saturday morning, and stay the night, and come back home Sunday afternoon."

*And you want me to watch Laquita?* Felicia thought, and sure enough that was what Sandra asked.

Felicia just knew that Sandra's visit was because she wanted a favor. "You're such a self-centered bitch," Felicia spat.

Scowling, Sandra said, "Come again."

"You heard me…My God, I just found out that I can't have children, and what's your response? 'Oh, you'll be all right.' You act like I just told you that Baskin Robbin stop making my favorite flavor of ice cream."

"Well, uh, shit, what do you expect me to say?" Sandra spluttered.

"Well, uh, shit, you know, Sandra, if I have to tell you, you're an incredibly stupid person," Felicia exploded.

"Hey, look, don't call me stupid," Sandra spat, throwing a hand on her hip. "I may not have been to college or write for magazines like you, but I'm not stupid, okay? Now, you can't have kids. What the hell can I do about it? I'm not God. I can't make it happen, you know."

"You could show a little compassion," Felicia snapped. "Or at least, make the attempt. I mean, most people would say, 'Warren still loves you. You can adopt. There are plenty of kids out there who need a good home.'" She blew out frustrated air. "But no, you're too self-centered to think to say that. You don't give a damn about anything that isn't about you. All you want to talk about is your damn self, and some asshole that you met."

"Look, I don't need this," Sandra snapped, exasperated.

"And that so-called Rock lookalike doesn't care anything about you. He just wants to take you up to Philadelphia to fuck you."

"Felicia, you can't have a child," Sandra snarled. "I assume that's the reason you're drinking wine at one o'clock in the afternoon, and looking like a bag lady, and acting like a bitch. Look, you just have to hang with it. Accept it," she said. "Now, what time do you want me to bring over Laquita?"

"Don't!" Felicia snapped. "You find somebody else to watch her. I'm not doing your insensitive ass any favors. And how dare you stand there and tell me to just *hang with it*…You, of all people?"

"What do you mean, *me*, of all people?"

"You were unhappy with your nose, and you didn't just 'hang with it.' Uh-uh, no sir. You found a doctor to cut some of it off…And you didn't like your hair. So, you went out and bought that shit." Felicia pointed at Sandra's weave.

Burning with fury over Sandra's cavalier attitude about her infertility, Felicia snatched at Sandra's fake hair, pulling a track off her scalp, and leaving another track dangling off the side of Sandra's face. Satisfied, she tossed the phony hair on the floor.

Sandra's eyes enlarged and her mouth became a gigantic o. "Have you lost your mind, you nutty ass bitch? Girl, you need to talk to a shrink. You need anti depressants."

"Get the hell out of my house, you whore," Felicia said and pointed to the front door.

"Oh, my God. No you didn't just call me a whore."

"Well, what would you call a woman who parades around shaking her titties at strange men?"

"Well, at least, this *whore* can have children. How you like that, bitch?"

"And you don't take proper care of your daughter, begging me for money to buy her school clothes and to keep a roof over her head. And while I'm at it, did you ever stop and think about why your hair looks different from ours?"

Gathering her hair off the floor, Sandra said, "Felicia, I know we have different fathers. So, you ain't telling me anything that I'm not aware of. I know Mama had an affair and I'm the product of it." Standing to her full height, she said, "But I don't care. And I don't need you, Felicia Yvonne Wainwright. You can go straight to h e double l." Sandra snapped her fingers and stormed out the house, leaving the door ajar.

Felicia slammed it shut. "Oh, shit," she muttered when she spotted the fingernails on the hand she had used to attack Sandra's head.

Three of her nails had broken off. They were jagged and one finger was even bleeding.

In the bathroom, Felicia got the nail clippers and trimmed down the broken nails, leaving two medium length nails.

And on the hand that did not get caught up in the fracas, all five medium length nails were intact.

So for fingernails, she had three nubs, and seven medium-length nails. Thinking they looked absurd, she reluctantly clipped down all her nails, making them the same length. Now, they were as short as Warren's. It would take forever for them to grow back.

Oh, well, looking at the sunny side, she wouldn't have to fool with manicures.

Felicia could not believe that she carried on like that with Sandra. Oh, sure they had scrapped in the past.

Sisters fight.

But it was always verbal.

But that vicious comment Sandra made about Felicia's inability to have children made Felicia explode with fury. Oh, she could never forgive her for that. But she got her back when she yanked that phony hair off her head.

Felicia caught a glimpse of herself in the mirror. She looked a mess and she needed to pretty herself up. But she didn't have the energy to bathe, put on lotion, apply cosmetics, and style her hair. The thought of going through all that exhausted her.

Taking a deep breath, she scuffed to the unmade bed, climbed in, and turned on *Bold and the Beautiful*. She watched a few times a week. Brooke was on screen, weeping. What else was new? She sobbed every other episode. And she was the biggest ho. She had been married to every man in the Forrester family, and even got pregnant by her son-in-law, Deacon.

Felicia absent-mindedly watched the show. Another character, Amber was crying a lake because she lost her baby.

*Poor thing.* Felicia's heart went out to the fictional person.

Felicia had never lost a baby. Hell, she couldn't even get pregnant with one.

# Chapter 11

She must have dozed off during the soap opera because when she was alert again, it was going on four, and Whoopi Goldberg was on *Hollywood Squares* answering a silly question.

Felicia loved Whoopi. She was such a versatile actress. She had the ability to make a moviegoer laugh or weep. She was hilarious in *Sister Act* and brought tears to Felicia's eyes in *The Color Purple.*

In about an hour, Warren would be arriving. And he'd expect a hot meal. Well, he wasn't getting it because she was in no mood to play cooking segment.

Besides, there was food in the fridge, so he could grab something. If he didn't want what was in the house, he could order pizza or Chinese.

He might be disappointed. Felicia and Warren did things the traditional way. He brought home the bacon and she fried it up in the skillet.

The past week or so, she hadn't been living up to her end of things, though. She hadn't been cleaning, or cooking as much. Her thoughts had been elsewhere.

Maybe, tomorrow, if she was in the mood, she'd spruce up the place, and make a mess of vittles. *I can at least do something to my hair,* she thought, going to the bathroom and running a comb through it.

In the kitchen, she poured a glass of Chardonnay, and took the bottle and glass to the sofa.

By the time, Warren came in from work, she was tipsy, on her third glass.

Looking at the bottle of wine on the coffee table, he asked, jocularly, "What? You threw a party and didn't invite me? I feel snubbed."

"Hi," she said dryly.

"Want some company?" He put his briefcase on a Queen Ann chair.

She patted a cushion of the couch. "Take a load off."

"I'll be back in a minute." He went to the kitchen, got a coffee mug, which he filled with wine. He sat next to her and quaffed the liquid in two gulps and replenished his cup.

He told her about his day.

She had nothing to contribute to the conversation. What could she say, Oh, I spent the day, drinking wine, and napping? And she had no desire to talk about her showdown with Sandra.

"Hey, this is a party, we need music," he said cheerily. He put on a CD by The Temptations. "Can I have this dance, madam?" he said, standing above her, extending his hand like they were in a nightclub and he had spotted her at a table.

She couldn't help but giggle. They twirled and gyrated to *My Girl.*

She was so touched by Warren's kindheartedness. For the past several days, she had been feeling deflated, and dreadful, and he was trying to elevate her spirits and she loved him even more for it.

She was so lucky he was her husband. A slow tune came on, and she laid her head on his chest. "I'm sorry, Fefe," he whispered in her ear.

"Let's not talk about it," she said, having no desire to discuss her blasted infertility.

So, they danced and eventually, returned to the sofa, and drank more wine and he replaced the Temptations with music by the Supremes.

They loved the oldies. And the current stuff too. But yesteryear's music—The Temptations, Sam Cook, The Supremes, The Carpenters, Martha and the Vandellas was simple. And sometimes, when one was feeling down, simple could be soothing.

Regarding the modern stuff, they enjoyed Kirk Franklin, Baby Face, Audra McDonald, Macy Gray and Luther.

Audra McDonald could bring Felicia to tears with her moody, operatic voice.

Eventually, there was no Chardonnay left to pour, so Warren made a quick trip to the supermarket.

And while he was gone, she listened to Audra McDonald's, How Glory Goes. Man, did she love *I Don't Mind* and *The Man That Got Away.* Felicia wished she could sing, but her bailiwick was writing.

About twenty minutes later, Warren returned, carrying a plastic bag. "I also got frozen pretzels," he said. "I know how much you like them with mustard. I'll put them on." He went to the kitchen and she heard pans clanging, and the oven door squeaking open.

Warren was so attentive.

On her birthday, he served her pancakes in bed, and when she was ailing, he provided Nyquil, orange juice and chicken noodle soup.

Eventually, they were drinking wine, and eating hot pretzels while Jennifer Holliday screamed out *And I'm Telling You I'm Not Going.* "She has such a powerful voice," Felicia said.

"I bet she used to make the church walls rattle," Warren said.

Licking granules of pretzel salt off her finger, she said, "Ever notice how black people yell and hold notes when they sing?"

Dipping a pretzel in a puddle of mustard, Warren nodded.

"It's a legacy of slavery," Felicia said.

He chuckled doubtfully. "Where did you hear that?"

"I read it."

"I don't see the connection."

"Well, at one time, we had no rights. We were property. The overseers whipped us. The women were raped. We were torn away from our families. The abuse went on for years."

"What is this, a black history lesson?" he joked. "We're suppose to be having a good time, not discussing depressing topics."

"Oh, shut up," she kidded. "So, shouting during singing was a way of releasing all that angst and pent-up anxiety. It got passed down in the genes." She shook her head in awe of the chanteuse's powerful voice. "I wish I could sing like that. Maybe I could belt out some of the rage I'm feeling." Her expression grew faraway and reflective.

"What cha thinking about?" Warren asked.

"Those charlatans say there's nothing they can do for me, that my case is hopeless. Yet, doctors can change a person's sex...Make a flat chest woman look like, uh, Dolly Parton. So, why can't they make an infertile woman fertile?"

"We can adopt, or get a surrogate," he said.

She made a face. "Surrogate? That is so gross...just plain unnatural. I mean, you go in some room and masturbate and the doctor injects your semen into some woman who's as fertile as a cobra." She raised her upper lip. "Yuck. I'd rather adopt."

He chuckled. "What is your problem with a surrogate? I mean, I have no problem with an adopted child. But I'd like a child that had my DNA. And a surrogate is the answer. And we can afford it."

"It's disgusting," she countered.

"Why do you feel that way?" he exclaimed. "Make me understand. You're an open-minded person. You have no issue with gay people, or interracial couples."

"I think people have a right to do what they want to do," she said.

"So, then, I repeat, what is your problem with surrogate mothers?"

She shrugged. "I don't know. It just seems like a form of adultery." She sipped her wine.

"I think it could be a solution for us."

Felicia didn't agree with that at all. Deep down, she strongly disapproved of another woman carrying Warren's baby.

# Chapter 12

"Mama, can I have corn with my chicken leg?" Laquita asked excitedly.

"Sure, baby," Sandra replied. She and her seven-year old daughter were headed in Kentucky Fried for dinner. Sandra had a coupon for chicken, two sides, and biscuits.

She smiled at her cute daughter, who was so visibly overjoyed about getting some chicken. Didn't take much to please her.

Laquita had been pestering Sandra about taking her to KFC, and Sandra promised to do so that very evening, even borrowing a neighbor's car. Sandra would love it if she owned a set of wheels.

Imagine, no more bumming rides. *Yet, stripping pays so well,* said the voice in her head.

Exotic dancing, Sandra corrected.

And the pay was...okay, but a lot of her earnings went to buying sexy outfits and maintaining her weave and acrylic nails. Upkeep didn't come cheap.

On some level, Sandra knew she needed to get into a new line of work. Maybe she could become a dental hygienist or something.

But she loved the applause, the compliments and *handsome* men leering at her.

It did a lot for her ego.

But dancing had its downside. Some folks thought dancers were whores. And some of the girls were. For pay, they went home with guys. But Sandra was nobody's whore.

And in the apartment complex where she and Laquita lived, some of the judgmental women who knew about her vocation avoided her like she had horrible b.o.

She knew they thought she was trash.

And she also knew that some of those bitches were just green with envy because they didn't have what it took to be an exotic dancer.

Being shunned kind of hurt, but not badly enough for her to stop dancing.

When they reached the counter at Kentucky Fried, Sandra looked down at Laquita and said sweetly, "Now, baby, go over there and sit down while Mama orders the food." She pointed to a table. In the lobby was a handful of people sipping soft drinks, and eating chicken.

"Don't forget the corn, Mama," Laquita said and skipped off to the table. Sandra gave her order to a Chinese boy behind the counter. And while waiting for her food, she kept vigil on her daughter, who sat at a table, swinging her spindly legs.

Sometimes, Sandra thought she needed to relinquish dancing for her baby's benefit.

Laquita knew about Sandra's profession, and had been in a couple of brawls because of it. A few of her snotty playmates had called Sandra a whore, and Laquita kicked their little asses.

And because Sandra had been bullied growing up, she was glad Laquita whipped those FBA's—future bitches of America. They deserved to be smacked around for running their mouths about somebody's mama.

But Sandra gently lectured Laquita about not instigating fights. "Don't ever put your hands on anybody," she said. "But if they hit you, you have to defend yourself."

"All those playground scraps could be avoided if you'd stop the damn stripping," Felicia railed when Laquita explained how she acquired the scratches on her face.

In her heart, Sandra knew that Felicia had a point. But parents do shit that children get teased about. Daddy could be a drunk...Mama could be loose. And children get picked on because of it. That was life.

Sandra's thoughts drifted to the face-off she had had with Felicia earlier that day.

Ooh, she was still steaming about it.

She should have popped Felicia for doing that mess.

It cost her thirty-five goddamn dollars to repair the damage. Thirty-five dollars didn't mean a lot to Felicia, but it did to a single mother.

She couldn't believe Felicia acting like that, all because she can't have a baby. God didn't mean for her to have a child. Story over.

"Ma'am, your order's ready," the boy behind the counter said.

After trading her money and coupon for the food and drinks, Sandra went to the condiment table for napkins and salt for Laquita's corn. A woman appeared to her side. "Hey, girl," she greeted Sandra, like they were old friends.

Yanking an uncooperative napkin from the holder, Sandra eyed the woman curiously. "Do I know you?" Her tone was polite.

"We met once. My name's Angie Porter."

"Means nothing."

"Felicia Wainwright is your sister. I met you at her house one afternoon."

"Oh, yeah, yeah," Sandra said, recognizing. "I remember now. You do Felicia's hair. You dropped by her house one day when I was visiting."

"That's right," Angie said. "So, how is Felicia? I haven't talked to her in a few days."

Sandra rolled her eyes. "She's okay, I guess. She's not high on my list right now."

"Oh," Angie stated, curiously.

"Hold up a second, I've got a hungry seven year old over there." She nodded to where Laquita sat. "I'll be back in a minute." She sashayed to her daughter and placed the food on the table.

Watching Sandra swish off, Angie couldn't help but think how unlike Felicia and Sandra were. The old saying about being as different as night and day sprang to mind.

Felicia was educated and had style and class. And Sandra looked like a two-bit streetwalker. Via Felicia, Angie learned that Sandra was a stripper, and that Felicia strongly disapproved.

Angie would bet two week's worth of tips that Sandra did a little prostituting on the side. She looked like she'd drop her panties, or suck some guy's dick for money. And Angie could tell that Sandra was donning phony hair. It wasn't even the high-quality stuff. Angie wore a weave too, but hers looked authentic.

"Now, baby, it's hot," Angie heard Sandra tell that cute little girl. "So, blow on it before you bite it. You don't want to burn your little tongue. Mama will be right over here talking to this lady."

She returned to Angie, and revealed what happened at Felicia's house that afternoon.

"You're lying," she exclaimed in response to Sandra's revelation, thinking she needed to yank that cheap looking shit off your head. "That doesn't sound like Felicia."

"Well, she did it," Sandra said.

"What made her act that way?" Angie probed.

"She and her husband having been trying to have a child, and recently, the doctor told her that it wasn't possible. So she's all down in the dumps, and lashing out at people."

"That's so sad to hear," Angie said, not really giving a damn. "I know how much Felicia and Warren want children."

"Yeah, but that's no excuse for her to attack people," Sandra responded. "Well, girl, my fried chick chick is getting chilly, so I better get to it. It was nice talking to you." She sashayed off.

Felicia had a two-faced bitch for a sister, Angie thought. Sandra didn't know Angie, yet she freely badmouthed her sister and disclosed details about Felicia's private life.

The girl knew nothing about loyalty.

*So, Felicia could not have a child*, Angie thought, sneering.

*Poor thing must be just heartbroken.*

Felicia had everything, a beautiful home, and a handsome, successful husband. So what, she can't pop out babies.

Tough shit.

Angie was confident that the Wainwrights would go out and buy a brat.

Some people could buy any damn thing they wanted. She went to the counter and ordered a breast, a wing and a Coke.

*** 

A few afternoons later, Angie was in Felicia's living room. "Felicia, I was so sorry to hear your news," she said from the couch, appalled at the sight of Felicia. Girlfriend had really let herself fall into disrepair. She was dressed in a pink cotton bathrobe. Her hair was dry and harsh, looked like an auburn SOS pad. A shampoo and a conditioner would work a miracle.

"How did you find out?" Felicia sipped from her wineglass.

It was early afternoon, and already Felicia was drinking. And the minute Angie entered the house, Felicia had offered her a glass, but she declined. She never drank adult beverages before seven in the evening.

Angie was an occasional drinker. She loved her slim waist, shapely derrière and firm thighs, and she would not jeopardize it for mixed drinks or glasses of wine on a frequent basis. "I saw your sister a few evenings ago in KFC."

Felicia rolled her eyes.

"Felicia, you and Sandra are sisters. You should kiss and makeup and put the silliness behind you," Angie said, playing the devoted friend.

"I don't want to discuss Sandra," Felicia spoke in a tone that refused to be challenged.

Angie could not believe that this woman had allowed herself to fall apart like this because she can't have a dumb child.

Why was she even wasting her time on this person? But Felicia was wed to a prosperous attorney, and it stood to reason that a prosperous attorney would know other prosperous attorneys. And through them, Angie, a hairdresser could meet a man of means. And who knew, maybe she could find someone to buy her a beauty salon.

So, when she heard about Felicia's unfortunate news, she decided to drop by and play the role of the caring friend.

She uttered some bullshit lines about being sorry that Felicia couldn't have a child. "Do you want to talk about it?" she said, pretending to care.

Felicia shook her head.

"Okay. But girl, I have to level with you, your hair is looking a bit ratty," she said jocularly. "Why don't I pretty it up for you?"

Felicia made a face. "Thanks, Angie, but I'm not up to going out."

"I can take care of you right here," Angie said. "All I need is shampoo, a blow dryer and a curling iron. I'm sure that you have those things here."

Felicia nodded. "Yeah, I do,"

"So, why don't we hit the sink?"

Felicia couldn't recall the last time her hair had been washed, and this morning when she was in the bathroom, brushing her teeth, she caught a glimpse of herself in the mirror. And dreadful was an apt description of her hair.

Actually, her face, and entire body was looking puffy and bloated. And it wasn't hormonal, but from excessive wine sipping. And in order to restore her appearance, she'd have to cease drinking or cut back, but she just couldn't give it up.

The wine comforted her, made life more bearable. Lessened her pain.

Felicia and Angie went to the bathroom in the master bedroom. Angie beautified Felicia's hair, making her head feel lighter. "Your hair looks nice," Angie said after she was done.

"Complimenting your own work?" Felicia joked. The hairdo had improved her disposition. "Self-praise stinks, you know."

"Well, I couldn't have created that nice hairstyle if you didn't have the merchandise to work with," Angie said. "You have a beautiful head of hair."

"Thanks, Angie. I do feel much better. Let me get my purse and pay you."

"Girl, it's on the house. A little something I can do to make you feel better."

"Well, thanks again," Felicia said.

"Felicia, everything will be okay," Angie said and wrapped her arms around Felicia.

\*\*\*

But Felicia didn't know if everything would be okay. She didn't know if she'd be able to bounce back from the disappointment of this. Since the day she heard the words—*your fallopian tubes are damaged beyond repair*—it was like a part of her had died.

Her dreams of having children had been destroyed. Oh, people could wag their tongues about adoption all they wanted. And she would love an adopted child unconditionally.

But it wasn't the same as having your own baby.

And she wondered why had this happened to her.

She had always done the right thing.

At church, she gave generously...She bought Girl Scout cookies...When that appalling, history-making incident took place on September 11th, she donated money to the disaster relief funds.

When a little boy was shot in a drive-by shooting, and when the family went on television requesting money for the burial, she sent a money order for $100.

She donated to the Children's Hospital of the King's Daughter. On Thanksgiving and Christmas, she contributed food to the needy.

And her gestures were from her heart. She truly believed that giving a helping hand to those who were less fortunate was the right thing to do...the Christian thing.

And she believed that if you did right and acted right, God would bless you ten times over.

So why had she been denied the right to have the children that she wanted?

Yet, there were floozies who didn't want their children, who didn't take proper care of them, and they could have all the babies they wanted.

But she couldn't have one. Where was the justice? Why did this happen?

She hadn't had a good night's sleep in weeks. And every morning, she had to drag herself out of bed. She used to rise with Warren and prepare his breakfast. Now, she didn't bother.

She hadn't cooked a meal in weeks. Warren did a little cooking. But he was no Emeril Lagasse.

He had been buying double cheeseburgers, and having Pizza Hut deliver to the house. He had made a comment that his skin was looking different. "I think it's my diet," he said.

She didn't know if he was indirectly chiding her for not cooking or if he had simply made an innocent comment. His tone didn't sound accusatory.

And lately, she hadn't been doing much writing.

She had looked at a few of her short stories and articles, and saw areas that could have used sharpening. She could have replaced so-so verbs with more animated ones. But she didn't have the energy to make the repairs.

She hadn't gone back to class since she was told the heartbreaking news.

Mindy, a white girl she had met at school phoned. She liked Mindy. They had taken turns buying each other sodas and snacks during the break. "What happened to you?" Mindy asked.

"Family crisis," Felicia answered vaguely. Mindy didn't need to know her business.

"Oh, I'm sorry," Mindy replied. "Well, I've been wondering about you. A number of students asked about you. We love your insights."

Felicia managed a smile. In the class, they read their work and shared opinions on how they could improve it. "Well, that's nice to hear."

"When do you think you'll return?"

"I'm not sure."

Mindy prattled on about the wonderful poetry Marcus had written and how Hazel Crumpler thought she was the next Maya Angelou.

Felicia thanked Mindy for phoning, and told her to take care. Hanging up, she wondered if she would return to the class. It wasn't like she needed it.

She had a degree in English. And she wasn't getting any credit for the class, which was an advanced workshop filled with an astute group of people, many of who penned short stories, essays and plays. And when Felicia read her work to the group, they offered feedback, which she found beneficial to the work.

But who wanted to be bothered?

"What's up with you?" asked Lydia, a neighbor.

"What are you talking about?" Felicia asked.

"Well, where have you been hiding?" Lydia inquired. A few mornings a week, Felicia and Lydia got together for beverages (Felicia drank coffee. Lydia had sparkling water) and conversation. And when Lydia had doctor's appointments, Felicia collected her two elementary school aged sons, Adam and Shawn from the bus stop.

On Thursday mornings, she and Lydia took their coupons and shopping lists to Super Fresh and bought groceries.

But lately when Lydia called, offering lunch at a restaurant, or an exercise session, Felicia invented excuses.

"I haven't been hiding," Felicia responded. "I've just been busy."

Taking in Felicia's disheveled appearance, her rumpled jogging attire, Lydia made a confused face, "Are you feeling okay? You certainly don't look it."

Felicia wasn't up to being grilled. "I'm fine, Lydia," she said, scrupulously keeping the irritation out of her tone. "It's just that I didn't get much sleep last night." Lydia didn't need to know what was causing her insomnia. Felicia wasn't ready to discuss it.

And Lydia was not a gossipmonger, but like everybody, she chatted about others. And Felicia was not going to give her anything to discuss with the neighborhood women.

She could just see Lydia, sitting in somebody's kitchen...in between sips of water, flapping her gums about Felicia's inability to have children. "That is just terrible," she'd say, shaking her head sorrowfully. "She's so good with Shawn and Adam. She'd have made a great mom."

No, Felicia didn't want to be talked about, or pitied.

She assured Lydia that she was okay. But Lydia wasn't convinced. "Well, if you need somebody to talk to, you know, I'm just three houses away." She tapped Felicia on the shoulder.

But what was the point of talking? Talking wouldn't reverse what was what.

# Chapter 13

Warren was in his office, behind his desk, studying a document. His phone buzzed. He grabbed it. "Yes," he said. "Well, uh, yes, I'll see her."

As he stood to his height of 6'2, Angie, wearing a dress that looked painted on entered the lavish office.

In addition to the eye-catching dress, she gave extra attention to her hair and makeup, and sprayed on her favorite perfume. And she knew that she looked pretty damn fabulous. And Mr. Warren Wainwright's expression indicated that that was his assessment of her appearance as well.

Angie knew that lately, Felicia had been looking a fright, and no doubt smelling like a bottle of Chardonnay, so she thought she'd give Warren something nice to feast his eyes on, and a pleasant odor to whiff.

Also, her reasons for making sure she looked like a Miss America contestant was because she knew there was a chance that she could bump into one of Warren's lawyer chums. And maybe, he'd be so smitten with her, that he'd request a date right there on the spot.

"Angie, I'm surprised to see you," Warren said. He pointed to the chair facing his desk. "Have a seat."

"Thank you." She sat, slyly taking in the big oak desk, covered with documents, a phone and a computer.

Also, there was a bookcase crammed with thick law books, and on the wall were Warren's degrees from Hampton University and William and Mary.

Felicia had told Angie that for the most part, Warren had put himself through school, flipping burgers and bagging groceries. Watching Warren return to his seat, Angie said, "I know how busy you are, and I should have called before dropping by. But I uh…was in the vicinity and—"

"Don't worry. I wasn't involved in anything that couldn't wait. Can I get you some water, juice, or soda?" Off in a corner was a little refrigerator. And next to it was a table that held an automatic drip coffee maker, a stack of Styrofoam cups, sugar packets and a jar of non-dairy creamer. "I don't know about that java," he chuckled apologetically. "It's been sitting there for quite a stretch."

"I don't want anything. I'm fine."

"Well, what brings you here?" he asked, curiously. "A legal problem?" Warren really didn't know Angie. She was Felicia's pal and hairdresser, and she had attended a couple of backyard barbecues at their house.

Angie took a deep breath. "Warren, I'm concerned about Felicia."

"Is that right?" he said, playing it cagey. He suspected that she was referring to the infertility thing, but he didn't know for sure if Felicia had discussed it with Angie. And a good lawyer didn't volunteer information.

"I know that Felicia can't have kids," Angie revealed.

"How did you find out?"

"She told me."

"Well, she's broken up about it," he said, looking sad and stroking his hairless chin.

"I'm sure," she said, noticing his candy bar brown complexion, and bright, intelligent eyes. "Becoming a mother meant a lot to her. You know, I like Felicia and I hate seeing her so miserable," she lied. Her objective was to score points with these accomplished people. She was hoping that through them she'd meet an accomplished male. "She hasn't come by the salon in weeks to have her hair done. Several days ago, I dropped by your house, and did it for her there."

"I know. That was kind of you."

Angie smiled gently. "I think it picked up her spirits a little. Warren, I know that you and I don't really know each other, but how is this affecting you?" she asked, putting on a concerned face.

He took a deep breath. "I hate seeing my wife deteriorating. I mean, this news has really thrown Felicia for a loop. She used to take care of the house, and cook meals. On the weekends, we'd go shopping and dancing and dining; to the movies, the dinner theater—"

*Shopping, dancing and dining*, Angie thought...*and the dinner theater.* That sounded marvelous. Angie had never been to a dinner theater. Felicia was such an idiot, sitting around crying the blues over this baby crap when she could be having a blast with her hot looking husband. He was tall and broad, and Angie would bet he had a big dick swinging between his legs.

Warren was saying—" It's like she's lost all interest in everything."

Angie didn't respond. "Angie," he said, frowning.

"Um, huh?" she said. She hadn't heard a word he said. Her mind had been elsewhere. "I, uh, was just thinking, uh, doesn't Felicia realize that you and she can adopt?" she asked, offering a cover story.

He nodded. "We've discussed that. Also, we could use a surrogate. But Felicia isn't too crazy about the idea."

She frowned. "Why not?"

"She thinks it's unnatural. Some people are against using unorthodox means of doing things. I want a child, and I have no problem with the surrogate technique, but Felicia doesn't like it."

"Well, frankly, Felicia's being a little narrow-minded and unfair. I mean, you want a biological child, and she can't give you one, and since artificial insemination is the way to have one, why not go for it?"

He shrugged. "That's my feeling."

"Well, maybe you can convince her to see things your way." She stood. "Look, I've taken up enough of your time." Actually, she had grown bored playing Felicia's concerned sidekick. She deserved an Academy award for her performance. "I just want you to know that I'm worried sick about Felicia, and if you need someone to talk to, don't hesitate to call me."

"Thanks, Angie. That's very kind of you."

"Let me scratch down my number. Got a piece of paper?" He tore a slip of paper off a pad and handed it to her. She jotted down her phone number and extended the paper to him. "Now, if you need to talk, call. And take care of yourself."

As she exited the office, she could feel his eyes on her ass.

*** 

When she was in her car, Angie thought about what crossed her mind when she was in Warren's office.

Fuck this playing the caring friend shit in the hopes that she could meet a man through Warren and Felicia.

Scratch it. Toss it. Forget it. She had a new idea, a brilliant idea.

She'd have an affair with Warren and become pregnant with his child.

He wanted a baby, and she was confident that once she became pregnant, he would divorce Felicia and marry her, the mother of his child.

# Chapter 14

Puffing a Kool, Darnell Moody, sat behind the steering wheel of his Aunt Essie's Contour and watched Angie climb into her car. He had followed her to the law office and parked several feet away, and waited, and wondered what she was doing in a lawyer's office.

He figured she had gotten herself into some shit, and needed a mouthpiece to help her get out of it.

Whatever it was, he hoped it was serious, and that her ass would *fry* and be put away forever.

Darnell saw Angie's car go in reverse.

Fuck it. He wouldn't bother to follow her. He had plenty of information about her.

Off and on, for over a month now, he had been keeping an eye on Miss Angie Porter. And he had to give the bitch credit; she was still looking good.

She had a figure like one of the swimsuit beauties from *Jet* magazine. And her skin could be used in a makeup ad, and she was wearing a convincing head of hair. Angie's hair wasn't that long the last time he had seen her 'bout three years ago. So, yeah, the hair was purchased. But it looked nice.

He stubbed out his cigarette in the ashtray and immediately lit another. He knew that Angie worked at a beauty parlor in a shopping center on Montgomery Boulevard, and that for lunch, she alternated between Taco Bell, and the pizzeria next to the salon.

He had followed her home once, so he knew that she lived in an apartment on the corner of Ashton and Wilmington. And that she resided in apartment H. He looked at the names on the cluster of mailboxes and discovered that A. Porter dwelled in H.

She bought her sundries from Rite-Aid and her groceries from Food Lion.

Sometimes, he thought about approaching her and saying, "Hey, bitch. Remember me? Sure, you do. How the fuck could you forget me? Not after what you did."

And she'd deny doing it. But he knew she did it.

Yeah, he thought about having a face-to-face with Miss Angie. He'd loved to see her expression if she laid eyes on him.

But what would be the point of approaching her? What purpose would it serve? It wouldn't change what happened.

# Chapter 15

"What?" Felicia yelled.

"You heard me," Warren said.

"You think I need to see a therapist?" Her unkempt hair was secured with a barrette. She was dressed in a green jogging suit, which, of late, had become her uniform.

"I think it would help you." They were in the living room.

"Warren, I just recently found out that I can't have a child. So, I'm having a hard time dealing with this. That doesn't make me a mental case." She took a deep breath.

"I'm not saying that you are. But a therapist can help you come to terms with this."

She grabbed her wineglass off the coffee table and took a sip. The perpetually filled glass had become a prop like Sophia's straw purse on *Golden Girls*.

He stroked his chin. "You've changed. You've been unraveling. You don't keep the house clean…you don't cook…You—"

"Is that what this is about?" she snapped. "You're pissed because there's, uh, a little dust on the coffee table, or I'm not playing Betty Crocker? Is that what I am to you, a maid, and a chef?"

"You know that isn't true," he retorted. "I was merely pointing out that you don't do the things that you used to, and—"

"*Things* that you enjoyed."

"Why don't you stop being so damn defensive?" he hurled. "Yes, I enjoy a clean house. And hot meals, and an attractive wife." Looking disgustedly at the jogging suit she wore, he said, "And lately, you haven't made your appearance a top priority. You're always wearing that damn thing. And it smells."

"Oh, so not only do I need to see a therapist, but I also stink?"

"When I've hugged you, I got a whiff of it. And let me tell ya, it doesn't smell like fabric softener. You need to wash it…Better yet, burn it. I'm sick of looking at it. And every time I see you, you're toting a wine goblet."

"Look Warren, I'm going through a rough time," she said, pissed with his attitude. "Some mornings, it takes effort just to drag myself out of bed. Sometimes, it takes effort to even take a bath."

"And sometimes, you smell as though you didn't make the effort."

"I don't need your put downs and disapproval," she shrieked, on the verge of tears. "I need your *support.* Have you forgotten *for better or worse?* Well, this is an example of the worse."

He sighed. "Baby, I care about you."

"Doesn't sound like it."

"I love you with all my heart, which is why, I think you should talk to a professional."

She rolled her eyes. "What good would it do? Talking to some psychologist isn't going to make me fertile?"

"No," he conceded. "But a therapist can help you learn to cope with what's what...Felicia, I've read about depression. And you've got the symptoms. Counseling can help. Maybe, you can get anti depressants?"

"I don't need any anti depressants. That's what's wrong with people today. They use pills to deal with their issues. If they feel down, they pop a pill. If they're shy, they take a pill. People need to learn to cope on their own." She sipped from her wineglass.

He chuckled without cheer. "Man, you're contradicting yourself. You put down people for using anti depressants, when," He nodded to her wineglass, "you're using that to cope."

He had made a valid point, but she was in no mood to give him credit.

"Look, you've got to do something," he said firmly. "And therapy may help. It's time to get over it, and move forward."

"That's so easy for you to say. You're not the one with the problem. I wonder what your reaction would be if the doctor told you that you didn't have what it took to make a woman pregnant."

"This is my problem just as much as it is yours. It kills me to see you in pain. I wish I could make it all disappear."

"Well, you can't," she said flippantly, leaving the sofa, carrying her empty glass.

Warren was behind her. In the kitchen, she pulled a bottle of Chardonnay from the refrigerator and placed it on the counter. She put her hand on the cork.

He placed his hand over hers. "No more wine," he said.

Frowning, she said, "That's not your decision to make. And who the hell do you think you are telling me what I can and can't have?" She knocked his hand away, and pulled the cork out of the bottle.

"Give me the bottle," he ordered, reaching for it.

"Look, I need it," she said, stepping back from him, clutching the bottle. "It helps me to relax. It makes me mellow."

"So, it's your anti depressant, huh?"

"Whatever. I like feeling relaxed."

"Well, drink a cup of tension tamer tea," he spat. "You're cut off. No more wine tonight." He reached for the bottle.

"Man, go to hell," she growled, not relinquishing her elixir. "I'm not six years old. I can do any goddamn thing I want."

"So, it's like that now?" he stated. "You saying g d. when you know how much I hate that word."

"I don't give a shit," she tossed.

He snatched the bottle from her, and poured the wine down the drain.

"Hey, fine. I don't care," she yelled. "There's more in the fridge."

"Yeah, I know," he said, flinging the empty bottle in the wastebasket and moving towards the refrigerator.

But she beat him to it. She tore open the refrigerator with ferocity. Jars of pickles, salad dressings and olives on the side door clashed and rattled. Milk and juice sloshed in their containers.

Felicia grabbed the bottle of wine off the top shelf.

"Give it to me," he ordered, with his hand extended.

"So, you don't want me to have it?" she exploded, holding the bottle by the neck. "Well, fine." Like a pitcher for the Baltimore Orioles, she hurled it against the wall, shattering the bottle. Amber liquid rushed and trickled down the wall...chunks of emerald glass fell to the floor.

For some oddball reason, she thought of some VIP christening a liner. "Have you lost your fucking mind?" he hollered, looking at her as if she had grown an extra head.

"Well, you didn't want me to have it," she said, smugly.

Shaking his head, and looking at the mess she created, he blew out frustrated air. "You've flipped. Just get the hell out of here." He squatted to the floor and picked up the jagged pieces of glass and tossed it in the wastebasket. Watching him, Felicia suddenly regretted her behavior.

"Be careful," she whispered, sounding piteous. "Don't cut yourself."

He didn't respond. With her head lowered to the floor, she left him in the kitchen. She didn't see the tears that had formed in his eyes.

# Chapter 16

Angie was in bed, watching that Payless Shoe Source commercial featuring Star Jones from *The View*.

Star knew damn well that she didn't buy her footwear from no Payless. Somewhere, Angie had read that Star was a shoe-o-phile, which was undoubtedly why Payless commissioned her as a spokesperson.

The phone pealed. *Who the hell could that be?* She stretched to the nightstand and quieted the ringing. "Hello," she greeted.

"Angie?" a male voice said, sounding hesitant and unsure.

She frowned in confusion. "Yes."

"Uh, this is Warren"

*That was mighty quick.* It was just three days ago that she had given him her phone number. She sat up a little straighter. "Well, hi," she said, pleased to hear his voice. But making certain to keep hers neutral. She couldn't let him think that she was interested in anything but friendship. For now, anyway.

He took a deep breath. "You said if I needed to talk, I could call you."

"Is this about Felicia?" she asked, thinking, *What else? And who cares?* She was showered, snug in her favorite robe, with a bag of Doritoes next to her, waiting for *The Jeffersons* to return from commercial break.

He sighed. "Yes."

*Oh, lord.* She had no desire to listen to Warren go on and on about his barren wife.

But she had no choice but to listen. Providing him with a sympathetic ear was part of playing the goddamn confidante.

He said, "I...uh, was wondering if it we could get together tomorrow evening to talk?"

*Tomorrow evening.* So, she would be spared listening to the shit tonight. And she didn't have anything planned tomorrow, and if she had, she would have changed it. "Sure," she said. "Would you like to come here?"

"If it's okay?"

"No problem. What time do you want to drop by?"

"How's sixty thirty?" he asked.

"I'll be here."

"Thanks, Angie. You're a great friend. Bye."

Putting down the phone, for a fleeting moment, she felt badly hearing Warren call her a 'great friend,' when she knew she was plotting to destroy his marriage.

*Oh, well. Every woman for herself.*

\*\*\*

The following morning at work, Angie cancelled her late afternoon appointments. Portia, a 6'3, big-boned, department store security guard wanted to come in for a touch-up/roller set, followed by Mrs. Stapleton, a middle school Civics teacher who needed her ends trimmed.

Angie phoned them, explaining that an emergency had arisen, and she couldn't keep the meetings.

Miss Security Guard got huffy, saying that she was going out of town to a wedding, and it was crucial that her hair be done.

"Well, Bernice and Anne will be here," Angie said pleasantly. "One of them can give you a perm."

"I don't let just anybody put chemicals in my hair," Portia said sternly.

"Well, I'm sorry, I can't help you," Angie replied, remaining cordial. "As I said, I have an emergency."

"Well, you've lost a customer. I'll find a more reliable beautician."

The Amazon slammed down the phone.

*Kiss my ass, bitch,* Angie thought. *Emergencies come up, you know.*

She had considered just leaving early, and when the customers showed up, they simply wouldn't find her there. She had pulled that a few times previously, and the clients whined about it to Carolee, the proprietor.

And Carolee confronted her. "I'm the owner of this place," she said.

*Oh, I thought Vidal Sasson operated the joint,* Angie thought.

"And I want this salon to have a good reputation," Carolee went on, "and having customers arrive for an appointment and the stylist not be on hand is not the way to do business. So, if something comes up, please phone the patrons and let them know you will not be here. That is common courtesy."

When Angie married Warren, she was definitely going to give Carolee an earful.

She hated the tramp.

\*\*\*

Driving home, she mused about Warren's impending visit, which she intended to treat like a hot date, and she always took extra time to prepare for such events, which was why she called off those appointments.

She had to shower, and get dolled up.

That morning, she had tided the apartment, so the place was gleaming. For din-din, she was making lasagna and salad, and she had to swing by the supermarket to pick up some ice cream, just in case Warren wanted dessert.

Of course, he was not expecting dinner, but that would be her pleasant surprise.

Warren had said that Felicia no longer bothered with cooking.

Angie wasn't that crazy about the activity herself, but Warren Wainwright was a worthwhile man, and worthwhile men were worth the extra while.

Waiting at a red light, she giggled at her quip.

She was going to supply Warren with everything that he wasn't getting at home, a clean house, a tasty meal, an attractive woman, and eventually, a bambino.

She made a face at the thought of taking care of a baby. Ugh, changing smelly diapers, and being burped on.

And giving birth to the little monster could destroy her figure. But during her pregnancy, she'd exercise. And the minute, that brat was born, she was hitting the spa.

But the inconvenience of pregnancy and motherhood would be worth a handsome, successful husband.

Angie came from a poor family. Her father was retired from the Navy, and for years, he had been cohabiting with Bobbi, a beer drinking Hausfrau. Yeah, a beer drinking German was a cliché, but Bobbi, had been having a sizzling love affair with Budweiser for as long as Angie had known her.

All Angie's boyfriends had been losers. Jerks with no goals, ambition, drive.

But that would hardly characterize her future husband, Warren Wainwright.

# Chapter 17

When Angie opened the door, Warren took in her appearance, and she could tell by his expression that he was impressed. She had played it subtle, putting on just a tad of makeup, styling her hair and adorning Capri pants and a sleeveless tunic, displaying her slender, firm arms.

"You're cooking," he stated, commenting on the aroma wafting from the kitchen.

"Yeah, dinner," she answered.

He looked pleased. "Smells nice. If I had known you'd be having dinner, I would have come at a different time," he said, apologetically.

"Oh, don't worry about it. Usually, by now, I'm done with dinner. And the dishes are put away. But when I was making sauce for the lasagna, which is on the menu," she said, noticing his eyes light up. "I discovered that I was out of basil," she lied. "So, I dashed to the store because I had already started the sauce." She feigned a dramatic sigh. "And the store was lined up. And when I finally got out of there, I got held up at a train track." She shook her head. "So, that's why I'm behind schedule."

In truth, she rigged it so that the lasagna would be going in the oven right when Warren arrived.

"I see," he said. He shrugged. "Well, perhaps, we can talk some other time."

He was having dinner with her, damn it. She didn't concoct that little song and dance for the hell of it. "Well, uh, have you eaten?" she asked.

"No."

"Then, have supper with me?" she suggested.

"Angie, I didn't come here for that."

"I know, but you're here, and the food's cooking, so why not? You can't turn down my scratch lasagna. I make a mean lasagna."

"Actually, it's one of my favorite dishes."

Yeah, she remembered Felicia saying that Warren was nuts about Italian food. "Well, then, that's all the more reason to stay," she chirped.

He shrugged. "Okay."

"So," she said, pointing to the sofa, "Grab some couch. Chow will be ready in about fifteen minutes. The lasagna has to brown."

"Well, it smells nice," he said, sitting on the sofa. "But I already said that."

He was a little nervous about this, she figured. "Would you like something to drink?" she offered. "I have water, sparkling and tap, Pepsi, vodka, gin, rum and cognac." She also had red wine, which would have gone great with the lasagna, but considering what his wife's favorite potation was these days, she wouldn't mention the w word. She didn't want to trigger bad memories for her dinner guest.

"A gin and tonic would be nice," he said.

She pointed at him. "Why don't you make it? My specialty is styling hair, not tending bar. And you know, just what quantities of tonic and booze to use." She wanted him to feel right at home. "The alcohol's in the kitchen." She turned to go to the kitchen and Warren followed her. She got the gin from underneath the cabinet and handed him the bottle. "The tonic's in the fridge. If you want lime, there's some in the crisper."

"Can I make you something?" he asked.

"I'd appreciate it," she replied, opening the oven door and checking the lasagna. It was bubbling and browning.

Warren caught sight of it. "Not only does it smell good, but it looks good," he said.

On the sofa, they sipped their beverages, and he told her that he suggested Felicia see a therapist. "But she didn't want to hear it."

Well, that was music to Angie's ears. The last thing she needed was for some shrink helping Felicia come to terms with her issues, making her go back to being the woman Warren married. That would screw up Angie's plan.

Warren said, "And of course, she was drinking wine, and she wanted to refresh her glass. I thought she had had enough, so I took the bottle from her and poured the stuff down the drain. She became seriously pissed off."

*Winos don't like people messing with their Chablis,* Angie thought.

He said, "She went in the refrigerator and took out another bottle, and—"

*Another bottle? How much wine did she have on hand? Their fridge must look like the beer and wine cooler at the 7-11.*

"Hurled it against the wall," he said, shaking his head.

"What?" Angie exclaimed.

"Man, I was so steamed, that I didn't sleep in the same bed with her last night."

*Glad to hear it. Wanna sleep in the same bed with me?* "I have to check the lasagna," she said and vacated the couch.

In the kitchen, she removed the pan from the oven and set it on the stove to cool. A jumbo grin broke out on her face. *Some heavy-duty drama went down in the Wainwright house yesterday evening. I wish I could have been a mouse hiding in a corner.* She fought the urge to cackle. She composed herself and returned to the living room.

"It'll be ready in a few minutes," she said sweetly, reclaiming her seat.

"It's astounding what this infertility thing has done to Felicia," Warren said.

"Lately, I've been thinking about more pleasant times. When we got married, I had just graduated from law school. So, I didn't have a bulging wallet, so for a temporary honeymoon we drove to Richmond, which is only seventy five miles away."

Angie frowned. "A temporary honeymoon?"

He nodded. "Well, that was all we could afford at the time. But a few years later, when our finances improved, we went to Europe, saw Paris, Brussels and Amsterdam."

*Oh, my,* Angie thought. She had never stepped foot out of the United States. And she had only been to the Big Apple, and Detroit. When she and Warren were man and wife, she'd suggest a European getaway. If he took Felicia to Europe, he could take her too.

"But the Richmond trip wasn't bad," he said, reflectively. "We saw a movie, went to the amusement park, ate at a Caribbean restaurant." He made a face.

Noticing it, Angie said, "What, you're no fan of Caribbean cuisine?" She really didn't give a damn. But she had to add something to Warren's boring conversation about his honeymoon.

He shrugged. "Oh, the food was fine. But later that night, in our room, we got buzzed off cheap champagne." Shaking his head, he chuckled. "We tried to make love, but I couldn't perform." He looked embarrassed.

"You couldn't perform?" she stated. *Lord, she hoped this man didn't have a problem with keeping erections. How much fun would that be?*

"Upset stomach from jerk chicken and the champagne," he said. "I tried to make love to Felicia, but I moaned, 'Baby, this isn't going to work.'" He chortled at the memory. "So, on my honeymoon night, I went to sleep because of a messed up stomach. Felicia told me that she sat up watching a *Mork and Mindy* marathon. Luckily, the hotel had cable," he joshed. "But the next day, I made it up to her."

Fucked her brains out, Angie thought.

"We laugh about that from time-to-time, but we don't have a lot to laugh about these days," he said.

Angie was getting sick of this damn mess. "Warren, I know that you're worried about Felicia," she said, making sure that her tone was stripped of the irritation she felt. "And so am I...But there's nothing we can do about it. Eventually, she'll get it together. So, why don't you just put your marital problems out of your mind at least for this evening, and just enjoy the dinner?"

"I think that's advice I'm going to take," he said.

After the yummy meal, they listened to music, gabbed about how flicks, television shows and music had changed since they were teens back in the eighties. Warren took a deep breath. "Well, I better get going," he said, standing.

"Oh, so soon?" she said. She did not want him to leave. It was going on ten, and for her that was early.

He sighed. "Yeah, I better get home." She walked him to the door.

"Thanks for the food and the conversation," he said. "It was a nice break from the usual. I feel more upbeat."

"I'm glad I could help."

He regarded her warmly and gave her a brotherly hug. And exited the apartment.

Closing the door, she thought, *Soon, you'll be mine.* She hadn't expected Warren to fall into bed with her the first night he was in her apartment. But that would come in time.

# Chapter 18

"You have nothing to feel guilty about," said Steve, an eleven o'clock newscaster at an NBC affiliate. Steve and Warren had been great pals since college. Steve was black and, his wife Bethany was white. Felicia and Warren had gone to dinner with them a few times. Bethany and Felicia never clicked. They had nothing in common. Bethany was career-oriented and Felicia enjoyed taking care of her house.

"Oh, really," Warren said. He and Steve were in the steam room, sitting on a bench with towels knotted around their waists. "How do you figure that? I mean, last night, I had a very enjoyable evening with a woman who is not my wife."

"And what's there to feel guilty about? Unless you had the woman for dessert?" Steve chuckled.

"No, that didn't happen," Warren said.

"And what would be the big deal if it did?" Steve waggled his eyebrows suggestively. He had bragged to Warren about his many affairs on the side. "I mean, things aren't so great between you and Felicia right now, and a side dish could be just the thing you need to make life more bearable."

"I hear you, man," Warren said, not agreeing. The last thing a person having marital problems needed was a 'side dish.' That would only complicate matters.

But last night at Angie's was a welcome diversion from dealing with the sight of Felicia, lying across the bed, staring off in space, with a wineglass on the nightstand.

After she had christened the wall, he hadn't said another word to her about her drinking.

And if she wasn't off in her own little world, she was going on and on about the injustice of her infertility, ranting about crazy people dumping babies in trashcans, or murdering their kids.

Yeah, yeah, yeah. He had heard it all, and he agreed that it was abominable. But he was bone-weary of hearing Felicia yak endlessly about it.

So, yes, the evening with Angie was a welcome change... but it had to be a one shot deal.

That kind of thing could lead to problems.

And he had only had a meal and some chitchat, and he agreed with Steve that he had nothing to feel guilty about.

But driving home from Angie's, he considered that Felicia might be awake, and that she might question him about his whereabouts, ask why he was coming in so late.

And he was prepared to tell her that he was behind with his work, and was putting in some overtime at the office.

But he didn't have to lie because when he came in, he found Felicia, asleep, in the dark, with an encore presentation of *Six Feet Under* blinking away on the big screen TV.

And, another thing, since his evening with Angie had been so innocent, why did he feel a need to invent a cover story?

Simple.

Felicia would not have understood. If Felicia had gone to some dude's apartment for food and conversation, he knew that he would not have understood.

# Chapter 19

Angie dropped by Felicia's house, feigning interest in Felicia's welfare. She asked Felicia if she was sleeping well, eating right.

Felicia mentioned that Warren had suggested that she see a therapist.

"You're kidding?" Angie exclaimed, pretending to be shocked. "He actually told you that you needed to see a shrink?"

She used *shrink* because it sounded derogatory.

"Yeah," Felicia said. "He thinks I'm loony."

"Girl, you're not *crazy*," Angie said, using another disparaging word. Crazy sounded nastier than troubled. "You received some devastating news, and you're having a difficult time dealing with it. I don't think you need to talk to a professional." The last thing Angie wanted was for Felicia to go flapping her gums to some psychiatrist, who could help her put this infertility situation into perspective. Angie needed Felicia to remain an unhappy wino who was not a joy to be around.

"Neither do I," Felicia said, removing her wineglass from the coffee table. "And this chases the blues away." She held the goblet aloft. "But Warren doesn't think I should have it."

"There's nothing wrong with you having a little something that makes you feel better," Angie said.

"He thinks I'm using it as a crutch."

"Girl, please. It's not like you're addicted to crack. Felicia, I'm sorry, but I have to speak frankly…Warren telling you to see a shrink, and that you shouldn't have something that makes you feel better, well, he isn't being very understanding about what you're going through."

"I don't think so either."

"And girl, you're my buddy, and I'm on your side, but—"

"What?" Felicia said.

"Well, um, I'd appreciate it if you didn't say anything to Warren about this little chitchat. If he attacks your drinking, or suggest you see a professional, please don't go saying, 'Well, Angie agrees that I don't need to talk to anybody, and she sees nothing wrong with me having wine.' Please don't say that to Warren."

Felicia frowned. "Well, what's wrong with me pointing out that I have a supportive friend in you?"

"I don't want Warren to think I'm taking sides. Now, I come here to visit you, and I don't want him to cop an attitude towards me. You know how men can be. I don't need Warren looking at me saying, 'That old evil

Angie is nothing but a troublemaker, dipping her nose in stuff that doesn't concern her.' That could make coming here awkward."

"I got cha." Felicia slurred. "I won't breathe a word."

Angie knew what that bitch's problem was, all right. Warren had spoiled her ass, providing her with a nice home, a nice car, beautiful clothes, and all she had to do was sit up in that pretty house, writing silly articles and dumb stories. Angie had heard Felicia boast. "Oh, I published a story in *Good Housekeeping.*"

Or, "I published a little romance in *Woman's World.*"

Or, "I sold two articles."

One afternoon in the shop while Angie was styling her hair, Felicia went on and on about readers' replies to an article she had published. She said that some people didn't respect other people's opinions. And that people wrote nasty responses in regards to her articles, attacking her opinions on this or that topic.

But that she had fans who admired her work.

*Fans,* like she was Toni Morrison or something.

Pampered bitch. Sometimes when Felicia got on Angie's last nerve, Angie wouldn't style her hair as well as she could.

And because Felicia was spoiled, she just didn't know how to handle it when things didn't go her fucking way.

Well, her inability to cope with her bad news and turning every hour into happy hour would lead to her losing her husband. Eventually, Warren would get tired of her 'woe is me' shit.

Last night, he admitted that an evening with her had put him in an *upbeat* mood.

So, surely, he'd prefer upbeat moods to what Felicia was offering. And when Angie became pregnant with the child that Warren wanted, he would divorce Felicia and make Angie the next Mrs. Warren Wainwright.

\*\*\*

Driving down Wyndham Boulevard, Darnell Moody was smoking a Kool and musing about what Angie was up to.

Earlier, he had been cruising down Monticello and Richneck, a busy intersection, just chillin', listening to Mary J. Blige's *No More Drama* on the car radio. Happy to be off from the submarine sandwich shop where he made hoagies. On the opposite side of the street, he caught sight of Angie, driving down the boulevard.

He instantaneously jumped in another lane, made a rapid U-turn, and surreptitiously followed her, keeping a discreet distance.

She was still an impatient driver, tailgating other motorists, switching lanes unexpectedly; neglecting to click on a signal.

But he kept up with her until she made a sudden turn into Bancroft Manor, one of the ritziest subdivisions in Willow Oaks. Only the affluent could afford to reside there.

Darnell didn't bother to enter the residential area. He just kept going straight because in the residential area, his car would not have been hidden in the crush of vehicles on the highway. And the last thing he needed was for Angie to casually glimpse in her rear view mirror, and spot him.

So, he cruised for a bit and when he figured she had parked, he drove onto the street she had entered, searching for where her car may be parked.

Eureka! He spotted Angie's Grand Am, positioned behind a Volvo in the driveway of a two-story colonial.

Slowly, Darnell drove past the house eyeing the columns in the front, the well-kept lawn, the perfectly sheared shrubbery, and the rock garden. It was a palace. Looked like something out of a magazine.

*Who could Angie know that lived in digs like that?*

He wondered if she was doing what his grandmother used to call—" day's work," also known as, working as a maid.

Angie, a maid? Naw.

He couldn't imagine Angie cleaning up after anybody.

But who did she know in that house? He'd bet she was screwing some rich son-of-a-bitch.

Darnell was intrigued by her activities. The other day, she was in a lawyer's office and now she was visiting someone who lived in a house in an exclusive neighborhood.

What was oh Ange up to? No damn good. Of that, Darnell was pretty sure. He wondered how he could screw it up?

# Chapter 20

Warren was in his office, reflecting about his troubled marriage, and growing miserable by the second. He banished the unhappy thoughts by remembering the nice evening he had had with Angie a few days previously, the food, the music; the lighthearted conversation.

From his desk drawer, he extracted the slip of paper that had Angie's phone number on it. *I should call her.*

It was Monday, her day off. The shop was closed on Sundays and Mondays. For some reason, a lot of privately owned salons in the area didn't do business on Monday.

He picked up the phone, pressed five numbers, and then put down the phone.

He didn't need to be calling her. But he wanted to see her. He was in the market for some carefree conversation and a joke or two. He had lectured himself about getting too close to Angie. But, hey, all he wanted was to talk. What's the harm?

So, he dialed her number, and on the fifth ring, she answered.

"Warren," she caroled, sounding delighted to hear his voice.

That made him smile. It felt nice to be appreciated.

"Uh," he stuttered. Damn, he felt like some gawky high school kid calling a cute girl he spotted at her locker. "Have you had lunch?"

"No. All I've had today is a bagel and some juice."

"Well, uh, why don't I bring over a pizza? Joey's, an Italian restaurant I like makes a fantastic pizza. Have you ever had it?"

"No," she said.

"Well, in my opinion, it's the best in town. On the box, they say, 'You've had the rest. Now, have the best.'" Man, he felt stupid, fumbling for things to say. And usually he was so articulate. In court, he had given eloquent summations some of, which were impromptu. But now he was stammering like some teenager who had got up the balls to ask the homecoming queen for a dance.

"Sounds like a good slogan," Angie said.

"I'm not sure if it's their slogan, since I've seen that on a number of pizza boxes. But anyway, would you like to share a pizza with me?"

"I'd love it," she replied.

"What do you like on yours?"

She told him, and he said he'd be over in forty-five minutes.

***

He arrived about ten minutes early, holding a pizza box, splotched with grease stains. Atop the box was an aluminum bowl of tossed salad, a pack of salad dressing, and plastic forks and knives wrapped in a paper napkin. "Make yourself comfortable," Angie said, taking the edibles to the kitchen. "What would you like to drink?"

"Soda," he said.

"One Pepsi coming right up." she replied like a friendly waitress.

At the dinette table, she smacked her lips. "This is scrumptious. What did you say the place was called?"

"Joey's."

"Well, when I want pizza, I now know where to go." Actually, she had eaten at the restaurant countless times.

Warren stabbed his salad and said, "I would have preferred taking you out for lunch, but…" he trailed off. "Well, I know a lot of people in this community and if they saw me in a restaurant with an attractive woman, they'd jump to conclusions."

She plucked a quarter-size piece of pepperoni off her pizza. "Well, we aren't doing anything wrong." *Not yet, anyway.* "Just two people breaking afternoon bread."

He nodded. "But people talk."

"I understand," she said. *Don't worry, sugar lump. When we're married, you can take me out to lunch as often as you'd like.* "'Sides, I like the privacy of my apartment. More intimate."

After eating most of the pizza, they gabbed about this and that. She brought up John Grisham's, *The Firm* and *The Street Lawyer*, ranting about the story lines. Once when she and Felicia were in Books-A-Million, Felicia picked up a John Grisham hardcover for Warren, saying he was nuts about the author/lawyer.

So, the other day, from the drug store, Angie selected a couple of Grisham paperbacks, and quickly read them. She figured they'd be a conversation piece for her and Warren. Make him think that an admiration of John Grisham was something they shared, when in truth, she detested the writer's far-fetched potboilers.

Warren was clearly having a good time chatting with Angie. He thought she was an effervescent, charming lady. For a moment, he eyed her.

"Why are you looking at me like that?" she asked, feeling paranoid. She wondered if he was going to tell her that he knew she was a phony.

96

"You're a special lady, Angie Porter," he said. "You're warm, friendly. And we've talked about a little of everything, but you've never mentioned a special man."

"That's because there isn't one."

"And why not?" He was flirting and he knew he shouldn't be, but he sincerely wondered why there was no man in Angie's life.

"Well, I broke up with somebody about seven months ago, and I've been boyfriend-less ever since."

"Well, you'll find somebody else," he said.

"I hope so. Gets kind of lonely…if you know what I mean."

Yeah, he knew what she meant, but he didn't want to get on the subject of sex with Angie. That went beyond flirting and would be a little embarrassing. For a moment, they regarded each other awkwardly. Sheepishly, Warren lowered his eyes to the tabletop.

Without saying a word, she left the dinette, leaving Warren with a befuddled expression. *Why did she just up and leave without saying a word?* he thought.

A few minutes later, his eyes dilated with shock when he saw her standing before him *naked.*

She had round, firm breasts, a flat stomach and slender thighs. He tried to pull his eyes away from the beautiful scenery, but her gorgeous body had him hypnotized.

He could feel a swelling take place in his pants.

Like a lap dancer, she straddled him.

She put her arms around his neck. He could not believe this. He was fully clothed and this woman was sitting on his lap, not wearing a thread.

Exciting.

After sensuously kissing her, he lowered his hungry mouth to her nipples whose peaks and color made him think of sweet, yummy Hershey kisses.

Greedily, he took them into his mouth and sucked them. "Lick my tits," she directed.

And after obeying her order, he pushed her breasts together, kissing, sucking and licking one and then the other. "Make love to me," she cooed.

Cradling her, he rose from the chair, and carried her to the bedroom like she was a bride being taken across the threshold.

Lying on the bed, and watching him undress; she played with her nipples and vaginal lips. "Mm-hmm," she said when he was in the buff, and his rock-hard cock was ready for playtime. He clambered on the bed.

"Look at what you do to me," she whispered throatily, taking his hand and placing it on her mound, which was warm and throbbing. "Put your finger inside me."

Again, he obeyed her instructions, and discovered that she was warm, slippery, and ready. "I'm so damn turned on," she said.

*You damn sure is...uh, are,* he thought. He was so worked up; he wasn't using proper English.

For about an hour, they fucked, sucked, moaned and panted.

***

Warren was lying on his side, gazing at the chest-of-drawers in front of him. Angie was next to him, on her back. The room smelled of sex.

He glanced at the bedside clock. It was 1:34, and the closed curtains in Angie's bedroom camouflaged the radiant sunlight.

He felt like shit.

He had never before betrayed Felicia, and he had had opportunities galore.

At the spa where he worked out, black, white and Hispanic women had come on to him.

So did some of his clients and the teller at the bank where he did business.

The women were attractive and they had praised his physique, flirted, dropped hints; the brazen ones openly checked out his crotch.

So, yeah, he could have had all the extramarital sex he wanted, but he was a happily married man, and his wife took care of his sexual needs and he took care of hers.

Until now, he had never been unfaithful.

Sighing, he sat on the edge of the bed. Angie rose and placed her hand on his shoulder. "You're so quiet," she whispered seductively. "What are you thinking about?"

Every cell in his body became rigid. And not more than an hour ago, her touch thrilled him. He had loved her hands, stroking his face, roaming his chest, and moving his penis up and down. But now her touch felt like a violation...He felt like he was being molested.

Not wanting to offend the woman, he controlled the impulse to jerk away from her. "I've never done anything like this before," he said. "I've never betrayed Felicia. I don't know if I'll be able to look her in the eye." He took a deep breath. "Why did this happen? Why did you come out in front of me, naked?"

"You're blaming me?" she said, incredulously. "I made you betray your wife? Is that how you see it?"

He turned to look back at her. "No."

"That's how it sounds."

"Look, I don't blame you, okay. I have control over my actions, but I just didn't choose to exercise it. I mean, you were standing there, looking...uh, enticing." He sighed. "And I gave in. I have no excuses. I can't blame it on what I drank because Pepsi can't make you drunk...or impair your judgement. I did what I did because I wanted to."

"Well, Felicia is to blame for some of it, you know."

He frowned. "How do you figure that?" Warren got off the bed, lifted his underwear from the floor and put them on.

"Warren...lately, your wife has been drinking, letting herself go. Throwing that wine bottle against the wall. And although, you never discussed your sex life with me, I'll bet the two of you haven't been making love on a regular basis. Or if you have, it probably hasn't been the same." *Who could enjoy having sex with a depressed woman reeking of wine?*

"The only thing that's been going on in our bedroom is sleeping," he said, now putting on his pants."

"So, don't you see how Felicia drove you to this?"

"Felicia's issues may have contributed to what happened here. But I shouldn't have let it take place."

"But it did," she stated.

"And I repeat, it shouldn't have. And Angie, it was wonderful. But...uh, let's just forget this ever happened, okay?"

# Chapter 21

*Fat chance,* Angie thought, the following morning over a glass of orange juice.

She won't be forgetting what happened any time soon. And neither would Warren.

What man could easily forget a woman traipsing out in front of him naked and climbing in his lap?

And she had done things to him that he had never had done before, such as licking his balls.

When she tasted them, she stole a peek up at his face and she could tell by his expression that he was pleasantly shocked by her actions. "Oh, wow," he had said appreciatively. "I've never had that done."

And Warren was a good lover, and as she had predicted, he was generous in the dick department.

It was a wild afternoon, and he wouldn't develop amnesia about it any time soon. No, uh-uh.

She knew what his problem was. He was feeling guilty. Warren Wainwright was a good man, and good men who are married tend to feel guilty when they engage in a little hanky-panky on the side.

Despite Warren's regret, Angie was confident that this thing would play out in her favor. He wanted a baby, and she could give him one. And being the good man that he was, well, naturally, he would be a father to his child.

He hated his own father for deserting him when he was a kid. So, that was in her favor.

When he called, offering lunch, she decided right then and there that she was going to fuck him. In fact, when she decided to seduce him, she had ceased taking birth control precautions.

The baby would bring her and Warren together. And also, she was attractive and great in bed. So, when she became pregnant, he would ditch the unhappy wino.

That's how it would all go down.

Speaking of *go down*, when he remembered all the sizzling fun they had, that guilty shit he was feeling would go straight out the window.

In a day or two, when he was feeling all sexy, he'd recall what they had shared and he'd come back for seconds and thirds.

She liked thinking of herself as something to eat.

Also, she had to do some damage control. After all, she was Felicia's "friend," and she had screwed her husband, so he could possibly think of her as a slut.

Now, she couldn't have her future husband thinking of her that way.

So, she went to the kitchen phone and called Warren's office.

His receptionist put her through. "Angie, what is it?" he asked, practically whispering. Voice of shame, she figured. *Get over it, man.*

"I have to see you," she said.

"About?"

She visualized him frowning. "Well, what happened."

"I thought we agreed to just forget it."

"I know...But, uh..." To make it sound like she was confused and in agony over the whole thing, she peppered her speech with an uh or two. "I, uh, have to make something clear to you. So, can I see you?" She rolled her eyes. This begging a man to give her a few minutes of his precious time was not for Angie. Yeah, she knew it was play-acting, just part of a scheme, but still, she didn't like doing it.

"Well, can you come here?" he inquired.

*What's the matter, buddy boy? Scared if you're alone with me, that things will get pornographic.*

"Well, yeah, I can," she replied.

"How's two?" he asked. "I have some free time at two."

*I don't think so.* Everything was not going to be at Warren's convenience. "I can't make it at two," she lied. "I'll be in the middle of a curl at that hour. So, how's three fifteen?"

"Fine. I'll be here," he said.

\*\*\*

"Warren, I have to let you know that I'm not a tramp who goes around having sex with other women's husband's," Angie said, from a chair facing Warren's desk.

"I never thought that of you," he said.

"I know it's cliché, but what happened between us was just one of those things...As I told you, I hadn't been involved with anybody in seven months and I've been lonely." She sighed. "And I don't know. You and I had food and conversation, and we were joking and flirting. And I felt excited and I took things to the next level." She took a deep breath. "But I regret it."

"We both do," he said.

"You said that you were going to have trouble looking at Felicia, well, so am I," she said. "Remember, she and I are friends, and being around her is going to be difficult for me." Another sigh. "I've considered not going to your house again, and referring Felicia to another stylist if she calls requesting an appointment.

"Well, however, you chose to handle it, is your decision," he said. "But Angie, we can act as if it never happened."

"Well, I don't think that I can put what happened out of my mind like one, two, three. For me, it was a fantasy come true."

He frowned. "What do you mean?"

She sighed. "I don't know how to put this," she said, pretending to be formulating her ideas, when she had thought her entire spiel out. "Warren, you're handsome, warm and intelligent…" She put her hand on her heart. "And I'm drawn to you and I allowed myself to become carried away…forgetting or not caring that you were married. Or that Felicia was my friend, and I owed her loyalty." She took a deep breath. "But I care for you. And your opinion of me matters. I don't want you thinking I'm some whore who goes around screwing married men…This is the first time, I've been with another woman's husband. And if I didn't have feelings for you, I wouldn't have done it. Because, well, I, uh, like you a lot, I had to make sure that you understood that."

"I got you," he said, uncomfortable with the discussion.

She sighed. "So, take care. And have a good life." She put on a forlorn smile. "I sincerely hope that you and Felicia work things out."

She vacated the office, drove off in her car, and when she was at a stoplight, she burst out laughing at the load of bull she had fed Warren.

*This is the first time I've been with a married man,* she had said. Please. She had a three-month affair with Walt, a white, middle-aged owner of a Pontiac dealership? And she could never forget her steamy romps with Brucie, husband of Tasha, one of the hairdressers at the salon where Angie worked.

It was nothing serious. Brucie managed the health spa across the street from the salon and he'd come in to say hey to Tasha or to take her to lunch, wearing sleeveless shirts and skimpy short silk pants displaying his muscles and firm legs.

Angie thought he looked right tasty, and she wanted to find out if he could fuck. So, she visited the gym and did a little flirting, and for two months, she and Brucie had an affair. Ooh, that boy could eat pussy.

And dumb ass Tasha was not the wiser. On Angie's birthday and Christmas, Tasha gave Angie a card and a tin of home baked cookies, respectively.

Dumb bitch.

There had been other married men, but it was time for Angie to settle down. But after she and Warren tied the knot, if she got in the mood for something different, she'd find some extramarital sex on the side. Why should men have all the fun?

# Chapter 22

Felicia unscrewed her eyes and squinted at the clock on the nightstand. Oh, God, it was 11:13 in the morning, and she was just waking up. That was okay for some heiress whose life was about lunching and shopping. But that wasn't the life for Felicia Wainwright.

Warren had long since left for work. Sighing, she sat up, and frowned when there was a banging in her head. *That's what you get for drinking wine before going to bed,* chided her inner voice.

Usually, when she had wine late at night, which had been a frequent occurrence lately, she took two aspirin to avoid waking up with a headache.

But last night, she forgot to do so.

And it had been a rough night. She had gone to bed shortly before ten, woke up at 3:15, went to the kitchen and gulped two glasses of water. She returned to bed and just stared in the dark, unsuccessfully trying to return to dreamland.

At some point, she drifted off, sleeping fitfully.

She sighed and muttered, "Lord, lord. I've got to do something about my pitiful life. This can't go on much longer."

For over three months now, she had had no damn life. She had ceased living. She had become nothing but an entity that took up space and air, doing nothing but drinking wine.

And sleeping during the day, something she never used to do.

And she had not been taking proper care of the house. At least, not in the same manner before hearing the devastating news.

Here and there, she had pushed the vacuum, mopped, sprinkled Comet in the sinks; squirted some toilet bowl cleaner.

She couldn't recall the last time she had cooked a meal. When she became hungry, she grabbed a burger from Wendy's, or microwaved a dinner. Warren did the same thing.

God, her *damaged fallopian tubes* had changed her life.

She had not been doing any writing. She quit going to that workshop. By now, it was over. Her sister was trying to lose weight, and Felicia had planned on penning an article about the difficulty of weight reduction, but she hadn't written a sentence, nor had she crafted a short story or article, or done any work on the ones in her computer.

And she had been neglecting her girlfriends, inventing excuses to avoid seeing them socially. They didn't know what was going on, but they had grown sick of having their offers for lunch, or shopping declined, so they ceased calling or visiting.

Exercising.

Felicia had been avoiding it.

And boy, did she need it. Her stomach, arms, and thighs had become bloated from all the wine.

Lord, she really loathed what had become of her life.

She wiped her eyes, sighed, left the bed, and got a crammed photo album off the bedroom shelf.

Wistfully, she gazed at pictures, of her and Warren, on Christmas, standing by the tree. Or on New Year's, dressed in their finery. Or in their backyard, in the summer, having picnics. She had taken pictures with his family and Laquita, and Sandra, and Denise. There were photos of her and Warren on vacation…pictures of them singularly and together. Pictures of the waterfalls in Hawaii. And in the snapshots, Felicia was smiling because she was happy, on holiday, with her wonderful husband.

Back then, she was a woman who liked herself, and enjoyed her life.

And even now, she had plenty to be proud of, to be thankful for. She had her health, her intelligence…her creativity, a loving husband, a beautiful home and solvency.

But when she was told about her defective fallopian tubes, she ceased caring about anything.

And she had read that losing interest in the things that once brought you joy, and difficulty sleeping were signs of depression.

So, now, she agreed with Warren that she had fallen into a depression. She certainly had some of the symptoms. Plaintively, she looked at another picture. "Where are you?" she whispered.

She'd like to rediscover that perpetually smiling woman, bring her back into her life.

Warren would probably like for her to come back as well. Felicia was sure that he missed the woman he married. He certainly could not be enjoying the wine drinking imposter who had shanghaied Felicia, stashed her somewhere and took over her life.

With her eyes closed, she remembered the time she hurled the bottle of wine against the wall.

She shook her head sorrowfully. That man did not deserve that. He was only trying to help her when he took it from her.

Yes, she was depressed. But she didn't need to see a psychiatrist, or take drugs, or drink wine.

When her mother committed suicide, she dealt with it without drinking wine.

As painful as her mother's death was, she coped with it. And she could deal with this without substances or counseling.

She wanted children, and she can't have them, so what was there to discuss? She simply had to make her peace with it.

And she wanted the Felicia she used to be to return.

She wanted to clean her house, and cook meals. She wanted to write her articles and stories.

But the Felicia that she had known and loved all these years had been away on vacation. How did she go about banishing the Felicia she had become and bringing back the one she liked?

Taking a deep breath, she climbed out of bed, went to the kitchen, and removed the two bottles of wine from the refrigerator.

One was half full, and the other hadn't been unsealed. She yanked the cork out of the opened bottle and poured the liquid down the drain.

She uncorked bottle number two and did the same thing.

Now, there was no wine in the house. And she would get through this day without that damn shit.

Next, she pulled out the vacuum cleaner, and cleaning supplies and made the house spotless.

While dusting, she thought about dinner. When Warren came home tonight, he'd receive a delicious, piping hot meal. She inspected the fridge and the pickings were slim.

She hadn't shopped in weeks.

She washed her face, put on a little lipstick, dressed casually in jeans and sneakers, and climbed in her Volvo and drove to Super Fresh to buy groceries.

After cooking, she wanted to spruce herself up and she remembered that her lip paint was almost history. So, she made a sudden left and pulled into her favorite department store to buy a tube.

En route to the cosmetics department, she took in the smell of leather and fragrances. Out of the corner of her eye, she spotted the beauty salon.

A young black woman was sitting in a swivel chair, reading a tabloid looking magazine.

Without thinking, Felicia touched her hair. She knew it looked a mess. She couldn't remember the last time she had washed it. She should buzz Angie, but more than likely, there would be waiting involved. And the department store salon wasn't busy. The only customer was a wrinkled white woman, sitting under a dryer, reading a Belva Plain paperback.

Felicia entered the salon.

"Can I help you?" asked the girl, who was reading the magazine. Felicia discovered that it was *Soap Opera Weekly.*

"I hope you can," Felicia said. She touched her hair. "I'd like to get this done. I don't have an appointment."

"Oh, that's not important," the girl said. "I can take care of you. My name is Zora Neale. But everybody calls me Z." Another stylist, off in a corner, eating Chinese food smiled at Felicia. Felicia figured that she was taking care of the Belva Plain fan.

"Your mother named you after Zora Neale Hurston?" Felicia asked.

"Yeah, she's an English teacher. But my last name is Lawson."

"Oh, I was an English major," Felicia said.

Z shampooed, conditioned and styled Felicia's hair.

And Felicia was most impressed with Z's work. It surpassed Angie's. She felt disloyal even thinking that, but with Angie she had to wait a few days before she appreciated the look.

The bill was 34.75 and Felicia gave the hairdresser a fifty-dollar bill and told her to keep the change.

She bounced to the cosmetics department, and after buying lipstick, she drove to the grocery store, filling a cart with fruits, vegetables, meats, juices, milk, coffee, potato chips, canned cashews, cookies, and a block of baking chocolate to make a cake today or tomorrow.

She felt magnificent and it had been a long time since that was the case.

# Chapter 23

At home, she bathed, applied a little makeup, and dressed casually in pants and a blouse. Warren looked perplexed when he entered the house, and found her in the kitchen, slicing mushrooms instead of lying across the bed, with a glass of wine nearby. "Hey. How you doing?" he asked, opening the fridge and getting a pitcher of tea that she had made that afternoon. He poured a glass.

"I'm great," she said. "How was your day?"

"Hectic. But you know, I like keeping busy." For a few minutes, they discussed his day, and how he knew he was going to lose a case because his client was clearly lying, and the judge will see right through it.

Dumping steaming egg noodles in a colander, Felicia suggested Warren grab a shower. "Dinner will be ready in about fifteen minutes."

He drained his tea glass, left the kitchen, and when he returned, he was dressed casually and smelling of Ban deodorant and Dial soap.

She served dinner in the kitchen. She had thought about doing so in the dining room, but she decided to take baby steps at trying to restore their life to normal. They ate roast chicken, noodles in a Parmesan cheese sauce and broccoli with mushrooms.

To some people, Felicia and Warren's traditional marriage might seem like something out of another era, but it was the home life that they both wanted. She stayed home and took care of the house and he went to work.

But her girlfriends had ridiculed her about being the little wifey and a black Betty Crocker and she couldn't understand their jibes.

For heaven's sake, to avoid smog, traffic jams and school violence, some people relocated to more rural settings. She and Warren simply wanted a more conventional family life. Story over.

"This food is magnificent," he said, scooping a second helping of noodles from the serving bowl.

She smiled. "Glad you like it."

Sprinkling salt on the pasta, he said, "It's been a long time since we've had a moment like this."

"I know."

"I've missed it." Frowning, he added, "But I'm confused. What gives?"

Putting down her glass of ice tea, she shrugged. "As old hat as it may sound, I woke up this morning, and I said, 'Enough.' I didn't like what had become of my life. And I wanted to be my old self again. So, I threw out the wine, not against the wall," she joked. "And I spent the day cooking and cleaning and having fun while doing it."

"And you fixed yourself up," he said, looking at her admiringly.

She blushed. "Yeah."

"You look lovely. Like your hair." Mentioning her hair made him think of Angie, and she was the last person that he wanted to think of at this moment. Actually, he didn't want to think of her at any time.

"I went to the salon," she said.

"You saw Angie?" he asked, playing it cool.

"No. To a department store."

"Oh," he said, relieved. He wished that Felicia would cut all ties with Angie, never go around her again. Women were very intuitive. They could pick up on things. He didn't want Felicia in Angie's company, and sensing what happened. "Well, it looks better than it does when Angie styles it." And he meant that.

"Yeah, I think so too."

"You should have the other person do it all the time." *Man, I'd really like that.* It would keep Felicia away from Angie.

"Oh, I couldn't do that," she objected, stabbing a spear of broccoli. "It would be disloyal to Angie. I could never turn on her. I believe in being loyal to my friends."

*Talk about an appetite suppressant,* Warren thought, feeling like a heel.

After dinner, she washed the dishes and he dried, and it was a little awkward between them. They were like two people becoming acquainted, not sure of boundaries, or what topics were okay and what was considered intrusive.

Later, they watched some TV. He was going to look over some briefs, but the documents weren't pressing, and he'd prefer to spend time with Felicia.

And that night, they made love and it was sweet and satisfying. And afterwards, he didn't feel guilty, unlike he had with Angie. When he left her apartment, he felt like a shoplifter with merchandise crammed in his pockets, shifting his eyes from left to right, feeling self-conscious about who may see him.

And after making love to Felicia, he lay awake, in the dark, while his beautiful wife slept quietly next to him. He was glad she was back. But he cringed when he considered that he hadn't been with Angie just that one time.

Oh, no. He had been with her several times afterwards. He had been going to her apartment in the afternoon, and having sex with her, and enjoying her tongue on his balls. And using her body to take care of his needs.

And so that she wouldn't feel like he thought of her as some pick up in the red light district, a few times, he sent her flowers and took her to a faraway place for lunch.

She had fretted about being short of the rent money, and he gave her $300 to add to what she had. It was the least he could do. Sometimes he felt like he was using her, which made him feel guilty.

She had said that she had feelings for him, but he didn't feel the same. He liked Angie, but he loved his wife, and despite enjoying sex with Angie, he never stopped loving Felicia. He had seriously considered giving Felicia an ultimatum, telling her to clean up her act, or he was out the door. He was going to rent an apartment, which would have given him the freedom to do as he damn well pleased, guilt-free.

But how could he walk out on his wife when she needed him?

And he wanted to get out of that situation with Angie. He wanted to end the affair. He was going to end it.

# Chapter 24

Angie was at work, sweeping sheared hair into a dustpan and dumping it in the wastebasket. She didn't have another appointment for forty-five minutes. So, she decided to go to Uncle Sam's, the little hot dog place in the shopping center and buy a bottle of water. Out of courtesy, she asked the patrons and the other stylists if they wanted anything. Nobody did.

Walking to the store, she wondered about Warren. She hadn't heard from him in over a week. And they had been fucking a couple of times a week. And he had taken her to lunch and bought her flowers, and soon, he would be hers.

As Angie was emerging from the hot dog establishment, a Contour drove by and when she made eye contact with the driver, he quickly switched his eyes in the opposite direction.

She frowned. There was something familiar about that person. Crossing the pavement to the salon, the name Darnell popped in her mind.

Was that Darnell Moody?

Hmm. Maybe it could have been someone who resembled Darnell. Darnell wasn't a bad looking dude, but his looks didn't stand out in a crowd. Men who looked like Darnell were as commonplace as chewing gum in a vending machine.

But then she considered how rapidly the driver had turned his head when they made eye contact.

Maybe, she was just being paranoid, and even if it was Darnell, who gave a shit?

# Chapter 25

"Well, you sound chipper," Denise said to Felicia. It was a Sunday afternoon and they were chatting long-distance.

"I am," Felicia replied. The other times they talked, Felicia hadn't felt chipper and evidently, Denise picked up on it. Denise knew that Felicia was having trouble dealing with her infertility, but she didn't know about the excessive wine drinking, or that Felicia had distanced herself from Warren.

Denise said, "So, what's put you in this good mood?"

"Well, I can't have children. And I'm making my peace with it. I have a lovely home, a wonderful husband, talent, a terrific sister; some great friends."

"So you've been counting your blessings?" Denise stated.

Felicia nodded. "Yeah. When we're hurt and disappointed, we tend to zero in on what's hurting us, and asking ourselves, 'Why me?' We forget about our good fortunes, and what we have to be grateful for. And that's what we should concentrate on."

"And you do have a lot to be grateful for," Denise said.

"I know," Felicia replied.

"And you and Warren can adopt, or get a surrogate."

Surrogate. Felicia raised her upper lip at the thought. "Warren and I will get around to discussing adoption."

"You'd make a great mom, Felicia. You were, so good with Laquita. And speaking of blessings, some little angel out there who will get you and Warren as parents will receive one."

Denise's sweet words made Felicia choke up. "Enough schmaltz," she said, and sniffed. "So, what's happening with you? How's the diet going?"

"So far, I've lost twenty one pounds," Denise revealed, sounding happy.

"Yay," Felicia cheered like a two-year old that got what she wanted for Christmas.

"Yeah, but girl, that's just a drop in the proverbial pail. I have a lot more to lose."

"But you're making progress," Felicia said. "That's the point."

Denise sighed. "It hasn't been easy. You know, how much I love Kentucky Fried, and pizza…food, period. And girl, do I miss my Pepsis. Every time I got thirsty, I would grab one. And every afternoon, I'd have a Snickers."

"But you've stopped doing that?" Felicia asked.

"Sort of."

Felicia frowned. "I don't understand."

"Oh, I still have the foods I enjoy. I'm a whore for junk foods. What can I say?" she joked.

"Yet, you're still losing weight?" Felicia asked, frowning. Now, how could Denise still be eating high calorie goodies, yet still shedding pounds? *Oh, God.* "Denise, don't tell me that you're eating till your heart's content and then sticking your fingers down your throat to regurgitate?

Denise chuckled. "Girl, stop talking like a fool. You know, I wouldn't do no shit like that. White women do that mess. They're always striving for perfection."

Yeah, on second thought, Felicia should have known better. Denise was strong and sensible. "Then how are you eating yummy foods and still getting thin?"

"Well, for the most part, I eat fresh veggies, and baked fish. Love orange roughy. And instead of having a six pack of Pepsi a day, I allow myself one can. When I get parched, I drink sparkling water—the fruit flavored stuff. Comes in lemon, lime and orange, and has zero calories. It's a great substitute for soda." She paused. "And girl, for years, I've been having a passionate love affair with Colonel Sanders. I'm addicted to that white-haired old man. He ain't as good as he used to be, but he's still finger lickin' good."

Felicia cackled. "Niecy, you're a lunatic."

"So, once a week, I treat myself to Kentucky Fried, but instead of gobbling an eight piece bucket, now, I just have a breast and a wing. And I still have a Snickers bar everyday. But I have a fun-size bar instead of the size that is found at the checkout counter at the grocery store. I keep a bag of fun-size on hand. And I only allow myself one a day."

"So, you're still having the stuff you like only in moderation?" Felicia stated.

Denise sighed. "Yeah, and the pounds are dropping off."

"That's wonderful, Denise."

"My tops aren't as tight across the shoulders and back. My pants are looser. Even, my shoes aren't as snug."

"How does Eugene feel about what you're accomplishing?"

"He's not exactly throwing up pom-poms."

"Well, that's strange. You'd think he'd be happy that you were doing something positive for yourself."

"Yeah, you'd *think*. But Eugene feels that my weight loss is harming our relationship."

"How?" Felicia asked, totally baffled.

Denise sighed. "In the beginning, our relationship was about food and eating. For us, a good time was hitting all-you-can-eat-buffets, going back for fourths and fifths. At night, while watching TV, we'd each have a pint of Haagen Dazs and split a Sara Lee cheesecake. Girl, Eugene and I ate."

"Yeah, I've seen you two in action," Felicia teased.

"And eating is still important to Eugene. And I think it bothers him that I'm no longer his eating buddy."

"Well, I've heard of people drifting apart because one drinks alcohol and the other gave it up," Felicia said.

"That's what's going on here, but the thing that was keeping us together was food."

"*Was keeping us together*," Felicia said. "Are you saying that you guys may break up because you're trimming down?"

Denise sighed. "I don't know."

"Well, Eugene isn't a stupid man. I don't think he'd call it quits with you because you're losing weight." How dumb did that sound, Felicia thought.

"We'll see," Denise said doubtfully. "My goal is to become a size ten, and I'm not giving that up for anybody."

Eventually, Felicia and Denise said, "I love you...take care, and goodbye." As Felicia was putting down the phone, and feeling warm inside because she had spoken to her favorite sister, Warren entered the room, and suggested a trip to the movies. "Well, that sounds, nice," she said pleasantly. "What would you like to see?"

"You make the selection," he said.

She laughed. "Well, you know, I'm into 'chick flicks.' And you don't have to sit through a movie that doesn't interest you just to please me."

"Well, I crave action," he countered. "And you don't have to sit through a movie that doesn't interest you to please me." He playfully stuck out his tongue.

"So, we're at a stalemate," she said.

"Hey, let's compromise," he offered. "You pick the flick this time, and when we see another, I'll pick."

She nodded. "Fair enough." They agreed to see a movie with Jennifer Lopez playing an abused wife.

***

Things were getting better between Felicia and Warren. They were cracking jokes, going to movies...to dinner...getting together for

114

lunch…out shopping. He loved her taste in clothes and, he asked her to help him pick out shirts and ties.

One Saturday night, they went dancing at a nightspot.

Felicia was once again spending time with the neighborhood women, eating their coffeecakes, and cookies, and them eating hers. And she had resumed her writing. And her good spirits reflected in her work. She was her worst critic, but even to her own ears, her work sounded animated, enthusiastic. Crackling.

She told Denise to take snapshots of her weight loss journey. Felicia was going to roll up her sleeves and finally get around to penning that article about what Denise was going through, losing weight but not completely eliminating the things she enjoyed.

Her sister's experience could benefit a lot of women. So, Felicia would write the piece, and send it to one of the women's magazines, which offered nonstop articles on taking off pounds.

*It feels magnificent to be back,* Felicia thought, to be taking care of her house, writing, and loving and enjoying her husband.

It was like she had been on a vacation, and she was back home. And it felt great.

# Chapter 26

Felicia and Warren were in the dining room, eating by candlelight. No special occasion, just her way of keeping romance in their marriage.

Marinated vegetables, pasta and chicken Normandy was in front of them. He pushed a piece of zucchini around his plate, clearly in no mood for food.

And Felicia thought the meal tasted divine.

His lack of appetite reinforced her feeling that something was troubling him. Since coming in from work, he had been unusually quiet, offering no stories about a client, or how his day went. He just came in, mumbled a greeting, went upstairs and showered.

When she moved her lips to ask him what was on his mind, he said, "Felicia, we need to talk." His tone was solemn. What was going on?

Horrible thoughts raced through her mind.

Were they on the verge of bankruptcy?

Was Warren or a member of his family diagnosed with a horrible disease? "Wh-what's going on?" she asked anxiously.

He blew out the flames, rose from the chair, clicked on the light, bringing the beautifully decorated room into view, making her squint from the brightness.

Back in his seat, he took a deep breath. "Angie dropped by my office today."

Felicia looked baffled. She shrugged. "Well...uh, does she have some legal problem that she needs you to handle for her?" But why would Warren be upset about that?

He laughed cheerlessly. "I wish that was it."

"Warren, what's going on?"

"Angie's pregnant," he said, practically blurting it out.

Felicia frowned. "Well, that's some tidbit. I didn't realize she was seriously involved with anyone." But until recently, Felicia had cloistered herself from the world, not being much of a friend to Angie or anybody. "I guess I don't know everything about her. But I don't understand, why did she tell you that she was pregnant...what does it have to do with you?"

Wearing a hand-caught-in-the-cookie-jar expression, he looked down at his plate.

Felicia shifted her eyes from left to right, her thoughts working overtime. *Angie's pregnant. Warren is upset about it. Why? Could Warren be? No, uh-uh. No.* A lump formed in her throat.

In a quivering voice, he confessed, "I'm the baby's father."

*Oh, dear Lord!* Suddenly, her body started to quiver. To steady herself, she put her elbows on the table. "You and Angie had an affair?" she hissed, and grabbed her goblet of water and took a gulp, spilling some onto her chin. She wiped it off with the back of her hand. "Dumb question, Felicia," she said to herself. "Of course, you had an affair with Angie. She's carrying your baby." Her eyes became huge. "You son-of-a-bitch!" she screamed.

"Felicia, look, I—"

"What are you going to say, Warren?" she spat. "What the hell can you possibly say? But let me ask you something, do the words *forsaking all others* have a familiar ring to you? It was part of the vows you made to me on the day we got married. Or did they slip your mind?" She took a deep breath. "How could you do this? Why?" she shrieked, her face twisted with anger and confusion.

"We were having problems," he said. "The infertility thing. You weren't dealing with it very well."

"And that's your reason for betraying me?" she exploded. "And with of all people—a friend. A *supposed* friend. Oh, God!" She made a fist, and pounded the table, causing the forks, knives and spoons to clatter against the plates. "Oh, I've got to hand it to you, and Angie, that lowdown bitch...that whore. The two of you are good at hiding things. I never suspected a thing...She smiled in my face, played the caring friend. And you...gave me the loving, loyal husband routine." She shook her head. And for a moment, no words were spoken as she absorbed Warren's revelation.

He parted his lips to speak.

"I feel like a fool," she spat. "A first-class idiot." She sighed angrily.

Wearing a crushed expression, he stroked her hand with his fingertips.

The supposedly comforting gesture only strengthened her fury. This man had broken her goddamn heart, and now he was trying to *soothe* her. What was this? She felt like he was ridiculing her, jeering her. "Man, get the hell away from me," she yelled, snatching away her hand like she had touched a scorching lid.

Her face felt like it was on fire. Breathing had become a struggle. She sounded like an asthmatic gasping for air.

She wanted to claw the son-of-a-bitch, bang him with her fists, but she willed herself not to lash out. She had to get away before she did something she'd regret. Like commit homicide. She jumped up from the table. Her thigh pounded the edge, causing it to wobble. Cutlery and china clattered a second time. Water lapped precariously over the rim of the two goblets.

She stamped to the five carpeted steps leading to their bedroom. Warren was behind her, grabbing for her hand. "Felicia, we need to talk."

He managed to get hold of her wrist.

"Get your damn hands off me," she shrieked, yanking away.

"But we have to talk this thing out."

She wheeled around to face him. "There's nothing to talk out. You fucked my so-called best friend, and now she's pregnant with your love child. So, what's there to say?"

"Plenty."

She stormed into their bedroom, snatched her purse off the Queen Ann chair, and turned to exit the room. He tried to grab the pocketbook from her. "Where are you going?" he asked.

"None of your *goddamn* business," she snarled. She knew how much Warren loathed the word, goddamn. And right now, annoying him was enormously satisfying.

He made another grab for her purse, but she clutched it like an alcoholic refusing to release a bottle of vodka.

"I'm not letting you leave," he said, blocking her path.

"Oh, just try to stop me!" And his aggressiveness pissed her off even more. The jerk betrayed her, and she wanted to get as far away from him as possible. And fast. And he was telling her to listen to his garbage.

As if fighting off a mugger, she beat him over the head with her purse.

"Felicia, cut it out," he said, making an X with his forearms and using them to shield her blows. "This is childish."

"Well, leave me the fuck alone." She stormed out of the bedroom.

"Where are you going?" he repeated, trailing her down the carpeted hall.

Ignoring him, she descended the steps.

"We need to talk, Felicia," he said.

"You want a conversation, go talk to the mother-of-your child." She yanked open the door, flounced out in the muggy July night, climbed in her Volvo, and sped off, leaving Warren on the front porch, looking defeated.

***

Tears were in Felicia's eyes, but her pride refused to let them flow. At the house, she had wanted to cry, but she forced herself not to.

It was late summer, and twilight was approaching. The sky had been painted tangerine. With no destination in mind, she burned rubber down Jefferson Avenue, and like a racecar driver, jumped lanes, without bothering to signal.

Motorists responded with angry toots. "Go to driving school, bitch!" a man yelled from a mini van. In the backseat were two kids who appeared highly amused by the spectacle.

118

*Pull it together before you cause a pileup,* Felicia cautioned herself and began driving more conscientiously.

*Where the hell am I going?*

She certainly couldn't take this to any of her friends. In a heartbeat, they'd see that she was upset, and they'd bombard her with questions. 'What's wrong?'

'Talk to me.'

And her husband knocking up another woman was not a topic she was in a mood to discuss.

When she saw the bright red lights of a Hampton Inn beckoning lodgers to come in and take a load off, she slowed, made a left turn, pulled into a parking space, squeezing between a Jeep and a Honda.

Entering the lobby, she saw an old man sitting in a leather chair, reading a *Time* magazine.

She went to the front desk. "I'd like a room," she told the gum-chewing desk clerk who was white and looked about twenty and was reading a *Jughead and Archie* comic magazine.

She laid the funnies down. And in a who-cares attitude, asked, "For how many?" She blew a gigantic bubble.

Felicia frowned. "What?" Her mind was still on what happened back at the house.

The girl snapped the gum, startling Felicia. "How many people will use the room?" Miss Desk Clerk asked, annoyed.

"Uh, just me," Felicia said.

"For how long?"

Felicia scowled. "How long?"

The girl pulled a perturbed face. "Yeah. How many days do you want the room?"

Felicia didn't know. All she knew was that she wanted time away from her underhanded husband, and that the desk clerk was highly unprofessional and should be reported to the hotel's customer service department. "A few days." She shrugged.

"Can you be more specific?"

"Three," Felicia snapped. "And you know something, you're a rude little bitch that should be fired."

The girl's face turned the color of a cherry tomato. She ceased chewing her gum. And suddenly, began acting gracious and business-like.

After going through the credit card and signing in routine, Felicia received the key to her room and took the elevator to the sixth floor.

She located her room. It was the same old, same old.

*Pamela Hayes*

There was a queen-sized bed covered with a cheap, heavy blanket and a 19-inch TV perched on a cart.

Sighing, she dropped down on the bed. And after a few minutes in the impersonal space, she grew restless. She wished she had her laptop.

A little work would help take her mind off her troubles.

*I've got to get the hell out of here,* she thought, jumping off the bed.

Out in the hall, for the second time, she frowned at the oppressive stuffiness. The air conditioning must be on the lowest setting.

A black man was at an ice machine, scooping out cubes and tossing them into a bucket. He smiled at Felicia.

"How you doing?" she said like the gracious southern lady that she was.

Outside a door, she saw a room service tray. On a plate were the remnants of a meal. There was smeared steak sauce, a steak bone with a fly on top, a baked potato skin and a coffee cup containing a little cold coffee with curdled milk.

Disgusting.

In the dark, she walked to a shopping center behind the hotel. And entered a Giant Food store, picking up a ballpoint and a spiral notebook, and a Danielle Steel paperback.

God, she felt like shit. And wanting to eradicate that feeling sent her over to the beer and wine cooler. She regarded the stock. There was Glen Ellen, Turning Leaf, Kendall Jackson, Woodbridge, Korbel, in dark green bottles, in various sizes—four pack single-servings, 750 milliliters, 1.5 liters, and magnums.

And Glen was her preference. That boy had what it took to make her feel better. But at the same time, he brought her agony. He was like a lover who she knew was no damn good for her, but no one made her feel the way he did. She hated Glen, but at the same time, she needed him. She put her hand around his neck and lifted him from the shelf. But she didn't remove him. Frowning, she knew that she couldn't let herself start tippling again.

But she was miserable and the Glen Ellen would improve her frame of mind, would distance her from the heartbreak.

But she couldn't do it.

But, finding out that her husband knocked up another woman when she couldn't even have a child was sufficient reason to get buzzed.

But this revelation was different from ascertaining that she couldn't have a child.

She had desperately wanted to be a mother and it was physically impossible. And that crushed her. But she refused to let an unfaithful man drive her to the wine bottle. *Nah, honey, don't let no man drive you to self-destructive behavior,* counseled her inner voice.

120

She had to find another pick-me-up. She took her hand off the neck of the wine bottle and went to the produce section and threw her favorite pieces of allsorts—as the British called assorted candy—into a plastic sack.

When she was in college, and became overwhelmed by her course load, or when Sandra moved, taking Laquita with her, confections were a supportive friend.

So, maybe it could once again bring her the comfort she needed, but she knew that it would take more than a lump of butterscotch to make her feel better about Warren's betrayal.

At the check-stand, she paid for her items and went back to the room.

At the escritoire, she thought about a story she had in mind, and tried to do a little work on it, but she couldn't concentrate.

She took the novel to the bed and got as cozy as she could on the lumpy mattress, and started reading. But she couldn't make any sense of the words, sentences and paragraphs. It was like trying to read a foreign language edition of the book. Placing it on the night table, she thought of Angie...

Slut.

Liar.

Whore.

Tramp.

Two-faced bitch.

Pretending to be her friend, laughing with her, joking with her, lunching and shopping with her.

And a few times, Angie saw shoes or a purse that caught her eye, but she couldn't afford at that moment, so Felicia would charge the goods on her MasterCard and let Angie reimburse her when she could.

Felicia considered the bitch a friend, and friends did things like that for each other. And look where being a trusting pal got her.

She took a deep breath and twisted her face in confusion. *How could anyone be so duplicitous?*

"You're so lucky to have a man like Warren," Angie had said. "He's handsome and successful. Maybe, one day, I'll meet someone just like him."

"Ooh," Felicia muttered, shaking her head. She pounded a fist against the mattress. *God, that woman is terrible...a horrible human being. Human being? What a joke.*

Felicia recalled when Angie had come to the house and styled her hair, and refused payment for it.

Playing the good friend, wanting to do something to make me feel better.

And when Warren suggested that Felicia go into counseling, which had infuriated her, and Angie, the good friend, told Felicia that she didn't need to see a therapist. "Girl, you are not crazy," Angie had said. "You received some devastating news, and you're having a difficult time dealing with it. I don't think you need to talk to a professional."

*That bitch didn't want me to see a therapist because a therapist could have put me on the right road. And Angie didn't want that. No, sir. She wanted me drinking, depressed, so that I'd becoming disgusting to Warren.*

"You fucking bitch," she snarled as if her opponent was facing her.

Those stifled tears finally slid down Felicia's cheeks. She let them flow…And flow, they did, running under her chin and trickling down her neck, saturating the collar of her dress. She removed them with her fingertips, and crying brought a little relief.

She felt betrayal, exploitation; hurt.

She felt ridiculed, mocked. Laughed at. Oh, yeah, she'd bet Angie was laughing her head off at how stupid she was.

Sighing, she thought, *I have to talk this out with somebody, or I'll explode.* She grabbed the phone from the night table, depressed nine for a long distance call. After a few rings, Denise answered.

"Well, it ain't Sunday, or no major holiday, so what's going on?" Denise asked.

Felicia poured out the story.

"That no good motherfucker—" Denise yelled. "Felicia, I'm so sorry Warren hurt you like this," she said soothingly.

"You didn't do it, so you have nothing to apologize for."

"Girl, you're my sister and when you're hurting, I'm hurting." Her tone became hard. "And after I talk to you, I'm going to call that shit head, and give him a piece of my mind. I wish I were there to hug you," she said gently, "to give you some Kleenex. You poor darling."

It felt wonderful having Denise's support. Felicia took a deep breath. "There's more."

"More?" Denise spluttered. Felicia imagined Denise frowning up a storm. "What the hell more can there be? Did Warren's plaything give him a venereal disease? Did he pass it on to you?"

"Nothing like that."

"Then what? Is the home-wrecker pregnant?"

"Bingo," Felicia said.

"Lord have mercy. I don't believe this mess."

"And I thought she was a friend."

"Well, now, you know that she's a back-stabbing hussy. Ain't enough words in the thesaurus to describe how awful that tramp is. And Warren's lowdown too. If he had testicular cancer and had to have his balls cut out, I wouldn't feel an ounce of pity."

*That's strong,* Felicia thought. "Angie," she said.

"Who the fuck is Angie?" Denise snapped.

"The woman Warren had the affair with. She—"

"You mean, the slut, the tramp, the strumpet, the no-good piece of shit," Denise corrected.

"Well, she knows I can't have children."

"I assume she got this bit of info from Warren, maybe during pillow talk?" Denise asked sarcastically.

"Actually, Sandra told her and I confirmed it."

"Leave it to oh big mouth Sandra to tell something so private?" Denise stated. She firmly believed that you didn't share your problems with anybody but close family members.

Felicia sighed. "And Angie knows how inadequate and unwomanly I feel because I can't have children."

"Felicia, you're no less of a woman because you can't pop out a baby. I've told you that before."

"I know."

For a moment, there was silence, and then Denise spoke, sounding reflective. "Warren wants a baby?"

"Very much," Felicia said. "You know that."

"Mm-hmm," Denise said.

"What are you thinking?"

"I bet that tramp thought by getting knocked up that Warren would dump you and marry her."

"Yeah, that crossed my mind too…I wonder if that's what he wants to do."

"Don't be ridiculous," Denise spat. "That man ain't leaving you for that slut."

"But he wants to be a father," Felicia countered.

"I don't care what he wants. He ain't leaving you for that harlot. I mean, girl, as we teachers sometimes tell our students, 'Put your thinking cap on.' Angie has demonstrated that she's no damn good, that she's as worthless as a used postage stamp. Screwing her best friend's husband. Now, what man would want her? What man would trust her? The minute he turned his back, her panties would be off in a corner somewhere. Hell, nah, he don't want that floozy."

Denise's phone clicked. She moaned unhappily. "Hold on a second."

"No. I'm going to hang up," Felicia said.

"Sugar, if you want to keep talking, I can get rid of the caller. It probably ain't nobody but one of those annoying telemarketers, trying to sell somebody music from the sixties."

"Well, the hotel is probably charging me a bundle for this call."

"You're at a hotel?"

"Yeah. I had to get away from Warren."

"Have you walked out on your marriage?"

"Denise, I'm not sure if I have a marriage. I'm not convinced that Warren won't leave me for Angie."

"That's not going to happen."

"Well, I'm not sure I want to be with a cheater," Felicia said. "My head is so messed up right now."

"That's understandable." There was another click. "Girl, you and Warren may be able to work this out. Marriages have been known to survive adultery. Look, I'll be in touch, and any time you need to talk, just pick up that phone and buzz me. I love you." She made a kissing sound.

"Love you too," Felicia said and hung up the phone.

***

Out on the balcony, in the humidity, Felicia wondered, *Does Warren want to divorce me and marry Angie?*

He yearned to be a dad. His "sperm donor" as he called his father deserted the family when Warren was just four.

And during their courtship days, he had told Felicia growing up fatherless was difficult. "What kind of a man would walk out on his family?" he had said. "When I have children, I'm going to be there for them—monetarily and emotionally—from the time they're babies until they're old enough to fend for themselves."

And when they were in the mall, or the park, and Warren spotted a man carrying a tot on his shoulders, or playing ball with a child, Felicia saw craving in his eyes. He wanted to be in that man's position.

God, she despised Angie for being able to give her husband something she could not give him.

And she didn't necessarily agree with Denise's assessment of the situation. Men have left their wives for their mistresses.

And if that's what Warren wanted to do, did Felicia even give a damn? Who needed a cheating bastard for a husband?

She sighed. She was so conflicted.

# Chapter 27

Angie was in her apartment, musing about her future with Warren. Oh, they were going to have a marvelous life together. There would be vacations. She remembered Warren talking about taking Felicia to Europe. Well, she'd make sure that he did the same for her.

When they were husband and wife, she'd go on shopping sprees, buying clothes and anything that her heart desired.

And Angie couldn't wait to gleefully cuss out Carolee, owner of the beauty parlor where Angie worked.

She was going to do it on the salon's busiest day, a Saturday. "Carolee, you're nothing but a tub of lard," she'd say. "Honey, you should steer clear of those Dunkin Doughnuts." She'd tell her to kiss her ass, call her a whore, a bitch, and a slut.

The idea made her smile nastily. And she'd make sure to leave a weave partially done; knowing full well that Carolee or no one on her precious staff knew anything about weaving hair.

Carolee was so preoccupied with the reputation of that place. And a customer being stranded with a weave half done would not lead to repeat business, and glowing recommendations.

Oh, Angie couldn't wait. She'd like to do it tomorrow, but she'd have to put it off until she and Warren were happily married.

And the precise date of that event was anybody's guess. First, he had to unload Felicia.

Angie was going to suggest one of those quickie divorces.

She wondered if she and Warren would buy a new house, or move into the one he currently shares with Felicia. Of course, he'd have to toss Felicia out, literally kick her to the curb.

It was a nice house, and Angie would enjoy living there. Of course, she'd redecorate, give it her own touch.

She placed her hand on her stomach. Oh, yeah, the baby growing inside her was a passport to a better life.

A few days ago, she had told Warren that she was pregnant. She hadn't seen him in days, and she called his office and asked him to drop by.

"Now, isn't a good time," he had said.

"It's important that I see you," she countered.

"Uh, what's up?" he asked, sounding annoyed.

125

She wondered if he had been feeling guilty about their affair, which was why he hadn't been coming around. But she figured that the baby news would put a smile on his face.

"I'd prefer to tell you in person," she said.

"As I said, it isn't a good day. I'm swamped, and I have two appointments this afternoon. So please, tell me, what's on your mind?"

"I'm pregnant," she announced.

There was a lengthy pause. Finally, he sighed. "Wow!"

"How do you feel about it?"

"I'm, uh…thrown," he said.

Not surprising. He probably figured that he'd never hear a woman utter those words to him.

"Well, how are we going to handle this?" she asked, pretending to be scared and uncertain.

He sighed again. "Angie, I'm married to another woman, and you're telling me that you're going to have my baby. This is complicated, you know."

"Don't you want this baby?" she asked.

"Well, yes," he replied without hesitation. "We can work this out. As I said, it's complicated, but it can be worked out. Don't worry. I'll take care of things. We'll iron this out."

Coming out of her flashback, she nodded smugly. So, yes, he was going to tell Felicia aloha, and marry her. Isn't that what he meant when he said, 'We'll work this out.'

A knock on the door interrupted her reverie. She looked through the peephole and she wasn't surprised to see her visitor. She had expected the person to drop by. She opened the door.

"Come in," she said.

Felicia entered the apartment and stood in the middle of the room while Angie closed the door. "You know, I had a feeling that I'd hear something from you," Angie sang snidely. "And what do you want?" She took in Felicia's appearance, and was surprised by her look. Her makeup, hair and clothes were perfect. And she smelled of perfume instead of Chardonnay.

Angie guessed the wino had some pride, after all. Couldn't call on her husband's fiancée looking shabby and smelling like a wine bottle.

Felicia moved closer to Angie. "You bitch," she snarled.

"Now, why would you say such a thing to me?" Angie asked, unfazed.

"Warren told me," Felicia said.

"Told you what?"

"Stop playing these silly games," Felicia snapped. "Warren told me that you're pregnant."

"What of it?"

"Well, I wonder if it's Warren's child."

"I can assure you that it is," Angie said.

"And considering that you're a back-stabbing, two-faced liar, why should I believe a word you say? I mean, you pretended to be my friend, and you messed around with my husband. You're untrustworthy."

"Is that right?"

"Damn straight. So, it is possible that you were fucking another man at the same time that you were fucking Warren, and that that other man could be the father of that little bastard you're carrying."

"But at least, I can carry a little bastard," Angie said snidely. "Can you make the same claim?" She smiled nastily.

Felicia could not believe this. This was literally a nightmare. Who was this nasty woman standing before her? Angie had styled her hair, laughed and joked with her. They had gone shopping, and shared subs at the pizza place. Angie had sat in her backyard and listened to music and jabbered.

"And I'm sure you'd like for another man to be this baby's father," Angie shot. "But you see, wino girl...that isn't even a remote possibility. I haven't been with anybody but your husband. Now, I'm not stupid. I knew that after I became pregnant, that the baby's paternity would be questioned, which is why I avoided all other men." She took a deep breath. "So, a paternity test can prove that Warren is this baby's dear old dad. And besides, who gives a damn what you think?" She sighed extravagantly. "Warren believes me. That's all that matters. And he and I are going to be married."

Felicia frowned. "Is that your fantasy? Or are you using hallucinogenic drugs?"

"It's going to happen," Angie said. "Warren proposed."

"I don't believe you," Felicia snapped.

"I don't care what you believe," Angie said airily. "He wants this baby." She placed her hand on her stomach. "And I can give him this child and another one if his little heart desires. We're going to have a wonderful life together."

Felicia had to get the hell out of there before she smashed her fist in that vile woman's face, hurting her and her unborn child.

# Chapter 28

Yawning, Felicia opened her eyes, and looked at the clock on the bedside table. It was 9:17. She rose to a sitting position.

All night, she had tossed and turned, sighed and fluffed pillows, trying to become acclimated to the hotel bed, to different surroundings.

This was the second time in six years that she woke without Warren next to her.

When she threw that wine bottle against the wall, he had slept in the spare room.

Last night, in bed, she watched *Will and Grace* and *ER*, and during the commercial breaks, she hit the mute button on the remote control and read.

But her mind hadn't been on the TV shows or the book. She was merely trying to keep herself from going over the edge.

For a brief moment, she considered giving Warren a courtesy call, letting him know that she was safe and sound. But why would he care if she were lying in a ditch dead? After all, he was going to divorce her and marry his pregnant mistress.

But Angie may not be telling the truth? The woman was a damn liar and she could very well be yanking Felicia's chain.

Besides, Warren proposing to her could very easily be verified. All Felicia had to do was ask Warren.

But on second thought, maybe Angie was leveling with Felicia. Last evening, Warren was eager to talk to Felicia, and she refused to wait around and listen to what he had to say. Now, she wondered if he was going to tell her that he wanted a divorce so that he could marry Angie?

Sighing, she rolled out of bed, went to the bathroom, and peed. "Damn," she muttered when she discovered that there was no complimentary toothbrush or toothpaste. Well, she'd just have to go around with stale breath until she got near utensils to clean her mouth.

She flinched at her reflection in the mirror. Her eyes were bloodshot and her skin was drawn and haggard, making her looked a decade older.

She always looked a fright if she didn't sleep undisturbed for at least six hours.

And she needed fresh clothes, a toothbrush, and some Crest. But all that stuff was at home. She wanted to go and collect them, but she didn't want to bump into Warren.

It was Friday, so he would be at work.

But on the other hand, he probably skipped work, and was at home, waiting to talk to her, to tell her that it was over.

She dialed his private office number and when he answered, she hung up.

And laughed bitterly. She wasn't shocked to discover that he was at work. It proves that he didn't give a damn about her or their marriage. How else could he concentrate on depositions and bankruptcy petitions? So, that bitch was probably telling the truth that Warren wanted to marry her.

Well, fuck you, Warren Wainwright. I'll be okay.

Her grumbling stomach reminded her that she hadn't eaten since last night's aborted romantic dinner. Well, she had had a few pieces of the allsorts. The bag was on the nightstand. She thought about grabbing some, but she wanted some real food.

She took her funky breath and pasty mouth to the grocery store behind the hotel, and purchased teeth cleaning supplies.

After doing so, she went down to the gratis continental breakfast in the hotel's lobby, and found a table covered with doughnuts, muffins, single serving size boxes of cereal, pots of coffee, and ewers of milk, and juices. Continental breakfast always sounded so ritzy, making her think of crepes Suzettes, croissants, or eggs benedict. But alas, things weren't always as they sounded.

People milled about, enjoying the freebies.

Felicia grabbed a powdered doughnut, coffee and orange juice, hardly real food.

After eating, she drove to the house, put her makeup and some clothes into a suitcase; grabbed her laptop. Placing the stuff on the backseat of the car, she thought of Bernadine from *Waiting to Exhale*.

Bernadine's husband deserted her for a white woman, and girlfriend burned and sold some of his prized possessions.

Felicia considered taking a page from Bernadine's book, and strutting into the house and annihilating some of Warren's property.

She had been a devoted wife, creating a wonderful home, and because she couldn't become pregnant, that son-of-a-bitch went out and knocked up some whore and is planning on dumping her and marrying the bitch.

So everything he had said about not marrying Felicia for her reproductive system was just a bunch of gibberish to make her feel better.

Yeah, she felt like turning his property into a bonfire, all right.

Sighing, she shook her head. She had to remove these negative, though justifiable thoughts out of her brain.

She would be okay. She had assets, a college degree, which she would put to use. She had writing talent, and she had proven that she could make money from it.

She could survive without Warren.

\*\*\*

Back at the hotel, Felicia donned a one-piece bathing suit, and took her book out to the pool area, which was scattered with a few people.

The blazing sun was toasting a slim white girl, dressed in a barely there two-piece bathing suit, stretched out on a chaise lounge, her eyes concealed by sunglasses.

The girl's tan was lovely, the color of honey. A white woman told Felicia that by the time sun-worshippers reached thirty that their skin was as wrinkled as a shirt that needed ironing.

Felicia found an empty chaise in front of the pool. Splashing around in the chlorinated water was a black man in his twenties, and a chubby white woman and a little boy playing with a beach ball.

Eventually, the man emerged. He was tall, candy bar brown, with a lean, runner's body. He wore swimming trunks.

"Hi," he said, smiling down at Felicia, while drying off his attractive body with a blue towel and dripping water on her paperback.

When he realized what he was doing, he stepped back and said apologetically, "Wow! I'm destroying your book. Sorry." He was very articulate.

"It's okay," she muttered, not wanting to encourage conversation. She went back to reading.

"I'm Keith," he revealed, tossing the towel around his neck, and taking occupancy of the chair next to her.

*Do I care?* Felicia thought.

He explained that he was a computer programmer from San Diego and that he had moved to Willow Oaks just a few months ago. "The humidity here is a *bitch*," he said. "Are you a native?"

"Look, I'm not being rude," she replied politely. "But I'm, uh, not interested." She had considered just taking her book to another section of the pool. That would have given him the message. But she enjoyed her spot and refused to sacrifice it because some guy was trying to score a pickup.

He chuckled. "No offense, but neither am I. Just trying to make conversation."

What the hell was wrong with her? Her husband cheated on her with another woman, and now this guy had no desire to pick her up.

"I had a knock down drag out with my partner," Keith said. "So for a few days, this is my pied-a-terre."

Chuckling, and feeling stupid for jumping to conclusions, she said. "I didn't know. My name's Felicia ... I never would have thought you were...well, you know."

"Gay. It's not a cuss word," he said. "And why didn't you think I was gay? Is it because I don't swish or talk with a lisp?" he joked.

Keith talked about his troubled relationship with Robert. "Right now, we're fighting because Robert wants to play dress up in women's clothes. I have no problem with female impersonators, or drag queens. That is a part of the gay lifestyle, after all. But if I wanted a woman, I would have hooked up with one."

Felicia chuckled.

"You find my life amusing?" he asked.

"No, no," she replied truthfully. "People have every right to be who they are. I'm not laughing at you. I was just amused by this unusual subject matter. I mean, men just don't come up to me everyday, reveal that they're gay and say their boyfriend's want to dress as women."

He nodded. "Gotcha. But I've never hid the key to my diary, so to speak."

"Well, uh, we have something in common," she spluttered.

"Oh?" Keith sang. "Are you fighting with somebody about cross-dressing?" he joked.

She chuckled. "My husband got a so-called friend of mine pregnant." Hey, he opened up to her about his issues, so why not reveal what she was going through?

"Sounds like something off *Young and The Restless*," he kidded.

"And your situation sounds like something off *Jerry Springer*," she retorted, good-naturedly.

"Touché...But I think I have a little bit more class than the guests who appear on *Springer.*"

She rolled her eyes. "Believe me, you do."

"So, you've run away from home because of what happened?"

"Why hang around? My marriage is dead," she said sadly. "Six years down the drain."

"Well, it is possible for your marriage to survive what happened, you know," Keith said sagely. "And for my buck and a half, this is the last place you should be right now. You should be at home, talking this thing out with your old man. Find out where his head is, if he wants to stay with you, or make a life with this other chick."

"He wants to marry her. The bitch stood to my face and gloated that *my husband* proposed to her." Felicia sighed.

Keith shook his head. "I'll bet you wanted to put your fist in his mouth when he said he wanted to marry her."

"He didn't tell me. She did."

"And you believe her?" Keith said, shocked.

"Well, she has to be telling the truth. I mean, all I have to do is ask my husband."

"And that's what you should do. She could be just screwing with you."

But how much sense would that make? Felicia thought, when she could so easily verify what Angie said. And she enjoyed talking to Keith. It was easier discussing this highly personal situation with a stranger than it would be with any of her friends.

And he was right about her needing to talk to Warren. She had to find out where his head was because not knowing what was really going on was driving her nuts.

# Chapter 29

"Where have you been?" Warren asked the following afternoon. Felicia had just entered the living room, carrying her laptop and the suitcase. "I considered calling the police."

Putting her belongings on the floor, she snapped, "Oh, stop pretending to care about me."

"I do care," he said. "I've been worried sick."

"Right, right," she said, not believing a word. "You were so worried that you went to work."

"Felicia, I know you're a responsible person, and that you can take care of yourself. And instead of sitting around here driving myself crazy, I put in some hours at the office. If it makes you feel better, I wasn't working at my optimum. I asked for some continuances because I knew I couldn't give my clients my best."

"You want a divorce?" she blurted. "You want to marry Angie?" The question gushed out of her mouth like uncorked champagne.

He shook his head. "No! I love you. I want us to stay married."

She frowned. "Well, that doesn't jibe with what Angie said."

"You talked to Angie?"

"I went to her apartment. She plunged a knife in my back, so I had a few things to say to her. And the whore told me that you're going to divorce me and marry her."

He snorted. "Well, she's wrong. I want to keep our marriage intact, but she is carrying my child, and there are some things that we have to iron out. Why don't we sit down and discuss it?"

"Why don't we not," Felicia said and headed for the stairs.

He sighed. "Felicia, we're going to have to deal with this."

Standing on the first step, she turned around and said wearily, "I know, but not now. For the past two nights, I've been sleeping in a different bed. The mattress was lumpy. There's a crick in my neck. Right now, I'm not up to having an industrial size discussion about Angie and your illegitimate baby. I just want to go upstairs and relax." Sarcastically, she added, "I'm sure the topic will still be around a few hours from now. Or tomorrow morning."

She entered the Master bathroom, twisted the hot and cold knobs and while the tub filled, she added two capfuls of Summers Eve moisturizing bath. When the tub was a warm froth, she stepped into it.

Heavenly, she thought, sighing extravagantly. She closed her eyes and put her head against the wall behind her.

Angie.

She shook her head. She was not going to think of that tramp. Right now, she was going to delight in the warm, sudsy water.

*God, it's good to be home,* she thought. Dorothy wasn't lying when she said there's no place like home.

After her bath, she got cozy on the king-size bed, and eventually, drifted off to sleep.

\*\*\*

A few hours later, she opened her eyes and sat up, thinking about nothing in particular. Warren appeared in the room. "Hi," he said.

"Hey," she replied, disinterested.

"I made dinner," he said. "There's salad. The cucumbers and tomatoes are great. They're from Mama's garden. And corn on the cob and steaks. Why don't you come downstairs and eat with me?"

"Your menu makes my mouth water," she said. She hadn't had a morsel that day.

"Well, then, that's all the more reason for you to join me."

She wrinkled her nose. "I'll pass."

He frowned. "You just said that you haven't had a bite today, so you must be hungry, yet you're turning down food?"

"Well, what do you expect?"

"I'm not following you."

"I can't just sit there and eat with you, and act as if what happened didn't happen."

"Well, if you want to go on a hunger strike, fine," he said, peevishly. "I was just trying to be nice."

He slumped out of the room, clearly hurt by her rejection.

And she felt badly for hurting his feelings. And she shouldn't. He deserved her icy shoulder.

But wasn't rejecting his offer, self-abuse? After all, she was starving.

But she'd feel awkward sitting at the table with Warren.

*Yeah, but ain't a steak, corn on the cob dripping with butter and salad drizzling with your favorite vinaigrette worth a little awkwardness?*

Hell, yeah, it was, Felicia thought, getting off the bed and taking her salivating mouth downstairs. She entered the kitchen, and found Warren at the table, eating. She got a plate from the cabinet, and put a steak and a steaming ear of corn on it.

The salad was on the table in a wooden bowl, and when she sat, she helped herself to some. For a long time, they ate in awkward silence.

It was like being in a crammed diner and sharing a table with a stranger.

"You're right, the salad is great," she said, having no desire to talk to Warren, but sitting there not saying a word made her feel stupid.

"Yeah, it is," he said.

"Where did you get the corn?" She did all the food shopping and she hadn't purchased any fresh corn.

"A lady from church gave Mama a basketful," he said. "She gave me some."

"It's sweet."

"Yeah, like it's been rolled in sugar," he said.

This was bullshit. "Why did you do it?" she snapped.

"We were having problems. You had found out that you couldn't have children," he answered.

"So you had an affair?" she exclaimed, taking a bite off her ear of corn.

"It wasn't like that."

"Well, what was it like?" she demanded.

He sighed and put down his fork. "Felicia, you were messed up. Devastated. Drinking wine, nonstop."

"I was trying to distance myself from my heartache."

"And you weren't taking care of yourself. You weren't having your hair done, or bothering with fixing yourself up."

"And hey, you boys like looking at pretty things, so your eyes moved in the direction of Angie Porter," she said sarcastically.

"It wasn't like that…You lost interest in yourself. You lost interest in this house. You weren't bothering to clean it. You stopped cooking. You didn't want to go out. You didn't want to do anything but wallow in your disappointment. And you lost interest in me." He paused. "You know, when women come in asking me to handle their divorces…I frequently hear, 'I felt unappreciated. He never took me out. He never complimented me.' Well, guess what? Women aren't the only ones who need to feel appreciated…Men like being told that their tie or sweater looks nice, that their cologne smells nice. Men need to hear their wives tell them that they love them."

She made a face. "What does that have to do with you having sex with Angie?"

"Felicia, you had left me. You didn't pack a suitcase and literally leave this house. But you weren't here. You didn't seem to care about anything but your pain."

"Learning that I couldn't have children was very difficult for me," she said in defense of herself.

"I understand. And I tried to get you to talk to a professional, but you refused to." He took a deep breath. "I didn't know how to handle it."

"So you turned to Angie?" she said.

"I shouldn't have," he said in a tone that barely went above a whisper. "I wish I hadn't, but I did."

"And now she's pregnant?"

Sighing, he took his glass to the refrigerator, and threw a handful of ice cubes into it. Back at the table, he grabbed the pitcher of tea, and poured some over the cubes.

He sipped the drink. "I've thought it all through. And I want to be a father to the baby," he said, back in his seat. "I'm going to support the child...visit the child...Share custody with Angie."

"So you and she will act like a divorced couple raising a child?" Felicia stated sarcastically.

"I guess you could put it that way."

"And you expect me to go along with that?"

"I hope you can. I'm hoping that you can forgive me. Felicia, I want to save this marriage. A marriage can survive an affair if the person who's been betrayed can forgive."

"Well, I want us to stay married?" she stated. "If I didn't, I wouldn't have come back here. So, I'm going to work on forgiving you." She sighed. "But the baby will be a constant reminder of your moments with Angie."

"I know."

For a long time, she looked at him. "What if I asked you to choose between me and the child, who would you pick?"

The question threw him. "Well, uh, Felicia, I want us to grow old together."

"Yeah, you said that, more or less."

"I also want to be a father to my child," he said.

"And I guess the child will spend nights here." Seeing him nod, she added, "The baby will become a permanent part of our lives?"

"Well, um, yes."

"What if I told you that I couldn't live with that, that I flatly refuse to live with it, that I wanted no parts of your child with Angie?"

He frowned. "What are you getting at?"

"Let's say that I told you that you had to make a choice... between me and the baby...Who would—"

"You. If I had to pick between you and the child, I would choose you."

Relief embraced her. She desperately needed to hear Warren say that *she* was uppermost in his life.

"You want me to choose?" he asked, looking scared.

And may God help her, but that mean-spirited part of her personality, the part that rarely emerged, derived pleasure from the sight of it.

But she shook her head. "I'd never ask you to make that kind of sacrifice. And besides, if you gave up your baby for me, eventually, you'd grow to resent me...What kind of a marriage would we have if you resented me?" She took a deep breath. "I don't know. I know how much you want a child. You even mentioned wanting to get a surrogate...So, I just wondered if you had to pick between me and your baby, who would you select?"

"As I said, you."

"Well, you don't have to worry about choosing." She sighed. "I'll treat the baby as if he or she is mine. And I'd never resent a child. That would be stupid. That baby is sweet and innocent, and the baby did not betray me."

"I'm glad you feel that way," he said. "Felicia, I'm going to do everything I can to make this up to you."

She resisted the urge to tell him to kiss her ass. It annoyed the hell out of her when the perpetrator of pain said, 'Oh, I'm so sorry. I'm going to make this up to you.' Those apologies always struck her as hollow and pointless. Maybe he meant it. *We'll see.*

She rose from the table, and began clearing the dishes, and the bottles of steak sauce and salad dressing.

"Well, I'll wash the dishes," he said.

"I don't mind," she remarked. "I need something to do."

"Want me to dry?"

"I'd like to be alone, if you don't mind."

Leaving the kitchen, he said that he was going to the den to watch a little TV. And several minutes later, when her gloved hands were in a sink of steaming sudsy water, washing a plate, she heard Archie Bunker say— *Now, you listen here, meathead.*

Warren loved *All in the Family,* and Archie was no doubt talking to Mike.

Rinsing a glass, Felicia wondered if she was being a meathead for agreeing to work on forgiving Warren. Should she have told the bastard to go to hell, and filed for divorce?

He cheated on her, and who's to say that this was his first affair. For all she knew, he may have done it before.

Why should she tolerate him being a father to an illegitimate child he had with another woman?

Felicia could not have children, and Angie could and Angie rubbed her nose in that. That baby would be an everlasting reminder of that.

But she couldn't resent a little kid. No way.

When she found out that she couldn't have a child, she was crushed. She truly thought she'd crack up, and end up on the funny farm, milking cows.

And Warren wasn't there for her. He was off fucking Angie.

*Oh, he tried to help you,* said her inner voice. Yeah, he did suggest that she talk to a counselor, and try to make peace with being infertile.

But still, he *betrayed* her. And yeah, yeah, she understood that she wasn't herself, and that he may have gotten lonely, and needed someone to talk to. But why didn't he leave it at talking? Why did he have sex with the tramp?

Felicia loved her husband, and she wanted to work this thing out. But a part of her wished that Warren would tell Angie and her fetus to fuck off, that it was her problem.

But deep down, she knew that she'd have zero respect for Warren if he turned his back on his flesh and blood. His father had done that to him, and her pathetic excuse for a father pulled it too. So, how could she make a life with a man, or respect a man who did that to his own kid?

*** 

Later that night, she was sitting in bed, and Warren came into the room, wearing silk boxer shorts and nothing else. His chest and arms illustrated that he worked out at the spa four mornings a week.

He had just showered. She got a whiff of his favorite deodorant soap. He climbed into bed next to her. "Could you hand me my book?" he requested, nodding in the direction of the nightstand. In addition to his John Grisham paperback, there was the novel she was reading.

Without budging, she said, "I wish you'd go away."

He frowned. "Come again"

"You heard me. Why don't you use the guestroom? The bed in there is quite comfortable." She shrugged. "If you like, I can go there."

He sighed. "I don't want to go there, and I don't want you too either. I mean, are we not on the same page here?"

"Well, I'm on page 117. Where are you, on 166?"

He rolled his eyes at her sarcasm. "Earlier, you told me that you had forgiven me. At least, that's what I thought you said."

"I said I was going to *work* on forgiving you. There is a distinction." Her tone was serene.

"Well, did you mean it?"

"I said it. I don't make it a habit of saying things that I don't mean."

"But you don't want to share the same bed with me? That doesn't sound like you're *trying* to forgive me," he stated.

"Warren, forgiving you won't happen in a day and a half. This is not one of those 'everything will be better in the morning' situations. This is going to take time." She took a deep breath. "So, I cannot sleep in the same bed with you. Not now, anyway."

"I don't understand. You say that you want to forgive me, but you refuse to even sleep with me."

"Not just yet," she said.

"Fine," he replied petulantly.

"What, did you think by apologizing and treating me to a steak dinner that things would magically go back to the way they were?"

He jumped off the bed, grabbed his two pillows. As he exited the bedroom, she could tell by his body language that he was angry.

"There are pillows in the guest room," she stated.

"I'm accustomed to these."

Watching him go away, she resisted the urge to say, 'Nighty night,' but she didn't want him to think that she was ridiculing him. She was not being hard-nosed just for the fun of it.

Honestly, she did not want to be in Warren's company. But irking him was fun.

***

In the guestroom, Warren lay in the dark, trying to get comfortable in the bed. It was a queen-size. He was used to a king.

There was nothing like sleeping in your usual bed. And because he wasn't in his customary habitat, he knew that he wouldn't be drifting off right away.

He was glad that Felicia was back in the house, where she belonged. And that was not some sexist 'a woman's place is in the home' bullshit.

This was a home that they made together and he wanted her there. When she stormed off, he feared it might be over.

During her absence, he hadn't slept a wink.

He meant what he said about wanting to make it up to Felicia. But God knows, he didn't know where to start. An expensive piece of jewelry or some flowers won't fix this.

How did he atone for making another woman pregnant?

That would be hard for any woman to stomach, but when the woman couldn't even bear a child, it was twice as hard.

God, he wished that he had never laid eyes on Angie.

But in fairness, this wasn't going to be easy on her either, being pregnant and alone. Financially he was going to support the child, and make sure there was proper medical coverage.

So, this could work out. A man could be married to one woman and have a child with another woman, and be a father to his child. This was not an unheard-of situation.

And his family and colleagues would learn that he had a child outside of his marriage. He loved his family, and he cared what they and his colleagues thought of him.

But the only person's opinion that really mattered was Felicia's.

And his mother's. He was no Mama's boy. But he cared what Miss Shirley thought.

When he put himself through college, and helped her pay bills when things got tight, she boasted to her friends what a good son she had in Warren.

And his mom admired Felicia, and she would probably knock Warren up side the head when she found out that he betrayed Felicia and was giving her an illegitimate grandchild.

Yes, he wanted to make this up to Felicia. But he wasn't sure if he could.

# Chapter 30

Felicia and Keith were in Fridays, having lunch. The place was crammed with all kinds of people, black, white, young, and ancient. Across from Felicia and Keith was a gaggle of women in their early twenties, laughing and talking and eating. They were dressed in office attire, so evidently they were on break. Next to them was a trio of men in business suits, one appeared to be mesmerized by the convivial women. He looked as if he wanted to join their little party.

That morning, Keith had called and extended the invitation.

In a short time, she had grown to like him a lot. She told him that she hoped that they could become great friends. "Yeah, maybe we can be an African-American *Will and Grace,*" he quipped.

She had laughed at that.

At the hotel, they had exchanged phone numbers, and a few days after she returned home, he had phoned, asking if she was okay.

He too had gone home, and he and his partner, Robert, were still butting heads over Robert's desire to wear women's clothes.

"I don't understand what your problem is with it," Felicia said, cutting off a piece of her Jack Daniel's pork chop and placing a forkful of au gratin potatoes on top of it. Eating the two simultaneously was divine.

"As I said at the hotel, if I wanted a woman, I would have gotten involved with one."

"Well, it's not like he's having a sex change operation. I mean, all he wants to do is slap on some makeup, a wig, some heels, and a dress." She shrugged. "Play woman occasionally. What's the big deal? When he removes all the finery, he'll return to being the guy you fell in love with."

"I understand, but the entire drag thing turns me off." He made a face.

"Do you loathe women?" she teased.

"If I felt that way, would I be sitting here with you?"

"I know. Just joking."

"I adore women, and perfume, and tastefully applied makeup and pretty dresses on *women,* not female wannabes. And you know, I have no problem with drag queens. I enjoy drag shows, but I don't want to be romantically involved with anybody doing that. You showed me a picture of your husband."

Nodding, she sipped her Coke. At the hotel, they had shown each other snapshots of their romantic partners.

"And your husband's a fine looking man," Keith praised.

"Thank you," she said, wondering how Warren would react to a man complimenting his appearance. Warren was not a homophobe, but she'd bet Keith's praise would make him uncomfortable.

"Now, how would you like it if you walked in the house, and found that fine looking man dolled up in women's clothes?" Keith inquired.

She frowned. "I wouldn't."

"Now, you know how I feel," he said triumphantly.

"You can't make a comparison."

"And why not?" he exclaimed. "We both like how our men look, and seeing them done up as women wouldn't exactly get us steamed up and ready for action."

"But drag goes on in the gay community, you said that yourself" she challenged.

"And it also goes on in the straight community. There are some straight men who cross dress. And a lot of heterosexual women don't want husbands and boyfriends who dress like they do, and most gay guys don't want their partners doing it either."

"Point made," she conceded. "As I said at the hotel, this talk about drag is weird. I can't relate…but what you and Robert are going through is just an issue in a relationship."

Looking perplexed, he said, "I'm not following you."

She shrugged. "Couples disagree about things. In a straight relationship, he may perform cunnilingus, but she is unwilling to go down. And they argue about it. Men and women square off about one or the other's choices in friends, family members. Couples disagree."

Cutting off a piece of carrot cake, he asked. "So, what's going on in your continuing story?"

"You mean, with Angie?"

"Does your hubby want to dump you and take up with his floozy?"

Felicia chuckled. She got a kick out of hearing someone else trash Angie. Yeah, it was immature, but it felt good. "The whore was lying about Warren proposing to her."

"Told you so. Men usually don't wed their mistresses."

"That's what my sis said."

"Your sis is a smart girl. I'm sure Warren apologized repeatedly and begged for your forgiveness."

"He did." She mentioned the steak dinner.

"And have you forgiven him?" Keith asked.

She sighed. "Working on it. Forgetting something like this isn't going to be easy."

"It sure won't be, and the baby will be a permanent reminder."

"I know."

"How is he going to handle the baby?"

She sighed. "He's going to support his child. In fact, he's drawn up an agreement, saying that when the baby is born that he'll provide X numbers of dollars each week for child support, and he's going to provide medical coverage."

Keith nodded. "He's a good man."

"And he's going to visit his child."

Keith said, "So, he's going to be a father in every sense of the word."

"Mm-hmm."

"Miss Lady, how are you going to deal with that? Your husband having a relationship with his love child?" Keith shook his head. "That is some heavy duty drama." He held up his hand. "I'm not trying to rub it in, but you can't have kids, and then Warren steps outside of the marriage and has a child. And he's going to deal with the child. I repeat, heavy."

Felicia sighed. "But people do it. I've invested six years into this marriage, and for the most part, they've been good years. I don't want to hurl it in the wastebasket. I want to work this out."

"Well, you can take pleasure in one thing," Keith said. "Angie's little scheme to steal your husband has been ripped to shreds. You can gloat about that. You deserve to gloat."

Yeah, Felicia thought so too.

***

"Fefe, that isn't necessary," Warren said.

"I want to be with you when you visit Angie," Felicia replied.

"Look, all I'm going to do is tell Angie that I intend to support the child. It's not necessary for you to be there for that."

"I happen to think it is," she said, not backing off.

He sighed. "Things could get ugly."

"Believe me, I'm up for it," she said. Angie seemed to think that Warren was going to leave Felicia to be with her, and Felicia wanted to see that little tramp's face when Warren told her that there would be no divorce.

He eyed her curiously. "What is this really about?"

"I just want to be there."

"Is it an issue of you not trusting me?" he stated bluntly. "Are you afraid that I may have a quickie with Angie?"

"Well, since you brought it up," she said.

Warren sighed. "So, you don't trust me?"

143

"Not really, and that really shouldn't come as a surprise to you. Under the circumstances, I don't think most women in my position would want you alone, behind closed doors with a woman whom you had gotten pregnant."

"Fefe, it's over with Angie."

"And also, as I told you Angie seems to think that you and she are going to become man and wife."

"Well, she's wrong. I don't know where she got that idea from."

"Well, when I saw her, she gloated about it. And I'd like to be there when she learns that it isn't going to happen."

"So you want to do a little gloating of your own?" he stated.

She nodded. "I think I deserve it."

"I think you're being petty and stupid."

"I don't give a shit," she spat. "Angie is a nasty, evil bitch."

"Oh, Felicia," Warren said, shaking his head, disapprovingly.

Hearing him oppose her negative description of Angie enraged her.

"Well, what the hell would you call her?" she snapped. "That lowlife pretended to be my friend, and got knocked up by husband. That isn't the behavior of a saint, you know."

He took a deep breath. "Did you stop to think that Angie got caught up in something that she shouldn't have? She was lonely, and that made her vulnerable, and she did something that she shouldn't have done. Angie felt guilty about the affair."

"Oh, I'll just bet," Felicia snarled, remembering how foul and bitchy Angie had behaved when she confronted her.

"She expressed sadness about betraying you," he said. "She was tore up."

She slapped his face.

Warren looked appalled. "Are you crazy?" he yelled.

"Don't you make excuses for that whore," Felicia snapped, eyeing him balefully. "Now, she was putting on a damn act. She didn't feel a bit of guilt about what she was doing. She's a rotten, no-good, untrustworthy tramp, and you're just as bad for getting mixed up with her."

\*\*\*

It was early evening, and Angie was in the bathroom, naked, rubbing on a little body lotion. She used just a small amount to make her skin supple. Too much lotion would make it sticky.

She considered all she had to do. She had already showered, and she had to, apply some makeup, and style her hair.

144

Earlier, at work, Warren had called and asked if he could drop by her apartment that evening. "It's crucial that I see you," he said. "We have to talk about how we're going to handle this thing."

*Crucial that I see you.* He was going to tell her that he was going to divorce Felicia and marry her.

She was looking forward to his arrival. She hoped he was in the mood to make love. She could certainly use a good fucking. It had been quite a while since she had gotten some dick. And the idea of him eating her pussy increased her body temperature and made her all tingly. She loved the way Warren ate snatch.

He greedily licked her and shoved two fingers in her simultaneously. Oh, she loved it. She was sure that Felicia would miss that tongue action.

Oh, well. Felicia was history. So, screw her.

# Chapter 31

Warren tapped on the door of Angie's apartment. Childishly, Felicia stood to the side, out of view. She figured Angie would glance through the peephole, and she didn't want Angie to see her with Warren.

No, Felicia's presence would be an unexpected surprise.

The door opened, and the enchanting fragrance of White Diamonds wafted into the hall. Angie's welcoming smile collapsed like a skyscraper slammed by a wrecking ball when she saw Felicia appear from behind Warren.

Felicia took in the sight of Angie. Her makeup looked fresh and she wore a sleeveless sundress.

Tramp got prettied up to see my husband, Felicia thought.

"You didn't tell me you were bringing *her*," Angie snapped to Warren.

"*Her* has a name," Felicia retorted, contemptuously eyeing her former friend.

"Can we come in?" Warren asked pleasantly.

Without uttering a word, Angie stepped aside and let them enter. She closed the door. Looking at Warren, she said, "So, what's on your mind?"

"Uh, can we sit down?" he asked politely.

She pointed to the sofa, and remained standing as the Wainwrights sat on the couch. "What's going on here?" Angie asked. "Why did you bring her?"

"Well, I haven't seen you in a while," Felicia sang sarcastically. "I wondered how you were doing?"

Angie shot her a dirty look.

"Angie, as I told you, I want to be a father to my child," Warren said. "I'll pay your doctor bills. And give you generous child support payments. Everything is in writing. I'll put the child on my health insurance, so in case, something happened, you'll have medical coverage."

Frowning, Angie asked, "Uh, what are you getting at?"

"Well, what I've proposed isn't that complicated," Warren said, unruffled, sounding like he was negotiating a lawsuit, and was explaining his position to opposing counsel.

Nervously, Angie licked her lips. "Well, I, uh, don't understand. I'm pregnant."

"We're aware of that," Felicia snapped.

To Warren, Angie said, "And you're talking like all you want to do is take care of the kid."

*The kid. What a lovely way for an expectant mother to refer to her unborn child.* Felicia's heart went out to the baby.

"Well, that is what I want to do," he said. "It is my child after all."

"Well, what about me?" Angie shrieked. "I mean, I thought when I got pregnant, that you and I would like get married."

"Well, you, like, thought wrong," Felicia crowed, loving the sight of Angie upset and confused. *Yippee!* The bitch deserved it.

He sighed. "Angie, I don't know where you got that idea from. I never once said that I wanted to marry you."

Ooh, this felt good, Felicia thought, giving Angie a sunny smile.

"Well, you said that you wanted a child, and I uh, assumed that you'd marry me when I became pregnant," Angie snapped.

"You were mistaken," Warren said. "I want to stay with my wife."

"What is this?" Angie shrieked.

Ooh, Felicia wished she had a bag of barbecued potato chips and an ice-cold Coke. This was some entertainment.

"Are you playing some kind of a sick game with me?" Angie snarled and stomped her foot like a five year old who wasn't getting her way.

"Angie, you're the one who plays sick games," Felicia said smugly. "You knew how much Warren wanted a child, and that his father deserted him when he was a kid. And you figured that he'd be there for his child. But you miscalculated when you thought he would leave me and marry you."

Eyeing Warren, Angie said, in a shaky voice, "When I told you that I was pregnant, you said we could work it out. You said it was complicated, but that we could work it out. Those were your words."

"And from that, you assumed I was proposing to you?" he stated incredulously.

"Well, what else was I suppose to think? It sounded like a proposal to me."

"You heard what you wanted to hear," Felicia said calmly.

"Angie, when I said we could work it out," Warren said. "I was saying that I'd take care of my child."

"So, you aren't interested in marrying me?"

"Are you dense?" Felicia said spitefully. "Haven't you figured that out by now?"

Angie's eyes were on Warren.

"Tell her," Felicia shouted to Warren, wanting to rub Angie's nose in it. "Since you have to spell it out."

"I want to stay with my wife," he said, looking as if he wished he were someplace else.

"But what about the times, we made love?" Angie questioned.

"You had *sex,*" Felicia interjected, suddenly pissed. "Don't try to romanticize a sleazy affair."

"And it shouldn't have happened," Warren said.

"I don't believe this," Angie stated, huffing and puffing. "I don't believe this fucking shit. You wanted kids. You said that. And you said it disappointed you that she couldn't have them, and I figured because she's half a woman—"

"Hey, don't talk about my wife like that," he spat in defense of Felicia.

"Oh, look at you," Angie sneered, "playing the devoted husband. Well, where was all that damn loyalty when you were on top of me? Where was all that loyalty when you were kissing me, sucking my nipples, putting your tongue in my pussy?"

Warren looked embarrassed. "Angie, come on, don't be crass."

Oh, God, Felicia thought, being told that your husband had an affair was one thing, but for the bimbo to tell you what they did was hard to swallow. She felt like she had been kicked in the gut.

Noticing Felicia's pain, Angie snarled, "Yeah, girl, he used to eat me good. He sucked my pussy dry."

"Angie, we know you're a whore," Felicia snapped. "You don't have to give us any further proof of it."

"Ah, go to hell," Angie hurled. "And you are half a woman. You can't get pregnant. And Warren used to sit in here whining about how sad it was being married to a barren wino."

Warren shook his head. "Angie, come on, don't act like this," he said wearily. "I never worded it like that and you know it. Now, I've explained that I'm willing to give you child support."

"Fuck child support," she snapped. "Keep it. Shove it up your ass." She pointed a finger at him. "And please don't make the mistake of thinking that I'm in love with you." She laughed derisively. "I don't love you. You're good-looking and shit, not the finest looking man I've ever laid eyes on, but you look good. I'll give you that. And you're successful. You make a lot of money. You have a big dick and you know how to use it...So, you were good husband material." She exhaled angrily. "But love you? No, uh-uh. Love ain't have a damn thing to do with my interest in you, buddy boy."

Warren looked at Angie in visible horror. Felicia wondered if he still saw Angie as an essentially good person who made a lousy choice by becoming involved with a friend's husband.

"I can't believe you're acting like this," he said in disbelief.

"Well, believe it," she snapped. "And you know something else, you're going to *pay*. Oh, man, are you going to pay."

He frowned. "What do you mean?"

"Just what I said. You think you can get me pregnant and then go off and live a happy life with that wine drinking half a woman?" she taunted.

Felicia was sick of the jabs. She jumped off the sofa and circled the coffee table. "Look, bitch, I'm getting fed up with your mouth."

"Then, why don't you hit me?" Angie spat. "So, I can go downtown and swear a warrant out on your infertile ass."

Warren went to Felicia's side.

Felicia laughed derisively. "If you weren't pregnant, I'd beat the hell out of you. The pleasure of doing that would be worth a jail sentence." She looked at Warren. "Let's leave. This freak is insane. There's no talking to her." They headed for the door.

"Go! I don't care," Angie hollered to their backs. "But I'm going to get even. You better believe that."

Warren turned around. "Angie, are you threatening me?"

"You're so smart," she sang sarcastically. "I bet you were the first one with your hand in the air when the teacher asked a question."

"Well, threatening a lawyer is a dumb thing to do, you know," he said.

"Oh, don't worry, lawyer man," she said. "I'm not going to shoot you, stab you, or burn down your house. But I'm going to ruin you." Her face was twisted with anger. "I'm going to cause you many sleepless nights. You can take that to the bank."

Looking at Angie, Felicia spat, "You're mentally sick."

"Fuck you," Angie responded. With her eyes on Warren, she said, "I wonder how everyone will feel about Warren Wainwright, respected counselor when word gets out what you did to me."

Frowning, he asked, "What I did to you?"

"It's bound to hit the newspapers. And the TV news. I wonder how it will affect your practice," she snarled.

Felicia was curious. "Speak your mind, Angie."

"Your husband's a rapist," Angie spat.

Felicia and Warren looked at her in aversion. "A rapist?" he said. "What the hell are you talking about?"

"You used me...you left me pregnant. So, I'm going to go to the police and tell them that you raped me."

"That's a damn lie," he shot.

"Oh, I know it's a lie; you know it's a lie. But the police don't. Oh, I'll tell them a lovely story about how your wife was infertile, and how she was depressed about it. And how she and I were friends and you needed someone to talk to, so I lent you my ear...You told me that your wife drank all the time, and you no longer found her attractive, and that you wanted sex from me. And one night, you tried to get in my pants." She ceased speaking.

"Only, I'd say, you suggested we make love." She took a deep breath. "I told you no, that I could not have sex with a friend's husband ... Or any woman's husband. Well, you refused to take no for an answer. So, you forced yourself on me, and after it was over, you arrogantly said, that if I wanted to go to the police, I could, but you were confident that a judge would believe a respected lawyer over a hairdresser."

"No one would believe you, Angie," Felicia hurled. "Anyone who knows Warren knows that he isn't capable of raping anybody."

"It'll be his word against mine."

"Well, if you make such a wild accusation, Felicia will be my witness," Warren said. "She heard every word of what you said here."

Angie caroled nastily. "Oh, *please*, she's your wife. Everyone will think she's lying for you." She panted angrily. "I mean, my lawyer is bound to argue, 'Your honor, Mr. Wainwright is trying to convince this court that my client, Miss Porter actually told him and his wife that she was going to make a false cry of rape. Now, Warren, everyone in this room knows that I'm lying, but who'd believe I actually came out and told you and Felicia that I was going to lie?"

With a confused expression, he said, "Angie, why would you even threaten to do something so sick?"

She laughed derisively. "You need to ask? You fucked up my life, and I'm just returning the favor."

"You're being unreasonable," he said calmly.

"Unreasonable?" Felicia said. "Talk about euphemisms. The tramp is a nut case. Let's get out of here before I vomit from the stench this demon is spewing."

As Warren and Felicia vacated the apartment, Angie spat to their retreating backs—" You're going to get yours. I promise you that."

***

"She's just angry," Warren said behind the steering wheel. They were motionless at a red light. "When she quiets down, she'll realize how unreasonable she's being."

"I'm sure that's what you're hoping for," Felicia said.

When the light became green, he transferred his foot from the brake to the gas. "Well, of course, it's what I'm hoping for. I don't want her to carry out that threat."

"I'm sure you don't," Felicia said, looking out the window, at banks, car dealerships, a Burger King, a Blockbusters, a Kroger food store zoom by. "But don't be too sure that she won't make good on the threat. She's already

150

shown that she's treacherous and back stabbing. I wouldn't be shocked if she said you raped her."

For a moment, they rode in silence. "Thanks for defending me back at Angie's. I'm not too sure I deserved it," he said.

Felicia smiled sheepishly. She was still furious with Warren about his betrayal, and an infinitesimal part of her thought he deserved what he was getting from Angie. And she hated herself for even thinking that. But she certainly didn't want to see Angie wreck Warren's life. The man had worked hard for his career, and no bitch should demolish it. She glanced over at him, and he looked shaken. She wanted to utter some encouraging words, but her pride wouldn't let her be anymore supportive than she had already been.

# Chapter 32

Two days, later, Warren was in his office, and the number to his private line buzzed. "Hello," he said.

"Can you recommend a good lawyer?" Angie whispered in a menacing tone. "I'm going to sue this guy for rape. And since you're a lawyer, I thought maybe you knew some good ones."

He hung up the phone.

It rang back immediately.

"Hello," Warren said, pretending to be unfazed.

"I don't like you hanging up on me," Angie said.

"This is harassment," Warren spat.

"File a complaint," she stated cavalierly. "All I want is the name of a lawyer who can take my case."

"You do what you have to do," he said and threw down the phone.

Since that bitch told him that she was pregnant, he had been sleeping fitfully. He had been consumed with thoughts about how he could make his marriage work, while at the same time, be a father to his child.

Now, she was threatening to rip up everything that he had worked for.

God, why did he get involved with that crazy bitch? And how had she managed to dupe him? He was an attorney. He was supposed to be able to see through chicanery and lies?

And usually he did, and he believed her when she expressed sorrow about Felicia's inability to become pregnant, and that she wanted to lend a sympathetic ear.

It never occurred to him that her goal was to try and destroy his marriage.

And that threat worried him. It wasn't true, but Angie had convincingly played the role of the trustworthy friend to him and Felicia, so, it was quite possible that she could persuade a court that he had raped her.

He could lose everything he worked for, as well as end up in a correctional facility for men.

# Chapter 33

"I have a problem," Sandra said.

*What else is new?* Felicia thought, with the kitchen phone to her ear. "What's going on?" she asked.

"Well, I know we haven't been talking, or anything, because of that disagreement we had a while back."

"Disagreement? You mean, your insensitive reaction to the news that I can't have children."

"Well, I should have shown more understanding."

"Yeah, you should have," Felicia said, getting a pitcher of tea from the refrigerator and pouring some in a glass containing ice cubes. And she knew that the only reason Sandra was apologizing was because she wanted a favor.

"Well, the whole thing is in the past," Sandra said. "So, we kosher again?"

"Sure," Felicia said and took a swig from her tumbler.

"Well, like I said, I have a problem," Sandra stated. "I need six hundred dollars."

Felicia rolled her eyes. "I knew you wanted something."

"Felicia, I'm in a jam," Sandra said.

"Well, if you need six hundred bucks, I'm sure you are. But whatever, the problem is, I can't help you." She stretched the phone cord to the kitchen table and sat down.

"You can't help me?" Sandra's tone was incredulous.

"That's what I said."

"You don't even know what the problem is," Sandra stated.

"Well, whatever it is, you'll have to resolve it."

"Felicia, I don't have my rent money."

"Not my problem," Felicia said, being tough.

"If I don't have the rent paid by Friday, they're going to start eviction proceedings," Sandra whined. "They've already put up a 'pay or vacate' notice. We've been to court. I would've called sooner, but because of the argument, well, my pride kept me from doing so. But things have reached a desperate point. I have till Friday to pay."

"I wish you success at getting the money."

"You can't do this to me," Sandra wailed.

"You did it to yourself when you didn't budget your money properly so that you could meet your obligations. You know when your rent is due, so

153

you have to put aside a little money every week to make sure you have the rent when that time of the month rolls around."

"I don't need you lecturing me," Sandra snapped.

"Look, I can't help you," Felicia said, fed up with the conversation.

"You're taking pleasure in this, aren't you? I'll bet you're over there grinning up a storm. You're still pissed because of those remarks I made about your not being able to have a child."

Felicia rolled her eyes. "Sandra, that's yesterday's news. A while back, I promised myself that if you asked me for another loan, I was going to say n-o. You have to learn to stand on your own two feet."

"Well, what about Laquita?" she said irately, her voice rising. "You claim to care so much about her."

"I love that child. You know it."

"Yet, you're willing to let me lose my apartment, which means the niece you claim to love so much will be out on the streets."

"Look, don't even try to make me feel guilty. Uh, you can bring Laquita here, leave her with me. I'll take care of her until you get your act together."

"Get my act together?"

"Find another apartment, and hopefully, another line of work."

"Felicia, I'm not giving you my daughter."

"I'm not trying to take your daughter. I'm simply offering you a solution to your problem."

"Separating me from my child is not a solution. Loaning me the six hundred dollars would be."

"Loan you? We know that I'll never see a quarter of the money again."

"Felicia, you have to help me," Sandra said desperately.

"Sorry. Now, if you want to bring the girl here, okay, fine. I'll take excellent care of her. But I'm not giving you—"

The phone clicked in Felicia's ear. She put it down, and replenished her glass of tea. She was not trying to be difficult. She felt bad about turning Sandra down. But she was not going to let Sandra use her as a crutch ever again. Sandra had to learn to fend for herself.

And who knows, now that she no longer had a safety net to fall back on, maybe she would be better about managing her finances.

***

That bitch, Sandra fumed. Turning her down that way. And she wasn't lying to Felicia. If she didn't get the money together by Friday, she and Laquita would be thrown out of the apartment.

She sighed deeply. Where in the world could she cough up six hundred dollars? She didn't know a soul who could loan her that kind of money.

But there was another way of amassing it.

She had pals, people she worked with, a few friends in the neighborhood. She could hit this person up for fifty bucks, and that one for sixty. And plus, she earned tips.

Sighing again, Sandra realized there was no one she could borrow even small sums from. She owed money to every Tom, Dick, Sally and Sue, people in the neighborhood, the bartender at the club, one of the other dancers.

Sandra had debts all over the place, so no one would lend her a nickel.

Damn Felicia.

*Money, money. Where can I get some?* she thought, pacing in her living room.

Pussy.

She had one, and she could sell some of it. There were guys at the club who bought her drinks, and they tried to sweet-talk her into going home with them. Some of them offered her money. Maybe, she could say, "For two hundred dollars, you can have an hour of my time."

She made a disgusted face.

If she did strict screwing, no blowjobs, and used a condom, it shouldn't be so bad.

In the dark, she could pretend that she was making it with Shemar Moore or Denzel Washington. That would make it bearable.

Violently, she shook her head. Uh-uh, no way. No goddamn way would she turn a trick. She was not selling her pussy. She had no problem with dancing, but her body was not for sell.

But she was already selling it by parading around in front of men. But that wasn't the same as fucking them.

And for quite some time now, dancing had lost its sparkle. It was beginning to make her feel cheap, and she knew that she needed to go into another line of work.

She took a deep breath. Some of her current financial woes were the fault of this freak working at the club.

The manager hired another black dancer, sometimes scheduling her and Sandra on the same night, making it so that Sandra did not stand out in the crowd. And if a dancer wasn't special, the guys really didn't pay attention, which didn't lead to a g-string crammed with tips.

She had warned the manager that she would hand in her thong if he hired another black girl. Evidently, he hadn't taken her threat seriously because that bitch was in there, twisting her ass to the music.

But at this exact moment, quitting wasn't an option for Sandra. One couldn't resign from jobs when they didn't even have the rent money.

Oh, God. Felicia made Sandra so damn mad. How would Sandra get out of this predicament?

# Chapter 34

Felicia phoned Keith's workplace, and was told that he had taken the day off. So, she called his house and learned that he was using up some vacation days.

"Well, do you have anything planned for today?" she asked, cheerfully.

"Not really. I was just going to lounge around here, read a little and mess around on the computer."

"Well, why don't we drive up to Williamsburg?" she suggested. "I need to get out of the house and a little junket up there would be nice. I'll buy you lunch."

"Now, that's an offer, I can't refuse."

So, later that morning, she dropped by his house, and in her car, they went to Williamsburg, and it was summer, so naturally, there were visitors galore. A tour bus pulled along one of the colonial roads spilling its cargo of camera toting sightseers.

On the village green was a revolutionary war reenactment. Thespians pretending to be British red coats fired canons and their opponents, the colonials blasted muskets.

Restaurants had lines of hungry tourists pouring out the doors.

They drove past the brewery, and the yeasty smell of hops filled their nostrils. They bought ceramics and knickknacks from the pottery, and lumps of hand crafted chocolates from the candy store.

Warren loved the cherry cordials. You bit into the dark chocolate and got a splash of amaretto liqueur on your tongue.

Felicia wasn't that crazy about them. And she was ambivalent about buying some for Warren. She was angry with him these days, and she had no desire to treat him to a bag of his favorite candies.

So, after purchasing what she wanted, she and Keith vacated the store. And en route to the car, she felt immature and mean-spirited for behaving that way. Warren enjoyed those candies and she was right where they could be found, and it was downright nasty not to pick him up a half-pound. "I forgot something," she told Keith. "I have to run back in. So here are the car keys."

She returned to the store, and a few minutes later, she reappeared holding a white bag filled with the candy Warren liked.

Keith was in the car, with the windows rolled up, and the air conditioning running. As she entered the vehicle, he said, "Hope you don't mind me turning on the air?"

"Of course, not. It's stifling out there."

She put the car in reverse and they headed out of Williamsburg, eventually hitting I-64. The traffic was moderate.

Felicia blew out frustrated air.

"What's wrong?" Keith asked. "Exhausted from all the walking, and the heat?"

"No, I needed the outing." For the past few days, she had been thinking about what Sandra would do if she didn't get the rent money, and Angie's threat, and if she'd carry it out. She told Keith what was going on.

"What? She threatened to say your husband raped her?" he exclaimed.

Felicia's attention was on the traffic ahead of her. But she was sure that Keith's eyes had increased in size. "And Keith, that crazy ass fool just may carry out that threat. She's treacherous enough to do it."

"Well, from everything you've told me about her, I wouldn't put it past her. But hey look, Warren has friends in the community. People who know that he's a decent person...incapable of raping anybody. So, *if* this damn thing went to court, once people heard the whole story, they'll know that Angie is a scorned woman out for revenge."

Felicia had her doubts. "But Keith, some people want to think the absolute worse. And who needs the aggravation, the gossip, the stares?"

He chuckled. "I know all about gossip and stares. I'm a gay man who lives with another man. And some people in the neighborhood look at us disapprovingly...Some folks have a prob with gay boys."

Felicia made a face. "People can be so stupid."

"I hope Angie doesn't follow through on that sick threat," Keith said.

Felicia got off at the Jefferson Avenue exit. "Warren said she called his office, f-ing with him."

"What'd she do?"

"She said that she was going to charge a man with rape, and she wondered if Warren could recommend a good lawyer."

Keith laughed. "Now, you know I'm not amused by what you're going through, it's just that she's such a whack job."

"I understand. I'd probably find it a little amusing if it weren't happening to me. She sighed. "Warren's going through a bad time. The worry is all over his face. And I want to be supportive. I want to tell him that everything is going to be okay, but..." She shrugged.

"Just can't do it, huh?" he stated knowingly.

She nodded. "I'm still angry about the affair...Angry that he got another woman pregnant. And it's hard to have somebody's back when you're pissed with them."

"The guy betrayed you in a major way," Keith said. "That kind of pain is not going to evaporate over night."

"I know." She caught sight of an Applebees, and nodded in its direction. "Hey, want to stop and get a bite? My treat." she suggested.

"Sure," he said. "But I'm payin'. You sprung for lunch, after all. You know what I find intriguing."

"What?" Felicia asked.

"How Angie managed to deceive you. I mean, you strike me as a savvy lady. So, when you were *friends* with Angie, didn't you see glimpses that she was on the shady side?"

Felicia had asked herself that same question. "Keith, she hid that part of her personality. Looking back, I now realize that the only reason she gave me the time of day was to meet a successful man through Warren and me. When we were pals—" She rolled her eyes. "She suggested that I introduce her to one of Warren's friends...And I guess when she found out, I couldn't become pregnant, and that Warren wanted a child, she concocted that scheme to get pregnant."

Keith shook his head. "I can't believe that she honestly thought that Warren would divorce you and marry her. If all he wanted from a woman was to make him a baby, he could have found a surrogate."

As she pulled into the lot of the restaurant and took occupancy of an empty space, Keith was saying, "Also, how did you, a writer, and Warren, an attorney end up chillin' with a hairdresser?"

"Well, there's nothing wrong with being a hairdresser," Felicia said in defense of beauticians. "They provide an *enormously* vital service." She shuddered to think what her mop would look like without her stylist. Since the blowout with Angie, naturally, she had someone else taking care of her hair.

"I know, and I didn't mean to sound snobbish. I just wondered how Angie ended up in your circle," he said.

"My usual stylist moved, and Angie started doing my hair. We chatted in the salon, exchanged phone numbers . . That's how it started. I wish to God that I'd never met her."

# Chapter 35

In the kitchen, Angie fixed herself a rum and Coke.

She knew that a woman in her condition shouldn't be drinking. On the back of the booze bottle, she had read the Surgeon General's warning about how alcohol could cause birth defects.

*The Surgeon General doesn't know every damn thing. A couple of drinks won't hurt me,* she thought, moving the glass to her lips. She had a nice little buzz going on, and she wanted to keep it alive and kicking.

Soon, her pizza from Papa John's would be arriving.

God, she hated Warren...*No good motherfucker,* she thought, going to the living room.

But Mr. Good Guy wanted to give her child support.

To hell with that. Even if she accepted his offer, she'd still have to punch a time card and deal with Carolee and those annoying customers.

And she had wanted to marry his ass, so she could avoid the nine-to-five routine. He offered her twelve hundred dollars a month. Shit, she made more than that, doing hair.

She couldn't become a lady of leisure off twelve hundred dollars a month. Screw child support. Give her some *wife* support?

She had been so convinced that she and Warren would become mister and missus. And he could deny it all he wanted, but he had led her to believe that they would be married. He had said that the situation was complicated, but that they could work it out.

Oh, she'd bet big money that Felicia talked him into staying with her. Probably did a little crying and begging.

Angie squinted balefully.

*Oh, you're going to pay, Warren Wainwright. And so is that barren wife of yours.*

Angie was going to shatter their dreams of a wonderful life as they had done to hers.

First she'd hire a lawyer, and have Warren charged with rape. She'd say that she had tried to put the horrible ordeal out of her mind, but now she was pregnant.

And this story would hit the *Willow Oaks Free Press*. Yeah, she could easily see a newspaper story about a hairdresser charging a local lawyer with rape.

She laughed when she considered that the paper would name Warren, but leave her name out of it.

Ha, ha, ha, ha. They never pinpointed rape victims, she thought, returning to the kitchen to make another drink.

Oh, yes, Warren's life is going to be ruined.

Son-of-a-bitch.

When she was screwing the top back on the rum bottle, there was a tap on the door.

*Pizza time.* To think of it, pizza marked the occasion that she and Warren started fucking.

As she was going to the door, she realized that she didn't get any money from her purse to pay for the food. It won't hurt Mr. Papa John to wait a second. Neglecting to look through the peephole, she yanked opened the door.

Her eyes enlarged when she saw that it wasn't a pizza deliverer.

"Hello, Angie," said her visitor.

"What are you doing here?" she said.

"Let me in, and I'll tell ya," he said.

"Well, I don't want to let you in. I'm not interested in talking to you."

"I don't give a damn what you want," he said and strutted in.

"Hey, who do you think you are, charging in here like that?" she yelled, slamming the door.

"It's been a long time, Angie," said Darnell Moody.

So she had been right. She did spot Darnell that day when she had gone to get something to drink. "Not long enough," she said. "Now, what do you want?"

"What, no hug, no welcome home kiss? Not even a congratulations?"

She frowned. "Congratulations for what?"

"For being a free man," he said. "I pulled my three years and now I'm out."

"Well, hooray zip for you," she said nastily. "Why are you here? How many times do I have to ask you that?"

"You're a real bitch, you know that," he said, eyeing her with disdain.

"I've been called worse."

"I can't believe that I ever loved you." He took a deep breath. "And I did love you, Angie. I did everything I could for you."

She rolled her eyes. "I don't want to hear this. Why don't you just get out? You're out of the slammer, good for you. Great, terrific."

"I bought you clothes, and jewelry," he said, ignoring her tirade. "I bought you a car. You were my girl, and I wanted to treat you right."

"And let's see," she said. "Being an ex con, you're having a hard time. You can't find a job, and you want me to help you out. You think I owe you?"

"I don't want *shit* from you," he snapped.

"Then why the hell are you here? There, I asked again."

"To let you know what you did to my life," he snarled. "I did everything to try and please you, but it was never enough. And in the name of making you happy, I even wrote rubber checks, passing them in banks and supermarkets, using fake names, and phony ID's. I gave you thousands of dollars."

She smiled wryly. "Like it was your money to give away. You stole it, Darnell. Writing all those fake checks was another form of robbery."

"I did it to please you," he retorted. "But the cops caught up with me. I was arrested and thrown in jail. But I got out on bail." He shook his head. "And I couldn't go back, so I ran. They put my face on TV, and wrote about it in the newspapers."

Frowning, she asked, "Why are you rehashing all this shit? Is it my fault that you were so stupid that you went out and broke the law to please me?"

"I know what you did, Angie," he snapped.

"What are you talking about?"

"When the police were looking for me, I went in hiding. They offered a thousand-dollar reward for any information leading to my arrest. That's how they worded it on Crime Line. I contacted you, and I told you where I was. And you called the cops."

She shrugged. "So you figured it out?" Her tone was snide.

He sighed and shook his head. "God, you aren't even going to deny it?"

"Why should I? Sure, I told the cops where you were, and I went on a little shopping spree with that reward money, bought myself a couple of nice outfits."

"You sold me out for a measly grand," he spat. "You greedy bitch."

"I'm sick of this," she snapped. "Now, get the hell out of my face."

"Do you have any idea what it was like being locked up in that damn place? Do you know the shit I had to put up with?"

"What did you have to put up with Darnell, crappy food, lousy cellmates? Do you think I care?"

"I was locked up with freaks, Angie," Darnell yelled, spittle flying out of his mouth. "This one guy bit off his wife's finger; another dude killed his grandfather. Some other weirdo got his kicks having sex with six and seven year old kids. And I was behind bars with those sick bastards, all because you sold me out."

"Look, I'm in no mood for your sob story, okay. So, get out, or I'm calling the police."

"I was *raped* Angie," he revealed, between clenched teeth. "This motherfucker who was built like a wrestler, used to fuck me in my ass and he made me suck his dick," he said, still spewing saliva. His face was twisted with disgust and fury.

*This bastard is crazy,* Angie thought.

"And it's all *your* fault." With ferocity, he pointed a finger at her. "Because of *you*, I was turned into a fucking punk, a fucking homosexual, all because you double-crossed me. Why did you sell me out like that?"

"I'm calling the police," she said, marching to the kitchen phone.

He blocked her path. "You aren't calling anybody."

"We'll just see." She circled him, and went to the kitchen phone.

He snatched it off the wall, leaving a hole in the wall that looked obscene. He tossed the phone on the floor.

This wasn't the Darnell Angie knew a few years back. That Darnell was mild-mannered, and compliant. But obviously, prison had turned him into a crazy fuck. And she knew she had better get the hell away from him. She turned to run out the door.

He grabbed her by the waist. "You aren't going anywhere."

Her back was to him. "Let me go, Darnell," she shrieked, trying to wiggle free.

"I want you to know what it's like to be fucked in the ass," he said nastily and wheeled her around to face him. He ripped open her blouse, exposing her beige lacy, bra. He grabbed her.

"Darnell, let me go," she ordered in a shaky voice. "I'm not playing with you." Gone was all the tough talk.

"I'll let you go after I've fucked you in the ass."

She tried to break free, but it wasn't working. He frog-marched her to the living room. "I'm going to give it to you right here on the living room floor. I'm going to tear your ass up."

"Help," she screamed. He slapped a hand over her mouth. She bit his palm.

"Shit," he yelped, pulling away his hand, and losing his grip on her.

She dashed for the door, but he tackled her, charging her to the floor.

She screamed and kicked with all her might. He threw his hand over her mouth. She slashed him across the face with her acrylic nails, causing him to cry out a second time.

She scrambled to her feet, and once again, tried to get to the door, but he snatched her again and they tussled on the living room floor.

*Bedroom,* she thought, breathlessly. *I'll go to the bedroom, lock the door, and scream out the window.* She managed to throw him off her, and clambered to her feet, and got half way down the hall, but he grabbed her.

*Pamela Hayes*

"Bitch," he said and punched her, sending her through the Sheet rock of the wall in the hallway, leaving a gaping hole, revealing the other side of the wall, the two by fours, nails, insulation that looked like pink cotton candy.

# Chapter 36

Carrying her shopping list and cents off coupons, Felicia entered her favorite supermarket, filling a cart with meat, fish, produce, Tide, fabric softener sheets, cereal, a twelve pack of Pepsi, and bottles of sparkling water.

When her hand was on a box of spaghetti, she heard, "There's Aunt Felicia. There's Aunt Felicia." She knew that the voice belonged to her sweet niece, Laquita.

Felicia turned and put the pasta in her cart. A huge smile appeared on her face. "Hey, baby," she caroled to the child, squatting and giving Laquita a hug and a kiss. "It's so good to see you."

Laquita smiled, displaying her snaggle teeth.

"Laquita, there you are," Sandra said, carrying a handcart on her wrist like it was a pocketbook.

Standing, Felicia noted that inside of Sandra's basket were oodles of noodles, peanut butter and some hot dogs.

"Hi, Sandra," Felicia greeted.

"Laquita, we have to go," Sandra said, ignoring Felicia. "Now, I told you not to break away from me when we're in the store," she admonished.

"But I saw Aunt Felicia," Laquita objected.

"I don't care," Sandra stated. "Now, let's go."

"I want to talk to Aunt Felicia," whined the child.

Since that weave yanking brouhaha, and her depression and wine drinking, Felicia hadn't seen her little niece.

Prior to withdrawing from life, she and Laquita got together once a week. Felicia took her out for a kid's meal at a fast-food joint, or to the children's section at Barnes and Nobles. She really missed the sweet angel.

"Look, we have to go," Sandra said to the child, never once eyeing Felicia.

Obviously, Sandra was still angry because Felicia refused to pay her rent. "Sandra, I'm going to make spaghetti tonight," Felicia said. "Why don't you and Laquita come and have dinner with me and Warren?" She was trying to make peace.

Laquita thought that was a terrific idea. "Yay," she said and clapped her hands. "Are we going to have meatballs?"

"If you like," Felicia said.

"I'm sorry, Laquita, but we can't do that," Sandra stated.

"What, you have to work?" Felicia asked.

"Yeah," Sandra chirped.

Felicia suspected she was lying.

And sure enough, the little girl said, "You don't have to work. You said we were going to look at *Snow White* tonight."

*Out of the mouth of babes,* Felicia thought.

"Well, I got my days mixed up," Sandra said, trying to cover.

And Felicia flatly refused to let Sandra off the hook so easily. Sandra was not keeping her away from Laquita.

So she played along with Sandra's lie. "Well, then, since you have to work, why don't you let this little angel come to the house for dinner. In fact, since tomorrow is Saturday, she can spend the night. Would you like that Laquita?"

"Oh, can I Ma?" Laquita practically begged. "I like Aunt Felicia's house."

"No, you cannot," Sandra snapped.

Felicia did not like how she was talking to the girl. Okay, she and Sandra had had a disagreement, but it wasn't fair to take it out on the child.

"Why not?" Laquita whined.

"You just can't," Sandra stated. "Now, come on, we have to get this stuff rung up, so we can catch our bus."

"Sandra, I can give you a ride home," Felicia said, still trying to make amends, though she had nothing to apologize for.

"We can take the bus," Sandra objected.

"I want to ride in Aunt Felicia's car," Laquita grumbled.

"Well, you ain't doing it," Sandra barked. "And girl, you're getting on my last nerve. We don't need nothing from Aunt Felicia."

Felicia frowned. "Girl, don't talk like that in front of the child. You and I are sisters and you don't want her to see us arguing."

"Oh, don't you hand me none of that 'you and I are sisters' mess," Sandra growled. "Yeah, I'm your sister, but that doesn't mean jack to you."

"That isn't true," Felicia said, keeping it gracious.

"If you cared anything at all about me, you would have given me the rent money."

"Sandra, paying your rent is your responsibility," Felicia said.

"I don't want to hear it. Now, let's go Laquita," Sandra said, grabbing the child's hand.

"Laquita, I'll call you," Felicia said.

The child turned around, clearly disappointed and heartbroken. "I don't live in the same house anymore," she revealed.

Felicia frowned. "Well, where are you staying?"

"None of your damn business," Sandra yelled down the pasta aisle.

An antiquated white man, wearing a straw hat, getting a jar of low sodium spaghetti sauce off the shelf, told Felicia—" Somebody's in a pissy mood."

\*\*\*

"I just can't believe her," Felicia exclaimed.

"I can," Denise responded. Of course, it was a Sunday evening, and Felicia was in the backyard on the cell phone.

"I mean, she's angry with me because I refused to pay her rent," Felicia said. "Sometimes, Sandra can be so stupid."

Denise chuckled. "You're just finding that out? I've known it for decades. On the day God was giving out brains, Sandra was off some place else."

Felicia made a face. "Denise, come on. Yes, Sandra has made some lousy choices, but she's not really stupid. That was a poor word choice on my part."

"Humph! Look at her track record. When she was in high school, she got pregnant by a married man twice her age. And now, she's a stripper. The girl isn't the brightest bulb in the chandelier. End of story."

Felicia sighed. "I'm worried, Denise."

"About?"

"Well, I don't know where she's living."

"Felicia, Sandra is an adult, a self-centered adult, so, believe me, she's taking excellent care of herself."

Felicia sighed again. "I care about Sandra, don't get me wrong. But mainly, I'm concerned about Laquita. If Sandra gets mixed up in something stupid—there's that word again. Well, that little girl will be affected by it, you know."

Denise moaned. "I know. But what could Sandra get mixed up in?"

Felicia rolled her eyes. "Who knows? But she lost her apartment. Now, what if she moved in with some man she met at that strip club? I mean, there's no telling what kind of a person she could be exposing Laquita to."

"Now, you know that Sandra cares about her daughter," Denise said. "She'd never do anything that could hurt that child."

Yeah, despite all Sandra's flaws, she loved her daughter. The child was always clean, and fed, and Sandra helped her with her homework. And throughout the years, she had taken her to the photographer's studio to have pictures taken. She took her to the y for swimming lessons.

But still Felicia was worried, but what could she do? She sighed and changed the subject. "So, how's the diet going?"

167

Denise puffed out air. "It's been a struggle. But I'm eleven pounds lighter."

"Well, congratulations."

"But girl, I have more to lose."

"How's Eugene reacting to there being less of you?" Felicia asked.

"That thing moved out."

Felicia frowned. "Moved out?"

"That's what I said."

"Because you're losing weight?" Felicia recalled Denise saying that Eugene was having a problem with her weight loss, but to move out sounded so extreme. She thought he'd simply have to adjust to a smaller Denise.

Denise stated, "He said, I'm not the woman he got involved with."

"Well, going on a diet does not change the kind of person that you are," Felicia said. She had read that people's attitude change; that they move differently.

"Felicia, as I said before, food is significant to Eugene. And in order for me to shed pounds, it had to become less important to me. But he said he was tired of going to buffets and me getting one plate, and not going back for fourths and fifths like I used to…like he continues to do. He said he was tired of eating cheesecake and ice cream alone at night. He told me that he wanted things to go back to the way they were."

"You overeating?" Felicia said.

"Yes," Denise replied.

"And of course, you refused," Felicia said. God, this was bizarre. Eugene had a problem with Denise because she curtailed her food consumption.

"Categorically. I like weighing less. So, one night, he finally said that he wanted me to cease dieting. I told him uh-uh. One afternoon, I came in from work, and found a note. He said, he was leaving, and if I decided to resume my old eating habits, he'd come back and we can celebrate with a German chocolate cake." She took a deep breath. "Well, he won't be coming back here, baby, because I'm going to continue losing the pounds."

Denise came across like she didn't give a damn. But Felicia wondered. She and Eugene had been together for a few years and losing him must hurt. "Now, Denise, tell the truth, are you in pain, and pretending not to care? How do you *really* feel about this? Now, remember, you are under oath," she joked.

"As Marilyn McCoo said in that song—'One less egg to fry.' In my case, it's five less eggs," Denise stated.

Felicia chuckled.

"Good riddance to the pudgy bastard," Denise said. "Losing weight is important to me, and if he truly gave a damn about me, he'd have celebrated my achievements, not bitched and moaned about losing his eating buddy. And also, the man likes his women big. I've seen pictures of his ex and she was a jumbo...And I know that a part of a relationship is making compromises and concessions, but I am unyielding when it comes to my appearance. How I look is my decision. No man is going to determine how much I weigh or how I style my hair, or if I do or don't wear makeup."

Felicia nodded. "I agree with you one hundred and ten percent."

"So, how are things going between you and Warren?" Denise asked.

Felicia sighed. "Okay, I guess."

"You don't sound so sure."

Felicia said, "We eat our meals together, and we've resumed sharing the same bed."

"Well, sharing the same bed is good."

"All we do is *share* it."

"No X-rated activity, huh?" Denise stated.

Felicia shook her head. "Girl, I just don't trust Warren. He has shattered my faith in him."

"The man made a mistake."

"Oh, listen at you," Felicia declared, "sounding like you're defending Warren."

"I guess I am."

"Well, it wasn't all that long ago, you said that if Warren had his testicles removed, you wouldn't feel an ounce of compassion."

"When I said that, I was intensely irate. He had hurt my sister. But after hearing the whole story, I think that you should forgive Warren."

"So you think because of my previous bout with incessant wine drinking, and the fact that I had let myself and this house go, that Warren was justified in having an affair?"

"Absolutely not. But the man made a mistake and he loves you, Felicia. You have a good, honest husband."

"Perhaps."

"What do you mean, 'perhaps'?"

She envisioned Denise frowning. "Denise, Warren said that he never played around prior to Angie, but I'm not sure I believe that. I just don't trust him anymore. He could have had other flings, and the only reason he came clean about Angie was because she became pregnant. And he wanted the baby."

"If Warren had been cheating, you would have known it," Denise stated. "We girls always know stuff like that."

"I didn't pick up on anything between him and Angie."

"Only because you were off in your own little world, mellowed out by the zinfandel, oblivious to what was going on around you. If you had had your wits about you, you would've known. Intuition would have told you. You ain't no dumb woman."

"Maybe," Felicia said.

"If you want your marriage to work, you're going to have to give it all you have and then some. And put what happened behind you."

***

But Felicia did not know if she cared if the marriage worked or not. Why did Warren have to smash her faith in him?

Oh, God, how their life had changed in a just a few months.

Prior to being told that her fallopian tubes were damaged beyond repair, everything was magnificent between her and Warren.

They had a loving marriage. Those who knew them envied their closeness. They dined out, went dancing, and visited friends.

They enjoyed cozy evenings, watching television and rented movies, playing Scrabble, Upword, or Chess.

He read her work, and gave his opinions, helping her to clarify her points.

And then came the fallopian tubes news flash, which caused her to fall into a depression.

But eventually, she got her act together, and they were getting back on track.

And then bam, Warren revealed all that business with Angie, totally demolishing the progress that they had made.

"But Angie is dead," Keith exclaimed. "So is the baby."

Felicia sighed. "I know. But that does not change what he did."

Felicia had learned about Angie's death in the *Willow Oaks Free Press*.

According to the story, a pizza deliverer went to Angie's apartment to drop off food she had ordered; he found the door ajar. He called the police, and Angie was discovered in a wall, dead. An autopsy revealed that she was several weeks pregnant and she had died from a head injury.

The newspaper insinuated that the father of the baby could have been Angie's murderer. There were quotes from Angie's family members, who said that they weren't particularly close to her and didn't know that she was with child or who could be the father.

For days, Felicia and Warren wondered if the police would knock on their door, with questions about their whereabouts the night Angela Porter was killed?

They knew that they hadn't committed any crimes, but who wanted to become embroiled in a murder investigation?

Luckily, a few days later, a Darnell Moody stepped forward and confessed to the crime. He said that he and Angie had gotten into a fight, and that in anger he threw her against the wall, but that he didn't mean to kill her.

Also, the newspaper account revealed that three years ago Darnell Moody had been romantically involved with Angie, and that he had written a series of bad checks and was wanted by the police. He went into hiding, and Angie disclosed his location to the authorities.

So, Felicia wondered if Darnell killing Angie was really accidental, or if he simply sought revenge.

Of course, she had no way of knowing what transpired in that apartment on the night Angie was killed.

Felicia would be a liar if she said she mourned Angie, because she didn't. She didn't care if Angie was dead. Why lie about it? The woman had deceived and double-crossed people, and played them for a fool and it caught up with her in a bloody, hideous way.

But it was heartbreaking that a sweet innocent baby had not been given a chance at life. When Felicia considered that, she felt terribly sad. That child was an innocent in the whole sordid thing.

*** 

It was a Sunday afternoon, and Felicia and Keith were in a gay bar at an AIDS fundraiser.

Dinners and drinks were for sell, and the money made from them would be donated to AIDS related causes.

Keith had told her about the event, and asked if she'd be willing to come out and show her support. So, she said yes, and enjoyed a scrumptious chicken dinner and was now sipping a soda.

The event was packed. There were effeminate gay men, mannish looking women, female impersonators, men and women who could be gay, but looked straight, and could have been as there were straight people in the mix.

Keith had introduced her to supportive mothers, brothers and sisters of gay and transgendered people.

171

Felicia enjoyed Keith's company, and his sexuality didn't bother her one bit.

And she felt safer discussing her marital woes with Keith than any of her *friends*. She no longer trusted her friends, and she and Keith didn't travel in the same social circles, so she didn't have to worry about him gossiping, and she didn't think he'd do that, anyway. He seemed trustworthy.

"You still want to smell baby powder, and have a brat burp formula on you?" Keith joked to Felicia.

"Oh, sure," she said.

"Then do something about it," he encouraged, biting off a cheesecake bar. Graham cracker crumbs fell onto the paper plate. "Financially, I guess you and Warren are doing okay."

"Yeah, we are," she replied, not about to discuss her finances with anyone. That information was between her and Warren, their tax preparer, and stockbroker.

"So, why don't you adopt?" Keith asked. "I'm sure that you and Warren would have no trouble getting a kid."

Pensively, she ran a finger around the tip of her straw. "I don't think now is the right time, Keith. Things aren't so rosy between me and Warren, and at this point, I wouldn't consider bringing a child into our lives."

# Chapter 37

Warren was sitting up in bed, reading a John Grisham paperback by the lamplight. Felicia emerged from the bathroom, naked.

When he spotted her, he smiled warmly. She climbed into bed next to him, rolling onto her side, her customary sleeping position.

He got his bookmark off the nightstand and slid it into the novel. She could tell from where he had placed the bookmark that he was almost done with the page-turner. He placed the book on the nightstand, and clicked off the brass lamp. In the dark, he snuggled against Felicia. "You smell nice," he cooed and covered her back with a zillion little kisses.

Before coming to bed, she had bathed, brushed her teeth, and rubbed on a little perfumed body lotion, a lagniappe for a cosmetic purchase she had made the other day at her favorite department store.

And evidently, the delightful scent had ignited Warren's passion. He maneuvered her onto her back. "I've missed you," he whispered in a husky tone, and put his lips on hers. They hadn't made love in weeks.

She luxuriated in the wonderful kiss. And when his lips moved to her neck, she oohed, and ahed.

She hadn't been with this mouth-watering piece of chocolate in weeks.

They kissed with fury, warming each other's face and neck with their steamy breaths.

He cupped her right breast and greedily sucked her hard nipple like it was a lump of peppermint. Eventually, he transferred his moist, hungry mouth to her duplicate, and savored the taste.

She thought the sensations were wonderful, delightful ... magical. The great feelings made her moan happily.

*He did this with Angie*, snapped her inner voice.

Oh, God, Felicia thought. Her excitement and exhilaration deflated as rapidly as a balloon pricked by a needle. She snatched her face from Warren's ravenous mouth.

"Uh, wh-what's wrong?" he stammered.

She imagined him frowning in the dark. "I don't want to do it," she stated.

"Oh, come on," he sweet-talked, kissing her neck.

"Stop it," she said firmly. "I'm not in the mood."

"I'll put you in the mood," he said seductively, stroking her hair. He kissed her cheek.

"Stop it! Or I'll slap your damn face." She pushed him away and rose to a sitting position.

There was total silence for a moment. She figured Warren had been shocked motionless by her statement. He rolled onto his side and sat on the edge of the bed, causing the mattress to squeak.

He sighed. "You'll slap my damn face. That's a bit strong, don't you think?"

"Considering the circumstances, no," she said.

"Considering the circumstances?"

"Why are you repeating every damn thing I say? You need a Q-tip?"

"My hearing is fine," he replied peevishly. "I'm just trying to figure out your bizarre behavior. You get into bed, *naked*, and smelling sweet. I thought you were in the mood for lovemaking."

"Well, you thought wrong. You know that I always sleep in the nude. And I got this new body lotion, and I wanted to try it. I wasn't out to seduce you."

"Sure about that?" he snapped. "Sure, you didn't set out to get me all worked up, and then reject me?"

"Oh, Warren, come on," she protested. "You know I don't play silly games."

He sighed. "I know, and I'm sorry for making the accusation…But when I was getting you in the mood, you were enjoying it."

"I was," she confessed.

"Then why did you put up a stop sign?"

"Because I thought about Angie," she hurled. "Remember her?"

He moaned. "Oh, God."

"And the things you did with me, you had done with her," Felicia stated. "Knowing that makes me want to vomit."

"Felicia, Angie is dead," Warren said.

"Well, my feelings about what you did with her aren't."

Wearily, he asked, "What can I do to make things right with you? God knows I've tried. I've suggested that we get together for lunch, but you invent excuses to keep from doing so…I've sent you romantic email greeting cards, and you didn't even mention receiving them. And what about my idea, that we take a trip to Hawaii? I figured a getaway would bring us closer. I don't know about you, but when we're on vacation, I always feel closer to you." He paused. "I guess it's about being in a different environment, and not knowing anybody but you. I figured a holiday would make things more intimate between us. But my Hawaii idea didn't appeal to you. You claimed it would be too hot." He sighed. "I tell you, Felicia, I don't know what to do."

"Warren, do you honestly think a lunch, or a gushy email card, or some trip is going to make me forget that you two-timed me?"

"No, but I've been trying to show you that I'm sorry about what happened and that I want this marriage to work, which is more than what you're doing."

"What do you mean by that?"

"You refuse to meet me halfway. You could have at least said that you received the email cards and that you thought they were cute. That's what you used to say when I sent them." He sighed. "It's like you don't give a damn, Fefe."

"If that was true, I wouldn't be here," she countered.

He lay down as if he was about to retire for the night, and for several seconds, he didn't utter a word. "All you know how to do is wallow," he said.

"What are you talking about?"

"When you found out that you couldn't have a baby, you became depressed."

"Well, it wasn't exactly music to my ears, Warren."

"I know," he said. "I was disappointed too. But we had options. We could have adopted, or used a surrogate. But you refused to accept what was what, and use our choices. Oh, no. You cried and lamented the fact that you couldn't have a child, going on and on about the no-good mothers of the world, how it was unfair that they could have children and you couldn't."

"You're being very insensitive," she said angrily.

"Well, in the beginning, I was very sensitive. I felt your sadness and hurt and outrage. I understood why you moped around. And that the wine made you feel better. I got it, Felicia. I even got buzzed with you and listened to music…So, yeah, I understood. But you know, Fefe, there comes a time when you have to accept the things that you can't do a damn thing about and go on with your life. People have lived with far worse than infertility."

"I eventually realized that," she said. "Which was why I poured out the wine and went on with my life."

"Yeah, eventually, you did. And maybe, you'll eventually forgive me for what happened with Angie," he said. "But who knows by the time, you get around to forgiving me, I may not even care."

\*\*\*

175

Warren and Felicia were barely speaking to each other, and it was depressing, but she had no desire or inclination to make herself feel better by drinking wine.

She kept the house spotless and spent time at the computer cranking out articles and stories, even selling a few.

In the past, when that happened, she'd gush to Warren about it, and they'd celebrate, but she didn't even mention the recent sells to him.

She was so ambivalent about her marriage. Sometimes, she wanted it to work, and other times, she didn't give a shit.

The only thing that she knew for certain was that she didn't trust Warren.

One day at lunch, she complained about it to Keith.

"Felicia, I'm your friend, you know that," Keith said.

"Why do I get the impression that you're about to say something that I won't like?"

"Because I am."

"Speak," she said.

"Warren's been through some shit too, you know," he said.

Felicia found that statement intriguing. "Oh, really. What *shit* has Warren been through?"

"That she-devil threatened to charge him with rape. And you said that he was losing shut-eye over it. And when she was killed, Warren feared that he'd become involved in a murder investigation…So, that must have cost him a little anxiety."

"He deserved it," she retorted uncharitably. "He brought it on himself."

"*And* he wanted that baby, and the baby died with Angie. So, you see, he's been through some heartache too. His affair with Angie didn't come at a discount price. He paid, big time, with his emotions and the loss of a child that he wanted. And he also lost the trust of his wife."

"I guess you have a point," she conceded.

"I know I do," Keith bragged. "Felicia, if you want the relationship to work, you're going to have to forgive and move on. And…if you can't, then maybe you should leave."

*Leave*? Felicia thought. She couldn't imagine a life without Warren.

But she couldn't keep going on like this.

\*\*\*

"This is like eating at a five-star restaurant," Warren said. "You went to so much trouble."

By candlelight, they dined on crab-stuffed flounder, baked potatoes, and asparagus—foods Warren enjoyed. She had thought about making something Italian, but she knew he admired the flounder dish, so she prepared that instead.

"Wasn't that much trouble," she replied. Her lips parted, but nothing came out. She was going to say 'you're worth it,' but the words caught in her throat. So, she said, "You know, how much I enjoy cooking."

Keith had given her something to ponder, so she decided to try harder at improving her marriage.

"Well, it taste great," he complimented.

She smiled her thanks. After dinner, they did the dishes, and repaired to the couch and watched a movie.

And for a few days, things were better until one Friday evening when Warren arrived home from work.

Felicia, stylishly dressed was in the living room, pacing. "Where have you been?" she snapped the second he appeared toting his briefcase.

He frowned. "I just got in from work."

"Well, work ends at 5:00, and usually you're home a few minutes after five thirty. Look at your watch. It's almost six thirty. And don't you dare say that you got held up in a traffic jam," she said, not letting him get a word in. "That excuse and running out of gas are as old as repeats of *I Love Lucy.*" She hated herself for behaving like a shrew, but she couldn't help it.

Warren had played her for a fool once before, and she was watching his ass like a department store security guard keeping an eye on a suspected shoplifter.

"I had a mineral water with a client," he explained, barely keeping the irritation out of his voice. "And I really don't like the way you're acting." Putting his briefcase on the sofa, he asked, "What's your problem?"

"You could have called and told me that you were going to be late."

"It's Friday night."

She said, "What's that got to do with anything?"

"It's the night we eat out."

"So?" she said.

"Felicia, you wouldn't have had dinner waiting." His tone was patient. "And usually we don't arrive at the restaurant till around seven thirty. Look, I need to shave." He looked at her as if to say, 'Who are you, and where have you stashed my wife?'

Sighing, she went to the kitchen and poured a glass of sparkling water. Sipping it, she wondered if Warren was telling the truth about having a beverage with a client, or maybe he was carrying on with some other bimbo.

\*\*\*

Slapping on some after-shave balm, Warren thought about what could have been a nasty showdown with Felicia. He knew what she was insinuating with the interrogation about his whereabouts.

And yes, he usually closed up the office at five, and if he came directly home, he arrived a few minutes after five thirty.

But he didn't always come directly home. Sometimes, he'd have a drink with a buddy, or an important client. And Felicia never got in an uproar about it. She had never asked him to account for his comings and goings.

But this evening she had, and he knew it was because she wondered if he was screwing around, when in truth, he had been with a client.

But he was a lawyer and he knew that when someone had committed a crime, and when they were suspected of another crime, that prior offenses were more often than not brought up.

So when he wasn't where he was supposed to be, Felicia would become suspicious of his activities.

He sighed and shook his head. *This is no way to live.*

# Chapter 38

It was night, going on ten, and Felicia was driving home from her night class, a writing workshop. A few weeks ago, she had joined a new one that was being held at the University of Willow Oaks, on Tuesday and Thursday nights from 7:00 p.m. until 9:45.

It was the same routine as the other classes. Budding and marginally accomplished poets, essayists, fictionists of short stories and novels discussed their manuscripts with their classmates, who offered feedback.

Felicia was working on a few short stories and she enjoyed the different perspectives on her mini tales. If she particularly liked an opinion, she wove it into the story.

She didn't care for the instructor, a fastidious, effeminate man, who was enormously critical.

She had assumed that he had written some stories, and she had asked to see his work, but he had nothing to offer. She believed his criticism stemmed from jealousy of the writing ability of others, and that he probably had zero talent, so he resorted to teaching.

How did it go—those who can do, and those who can't teach?

She never understood why universities employed instructors to teach courses that they really knew nothing about. Anyone teaching university-level writing, should be a published author.

A writing teacher should be a writer. A medical school would no sooner have a non-doctor teaching courses in gynecology.

She turned onto her street, and before she reached her house, she saw that Warren's car was not in the driveway. *Okay, Warren, where are you?*

Usually, when she returned from her class, he'd be in the bedroom, reading or watching television.

Still wondering where he could be at this hour, she pulled into the driveway, exited the vehicle, and entered the house through the kitchen door. The house was hushed and dark. No television or stereo was playing. Felicia flipped up the light switch, bringing the kitchen into view.

She wondered if an emergency arose with Miss Shirley and Warren had to go over to his mom's.

She placed her purse, and folder on the kitchen table, went to the sink, and washed her hands with antibacterial liquid soap.

After drying her hands, she went to the freezer to get coconut sorbet. She always treated herself to soda or sorbet after class. Taped to the refrigerator was a note from Warren.

*At the spa pumping iron,* he had scrawled.

Usually, he worked out in the morning.

Getting the frozen treat from the freezer, she wondered if Warren was really at the gym. Or. "Forget it," she muttered, wiggling her feet out of her flats and switching her thoughts to her story.

In class, she had read her narrative, and some of her fellow students gave great input, and she wanted to work their ideas into the piece, which she planned on marketing to *The New Yorker*.

She took the sorbet to her office, which was once a bedroom, but she and Warren transformed it into a workplace for her.

She cut on the computer, clicked on her story file, read the piece, and began inserting some of the students' suggestions into it, but…She couldn't concentrate on fictional people when her mind was on a real person named Warren.

Was he really exercising?

She went to the bedroom and discovered that his sneakers and sweats were not in the closet, which meant nothing. He could have removed the work out gear to throw her off track.

God, his betrayal had made her as suspicious as a private eye.

Was he off having an affair?

She didn't trust the bastard and she wondered if while she was standing in the bedroom, wondering about his whereabouts, if he was laid up somewhere, with his dick in some slut's vagina.

At the spa, huh?

She took the unfinished sorbet to the kitchen, screwed the lid back on it, put it back in the freezer, donned her shoes, grabbed her purse and left the house.

***

She was inching down a dark, almost barren thoroughfare. A sporadic car zoomed by.

She caught sight of her gas needle trembling towards e. She had planned on getting gas tomorrow morning. But it couldn't wait.

Out of the corner of her eye, she saw a gas station/mini mart, so she drove up to a pump. Taped to it was a handwritten sign that said, "Pay before fueling."

She took her purse into the store. "I'm going to get ten dollars worth," she told a chunky, black dude, shoving a handful of popcorn into his mouth.

He nodded and accepted her two five-dollar bills.

After gassing up with unleaded, she reentered the station and asked Orville Redenbacher for the key to the ladies room.

Ugh was her response when she entered the place and locked the door.

On the floor was a sheet of toilet paper, a dead grasshopper and in the commode, a piece of shit.

*Oh, Lord.* She raised her upper lip, and wondered if peeing on herself would be worse than doing it here.

She flushed the stool, wiped the toilet seat, and felt squeamish relieving herself in this atmosphere, cursing Warren the entire time.

After washing her hands, she returned to her vehicle, and resumed her journey to the health spa.

"Keep driving till I tell ya to stop," came from the backseat. The voice was male, nervously high-pitched.

*My God,* Felicia exclaimed inwardly, feeling something prod her in the lower back.

She twisted her head to look back.

"You betta turn around," he ordered.

She did as she was told, but she had seen the gun and his black hand.

*Uh, what happened?* Back at the gas station, while she was in the restroom, he must have climbed in the back and hid, obviously escaping the attention of the clerk inside the store.

What did he want?

Rape.

Her palms became moist as she drove down the deserted road.

Ladies magazines.

Articles about women encountering trouble.

Cooperate.

Don't fight.

Don't antagonize assailant.

Well, uh, if this were a holdup, she'd give him her money, and watch. That stuff can be replaced.

But rape?

Uh-uh.

She'd fight.

Bite.

Claw.

*But remember he has a pistol,* warned her inner voice.

Well, uh, she'd knock it out of his hand, and jab a finger in his eye and when his vision became distorted, she'd go for his balls.

Getting near his balls would shift the power to her.

*I will not be raped.* The only way he was having sex with her was if he was into necrophilia.

Across the street she saw a couple entering a Chinese restaurant. Her window was rolled down, half way.

*Scream,* she thought.

No.

Could get shot.

"Pull dis car over there," he ordered, pointing the gun in the direction of a building boarded with plywood. He returned the weapon to her lower back.

*Bet you feel mighty powerful with that gun,* she thought. *You illiterate asshole.* It crossed her mind to plow the car right through the building like some ballsy chick from an action movie. That would show his ass. But hell, she could end up injured or dead.

So, she drove onto the parking lot and when her headlights hit the building, she saw that it was sprayed with graffiti.

And the steeple told her that it had once been a 7-11.

"Get out," ordered the lawbreaker. "And leave da key in the 'nition."

She got her purse off the passenger's seat.

"Leave dat," he barked. "Now, get out, and stand by the car till I drive off, and don't be looking back."

*Bastard,* she thought, exiting the vehicle, frightened, yes, but pissed, wishing that she were a black Charlie's Angels, or a virtuoso in martial arts. She'd kick that little turd's ass.

In the night air, she climbed out of the car, and stood with her back to him. "Nice doing been ness with you," he joked and then she heard him slam the driver's door and speed off in her Volvo, a birthday gift from Warren last year.

# Chapter 39

"Are you all right?" Warren asked when he heard about Felicia's ordeal.

After the car thief raced off, she crossed the street to the Chinese eatery, and the friendly proprietor allowed her to use the phone to call the police.

And gave her a Coke gratis while she waited for an officer to arrive to make out a report.

Warren asked, "Did he hit you, or try to—"

Felicia shook her head. "No, no. I'm all right."

He breathed a sigh of relief. "Thank God. Well, come on, sit down," he said, ushering her to the couch. She got a whiff of his customary deodorant soap, which told her that he had showered not too long ago. She wondered if he washed off perspiration caused by a workout, or a sexual encounter.

"Why don't I get you a brandy?" he said, treating her like a damsel in distress from an old movie. When the heroine got upset, the hero poured her a brandy.

She said, "Warren, my bout with wine, remember? I no longer drink alcohol."

"I wasn't thinking," he said, apologetically. He took a deep breath. "You say the car-jacker took your purse?"

She nodded.

"And I'm sure your credit cards were inside?" She nodded again. "I'll call all the credit card companies and cancel the accounts, so that little shit can't go on a buying spree. They'll issue new account numbers."

"That's a good idea," Felicia said. "And my driver's license was in my purse, so he could find out where I live. And my house key is on the same ring as the car keys, so you better call a locksmith."

"I'll take care of it right away."

She sighed. "Warren, that asshole had a gun, and since he knows where I live, he could possibly come here and make trouble."

"I doubt it," Warren said, shaking his head. "He wanted your car and your money, and possibly the credit cards. He wouldn't be dumb enough to come here. He knows that you've reported him to the police."

"I hope you're right."

"I'm going to call the locksmith and the credit card companies." He left the room.

She went to the kitchen, and put a kettle of cold water on the stove. While it heated, she got a mug and her favorite herbal tea from the cabinet. The tea was a nice blend with orange rinds and spices.

When she was at the table, carefully sipping the aromatic, steaming brew, Warren appeared in the room.

"I made the phone calls," he said. "The credit cards have been cancelled, and the locksmith will be here in about a half-hour."

Felicia smiled her relief. Again, she smelled the soap.

Watching him remove a bottle of water from the refrigerator, she said, "I've made a decision."

Taking a swig of water, he eyed her curiously.

"I want us to separate," she announced.

He pulled out a chair and sat. "I, uh, don't understand," he stammered. "Why? Uh, what brought this on?"

"You know, that things haven't been perfect between us," she said wearily.

"Yeah, but we've been working on repairing things. There was the romantic dinner the other night, and last Saturday afternoon, we went to a matinee."

"I've been trying." She sighed. "But Warren, I don't trust you. And tonight when I was car jacked, it made me realize that I can't stay married to somebody that I don't trust."

Warren frowned. "A minute ago, you said you want us to separate. Now, you're talking like you want a divorce."

"I don't know what I want. A part of me sincerely wants to forgive you, and put what happened with Angie behind us."

"Then just do it?" he pleaded.

"It's not that easy. When you aren't in my face, I'm wondering if you're with some other woman."

He sighed. "Fefe, I told you that I was unfaithful just that one time."

"I know what you told me."

"But you don't believe me." For a moment, they sat awkwardly at the kitchen table, not uttering a word. "You said being car jacked made you decide to separate?"

She nodded. "I got your note, and I wondered if it was b s...if you were really at the spa. I mean, you usually work out in the morning."

"Well, because of extra work, I haven't been getting to the spa in the morning. And I need my exercise. It makes me feel better. So, I made a night visit to the spa." He shrugged.

"Well, I wondered if you were off having a fling," Felicia said. "So I decided to go to the spa, to see if your car was there."

"It was. Didn't you see it?" He sounded annoyed.

"I never made it to the spa. The Volvo bandit interrupted me," she said bitterly.

"Well, I was working out," he practically snarled.

"So, you say," she retorted. "You know, it even crossed my mind that if I found your car at the spa, that you wouldn't be inside."

He frowned. "What are you getting at?"

"That maybe you considered that I might question your story. So, you parked at the health club, and went off in your girlfriend's car."

"This is fucking bullshit," Warren exploded and pounded his fist on the table. He jumped up from the chair. "I was at the gym working out. My funky workout clothes are in the hamper. Why don't you go sniff 'em? Or better yet, why don't you call the spa tomorrow morning and ask them if I was there. They know me. Or would that be good enough? You'd probably think I bribed them to lie for me." He shook his head in disgust.

"You really resent being distrusted, don't you?" she said, calmly.

"Damn right I do."

"Well, you brought it on yourself."

"I was at the damn gym."

"It doesn't matter. I'm just lucky to have come out of that incident losing only my car and my purse. I could have been raped…pistol-whipped. Killed. And all because I don't trust you. My distrust of you was why I was out on that damn road."

"So you're going to leave because of what *could* have happened?"

"Warren, because I put a question mark behind everything you tell me, a tragedy could have occurred. We need some time apart."

"*You* need time apart. And you know, something, Miss Lady, you think it's been so hard on you. Well, it hasn't been an evening at the jazz festival for me. Living with your indifference, mood swings, and schizoid behavior hasn't been easy."

She frowned. "Schizoid behavior?"

"Yes. Pushing me away when I wanted to make love to you…and then turning around and preparing my favorite foods. Cracking jokes one day, and then the next, not uttering a word to me. One day, you're friendly, and I think, 'Hey, this is going to be okay.' But then, out of no where, you're as cold as a bag of ice. It's like you're playing mind games with me."

"Look, I *wanted* to put it behind me. That's the God's honest truth. And some days, I'd tell myself, 'I'll get through this. I love Warren, and I'm going to make this work.' So, I made your favorite foods and cracked a few jokes. But then something would trigger what you did, and I just didn't want to deal with you." She sighed. "I need time away…to heal."

"How long do you want us to separate?" he asked, sounding weary and defeated.

"I don't know."

"Where will you stay? And I'm in no mood to placate you. You want some time away, well, you can find a place to stay. I'm not leaving this house."

"Fine," she spluttered. I'll stay with Keith. At least, until I get my own place." Keith had told her that she could stay with him if she decided to distance herself from Warren.

"Who the hell is Keith?" Warren snapped.

"A friend."

"I know all your friend's, and the name Keith doesn't ring a bell. Have you met someone else?" He snapped. "Do you want to leave me so you can go lay up with this Keith?" His jaw clenched as he spoke.

Taking pleasure in his jealous outburst, Felicia said, "Keith is gay. I met him at the hotel where I stayed when I found out about you and Angie. He and I have hung out together, so I know him. He shares a house with his partner, and I'm going to use the spare bedroom until I find a place of my own."

"How do I know that you didn't dream up this story about Keith being gay?"

"Well, you know, Warren, at this point, if I was romantically involved with anybody, I wouldn't give a damn if you knew. And you wouldn't be so suspicious if you hadn't played around on me."

"Touché. I deserved that." He sighed. "Look, Fefe, I can't erase what happened, but I can work on making it up to you. But I can't do that with you living someplace else. So, why don't you reconsider leaving?"

She rose from the table, having no desire to hear it. They had been down that road before, made a left turn, and went down it again. She was sick of the scenery. "I'm going to pack."

"You're going to Keith's tonight?" he asked.

She nodded.

"Look, why don't you sleep on it? You may feel differently tomorrow."

"I doubt it. Besides, I called Keith from the restaurant and told him that I'm coming there tonight. He's expecting me."

"Well, call him and tell him you're staying here instead. And tomorrow, if your feelings haven't changed, I won't argue with you about it."

Felicia relented. She was drained, and Keith's house would be a new environment, and she wouldn't be able to rest, so a night in her own bed, surrounded by familiar things did sound more appealing.

\*\*\*

186

The next morning, Felicia rolled over in the king-size bed, wiping sleep from her eyes. She glanced at the digital. 9:47.

Wow!

Usually, she was up and active at 7:30. And by now, she would have had her customary two cups of Folgers.

She had trouble getting to sleep last night. Every little noise, the floor creaking, the air conditioner clicking on, alarmed her.

She feared Mr. Carjacker might pop in with his weapon and do a little home invasion.

"We have new locks," Warren had said, trying to soothe her, reminding her that the locksmith had replaced the locks on the kitchen and living room doors. "And I'm here," he said.

He wrapped his arms around her and finally, she drifted off.

How *weird* was this? She and Warren were separating. Yet, she had slept in his arms last night.

On the nightstand was a note from him. *If you reconsider leaving, give me a buzz at work.*

But her mind hadn't changed.

She went to the bathroom, took care of some things, and descended the steps to the kitchen and poured a glass of white cranberry juice.

Back in her bed, with the juice on the bedside table, she dialed Denise's number. It was a Friday, and she knew that Denise wasn't teaching a class until three that afternoon, so maybe she'd be home. Felicia really wanted to talk to her, and she hoped that she wasn't out running errands.

After four rings, Denise picked up the phone.

"You were carjacked?" Denise spluttered after Felicia told her what happened. "My God! Are you okay?"

"Thank God, yes. He stole my car, and my purse."

"Trash," Denise snarled. "Now, you changed all your locks and cancelled your credit cards?"

"Warren took care of it," Felicia answered. "And later today, I'm going to DMV to get a new driver's license." She had to unearth her birth certificate. Thank goodness her checkbook wasn't in her purse. At least, she didn't have to fool with changing that account.

"Girl, what color was the garbage dump dweller that attacked you?" Denise asked.

"Black."

"I was hoping that you wouldn't tell me that. You're black and so is he, and he's out there ripping off a black woman. It was a black woman who changed his diapers, and taught his stupid ass to walk, and he's terrorizing one."

"He shouldn't be violating anybody, male, or female, black or white," Felicia argued. "And who knows, it could have been a black woman who mistreated him, which is why he has no respect for us."

And why did women have to analyze everything? She was in no mood for introspection. She had been doing enough of that lately. For all she knew, the guy could have had a perfectly wonderful mother and simply turned out to be a piece of shit. "Also, I'm leaving Warren," she revealed.

"*Leaving* Warren?"

"That's what I said."

"As in filling a Samsonite with underwear, clothes and toiletries?"

"You got it."

"Felicia, why don't you forget what Warren did with Angie? I know that's why you're leaving. I don't even have to ask."

"I've tried to forget, but it hasn't been easy."

"Well, what made you decide to leave?" Denise asked.

Felicia explained what led up to her encounter with the car thief. "I don't trust, Warren, and as a result, I could have been seriously injured or even murdered."

"Well, you have a point," Denise said. "But what will leaving accomplish?"

She sighed. "I don't know. I only know that I won't be around someone I have no faith in."

"Felicia, your anger and distrust is understandable. But you and Warren have been together for a half dozen years. You don't pitch that in the wastebasket because he had sex with some slut."

"Sounds like a good reason to toss it in the wastebasket to me. He shouldn't be having sex with anybody but his wife."

"And you have a beautiful home, and the man keeps money in your pocket, and most of all he loves you. Some women wish they had what you do."

"Well, all that's just marvelous, Denise, but it's not sufficient reason for me to stay with somebody that I have zero faith in. That's the problem with a lot of women. Men betray them. And they say, 'All men are dogs' and look the other way. Or pretend to be unaware of what he's up to…Look at our mother."

"What about mama?"

"Daddy cheated on her left and right. And she let that man literally drive her crazy." She took a deep breath. "Well, not me. I want a husband who is completely faithful to me…a husband that I can trust."

"I think you can trust Warren. I think he's sorry about what he did."

"Maybe he is. And Denise, I do love Warren. But I need a break from this marriage," Felicia said. "I need to put things in perspective. I just can't stay here, wondering what Warren is up to when he isn't in my face…if he's getting it on with some tramp who claims to be my friend."

"Have you and Warren considered talking to a counselor? God knows, you could use a Dr. Phil," Denise joked.

"I can fix my own problems."

"Well, where will you be staying?"

"With a gay friend named Keith." Normally, Felicia didn't label people, but had she said she'd be staying with a man named Keith, Denise would have automatically assumed that she was having an affair. "Eventually, I'll get my own place."

"And what will you do for money? You need me to send you some? I can spare a couple of thousand, and you can pay me back whenever. I'll send it by Western Union."

"I don't need any money, thanks."

"Well, what are you going to do for cash? You said you might get your own place, so, you're going to need money for deposits and first month's rent."

"I have several thousand dollars saved up, in a savings account that is in my name alone."

"I'm not trying to dip in your business," Denise said. "But how did you manage to swing that?"

"Well, I sold some of my writing, and I put away some of that money. And for a few years now, I've been squirreling away fifty bucks a week." Felicia sent off the checks to the mortgage, electric, phone and credit card companies. And each week, she paid herself fifty bucks and deposited it in an account in her name only.

"Smart move," Denise said, sounding impressed.

"You never know what can happen in a marriage," Felicia stated. "Men can walk out, and if that happened to me, I didn't want to be without any money. Over the years, I've cooked; cleaned house, did laundry, and took the car in for inspection or servicing. So, for fifty bucks a week, Warren got a bargain."

Also, Felicia had a Mastercard and Visa that was exclusively in her name. She had read articles about women who totally relied on their husbands for support, naively thinking that their husbands would always take care of them and getting screwed in a divorce, or finding out there was no money when hubby died.

She read about former homemakers ending up homeless, or having to ask friends for handouts. Felicia loved being a housewife, but in her opinion, a wise woman should have her own credit cards and savings.

"And speaking of bargains, you have a good man," Denise said, "so don't do something dumb like divorce him."

# Chapter 40

Like an eager real estate agent trying to make a sale, Keith showed Felicia the room that would be her temporary digs until further notice. The spacious room had a queen-size bed, a bookcase, a 32-inch TV and a VCR. Lovely curtains with a matching bedspread.

"Some room," she exclaimed. "You really know how to make a guest welcome."

"Well, you're my pal, and you can stay as long as you like," he said.

"I appreciate your offer, but I have no intention of hanging around long. Two weeks max." She had had family members visit for vacation, totally unnerving her, upsetting her routine. She wouldn't subject anyone to that. But Keith insisted that she wouldn't be an inconvenience.

"I don't know how long I'll be separated from Warren," she said from the edge of the bed. "But I'm going to go apartment hunting. And I have to find a job."

Keith was beside her. "Do you have any interviews lined up?" She had told him that she wrote, and he had asked to read some of her short stories, and articles, and she had promised to let him do so.

"I wish," she said. "I'd love to work on a newspaper. Maybe, I'll look into that."

"Well, since you've been published that should help."

She switched topics. "You know when people leave their spouses, they're supposed to do something off-the-wall." She touched her scalp. "Maybe, I'll cut and dye my hair."

"I like your hair," he said, looking at her admirably.

"So do I, actually."

Keith chuckled. "Well, a lot of people get smashed when they ditch their spouse. But you want to steer clear of the hard stuff, so that's out. What about meaningless sex?" he joked.

She played along. "Yeah, I should go out and pick up some stud and screw his brains out. But seriously, an affair is the last thing I want right now. But I want to do something that Felicia Yvonne Wainwright has never done before." She paused. "I know. Let's go to dinner."

"Too radical," he teased.

"My treat, and afterwards, you can show me how your half lives."

Teasing, he said, "Are you suggesting that Robert and I put on a live sex show for you?"

She playfully punched his arm. "Cutup. I want to go to a gay bar. I went to that lunch with you, and I wondered what it would be like at night."

"Do you have some tendencies that I don't know about?" Keith said.

"Ha ha, ha."

"But hey, if you want to hit a fag bar, why not?"

She chuckled. "Will Robert be joining us?"

"He's spending the evening with his parents," Keith revealed. "Tonight, they'll sit around drinking scotch and water listening to Wilson Pickett and Otis Redding." He rolled his eyes.

\*\*\*

After the bath, makeup, perfume and getting dressed procedure, Felicia appeared in the living room, smiling and thinking she looked pretty damn good.

Keith whistled like a horny stud checking out a babe wearing skimpy shorts.

"If I was straight, I'd be all over you," he jested. And then looking serious, he said, "You look great, Felicia."

"Thank you, kind sir," she said. "And what do we have there?" She nodded to the two flutes Keith held. The bubbles in the amber liquid twinkled like diamonds.

"Ginger ale," he replied.

"Oh, how nice." She had thought it was apple juice, the sparkling variety. Keith was aware of her problem, so she knew he would not have poured her champagne.

"Here you are, lovely lady." He handed her a glass.

Accepting it with a smile, she thought it was a damn shame that Keith wasn't straight. He was easy on the eyes, big-hearted, and he knew how to laugh and have fun. He would have brought tremendous joy to a woman's life. But there was nothing wrong with him bringing joy to a man's life.

"Let's toast," he said, holding the glass aloft. "To friendship, good luck and forgiveness."

They tapped their glasses, and sat on the sofa. "I'm guessing that friendship is to us...good luck is to my job search...But why forgiveness?" She sipped her Canada Dry.

"Well, when you speak of Warren, I can see the love in your eyes. And I'm hoping that you will eventually find it in your heart to forgive the guy."

\*\*\*

192

After a yummy seafood dinner, Felicia and Keith hit *Mix and Mingles,* a hopping gay bar that was as jammed as a Wal-Mart on Christmas Eve.

Felicia sat at a table, sipping a Pepsi, enjoying the loud, throbbing music, and the festive atmosphere while Keith was off twisting and turning with Fred, a gay mortician.

Earlier, under the flashing strobe lights, she and Keith had danced a few songs.

Bobbing her head to the music, she looked at the female impersonators, marveling at the beauty of some of them.

Some were clearly men, but if Keith hadn't told her that this person or that person was a guy, she never would have guessed. You just didn't know what you were looking at these days.

"Hi," greeted a young woman who looked like Lauryn Hill's doppelganger. "Wanna dance?"

Well, Felicia had danced with her sisters, so she had no problem kicking up her heels with another woman, but she didn't want this woman to think that she was a lesbian or anything. If she tried to pick her up, she'd explain that she was straight and was there with a gay friend. "Sure, why not," she said and exited her seat.

The girl's name was BB, short for Brenda Braxton, and they hit the platform and carried on like they were on a gay version of *Soul Train.*

Giggling, Felicia wondered what would Warren, or her sisters, or her friends and neighbors think if they saw her boogying in a gay bar.

Eventually, she returned to the table, and found Keith, sipping a cocktail. "I got you another soda," he said.

"Thanks. I can use it," she panted.

"Having fun?" he asked.

"A blast," She took a swig of her beverage.

Later in the evening, drag queens hit the stage and lip-synched country/western ditties.

A tall, white queen wearing a peach chiffon gown and a puffy blond wig flipped at the bottom, lip-synched, *Rose Garden* by Lynn Anderson.

After Lynn finished her number, Miss Tammy Whynot took the microphone. Before she began performing, a female in the audience yelled, "Excuse me."

"Yeah, honey," Tammy replied, looking out at the crowd.

"Now, I've had a couple of Long Island ice teas and I'm kinda messed up. So, I may not have heard you right. But did you call yourself, Tammy Whynot?"

"That's right," Tammy replied.

"Well, don't you mean Wynette?"

"Nah, honey, I mean, Whynot. I'm a whore and when somebody ask me if I want to have a good time, I say, why not?"

The audience broke into hysterical laughter, applauding.

Tammy performed, *Stand by Your Man.*

And afterwards, "Dolly Parton" did nine to five.

Felicia suppressed the urge to cackle, not because she thought the queens were absurd. She simply found the spectacle absolutely hilarious.

It was such a delightfully kooky evening…just the Rx she needed to distance herself from her marital woes.

# Chapter 41

But six days later, she wondered if leaving Warren had been a goof, a blunder, a whopper of a mistake.

Oh Keith and Robert had been wonderful, obliging, treating her like a cherished family member. But she missed Warren, missed her house...missed her kitchen.

She was *homesick,* damn it. "Then call Warren and tell him that you're ready to come back," Keith said. They were at the kitchen table, drinking limeade Felicia had made just that morning.

"Oh, I couldn't do that," she said, shaking her head as if someone had asked her to go grocery shopping in the nude.

"But you said that you missed Warren," Keith stated, frowning.

"I do."

"Then why the hell can't you tell him you're ready to come back? After all, it is what you want."

Felicia sighed. "I know, but Keith I've only been away for six days. Six lousy days." She took a deep breath. "How would I look going back after such a short time away?"

"Like a woman who's madly in love with her husband, and who wants to be with him."

"I know, and I do..." She trailed off. "But I just can't go back right now." She sighed. "You know, it took this time away to make me realize just how important Warren is to me. There was never any doubt in my mind that I love him." She shrugged. "But being away, looking at new scenery made me put a lot of things in perspective, you know."

"Talk to me, girl," Keith said, pouring another glass of limeade.

"Keith, Warren has been a terrific husband."

"Yeah, you told me."

"And had I not been drinking wine and wallowing in my misery about not being able to have a child...if I had been the Felicia that he had married, I don't think he would have gotten involved with Angie."

"Probably not."

"Now Warren was wrong to betray me, but people make bad choices."

He shook his head philosophically. "It's part of being human. And I tried to tell you this."

She nodded. "And so did my sister."

"But you had to find it out for yourself," Keith said.

She sighed. "I'm not fickle. My opinions don't change from minute to minute, or day to day. But since coming here, I've been doing some late night thinking and I now see things in a different light."

"Then take your ass home," he said emphatically.

"I will. But not now. Maybe in a few months."

"Months?" Keith practically shouted. "So, despite coming to this realization, you still intend to rent an apartment and find a job?"

"I have to. If I don't, I'll look like a mindless six year old who can talk a good game, but not deliver what she says."

"Felicia, you're too damn proud," Keith spat, totally exasperated. "And not only are you excessively proud, but you're being a damn masochist."

She frowned. "A masochist?"

"Yes. You love Warren; you miss him and the home you two created. Yet, you refuse to go back because of some stupid pride. Girl, you should go home, and give Warren a good fucking, and resume your married life. And be done with it. Send your damn pride to the recycle bin," he joked. "I thought it was men who were supposed to be overly proud."

No, women have pride and big egos too, Felicia thought. And Keith was right, she was proud, and she wanted to go back to Warren. But no way was she returning after a mere six-day absence.

# Chapter 42

Felicia was washing a bundt pan. She loved bundt pans, but cleaning between those damn ridges was a pain in the bundt.

To show Keith and Robert her appreciation for their hospitality, she whipped them up an applesauce/cinnamon cake, filling the room with the fragrance of cinnamon. Again, Keith told her that she should tell Warren that she wanted to return, but still, she said, "The time just isn't right."

The phone rang. She dried her hands with a dishtowel. "Hello," she said in the wall phone.

"Fefe, hey, it's Warren."

She had given him Keith's number. And it was so nice to hear his soft, deep voice. God, how she had missed it.

"Hi," she said, hoping that he was calling to say that he missed her too, and that he wanted her to come back, and categorically refused to take no for an answer.

For show, she'd hem and haw for a few minutes, and then relent.

"It's Mama," he said solemnly.

She frowned. "What about Miss Shirley?"

"She's in the hospital."

"Warren, what's wrong?" she asked anxiously.

"Calm down, calm down," he said. "She's in a rehabilitation facility. She had a knee replaced."

Felicia felt immediate relief. Miss Shirley's hospitalization wasn't life threatening. She was in her seventies, and it wasn't uncommon for elderly folks to have new knees and hips installed. "How's she's doing?" she asked.

"Fine. Just misses her home and her own bed."

*Boy, can I relate to that,* Felicia thought.

Warren said, "I'm going to the hospital to visit her tomorrow. If you don't have other plans, I thought maybe you'd like to come with me. I'm sure she'd like to see you."

"And I'd like to see her too," she said without hesitation. She adored Miss Shirley. Also, Felicia liked the idea of seeing Warren.

"I'll pick you up around two," he said. "How's that?"

"I'll be here."

She immediately called her hairdresser to find out if she had anything available for early the following day. "I know it's unexpected," she said. "But an emergency has come up."

"Let me see," the girl said.

Felicia heard pages rustling. "If you can squeeze me in, I'll double your tip," she offered, as an enticement.

The girl chuckled and said she had a cancellation at 10:15.

Felicia grabbed the appointment and the following afternoon, when her hair was shining and pretty, she returned to Keith's to get dressed, taking extra time with her makeup and clothes. She wanted to look her absolute best for her husband.

And shortly before two, Warren arrived, smiling awkwardly, like he was going on a first date. Felicia introduced him to Keith, and they shook hands, and Warren complimented Keith's home.

As he pulled away from the curb, she asked, "Did you get flowers?"

"Not yet. I'm going to pick up some," he said.

They stopped at Kathy's, a local florist, and bought a get-well bouquet.

Back on the road, he said, "Can I ask a favor?"

"What?" Felicia asked, hoping that he would say, 'Come back to me, please. I miss you.'

"Don't mention to Mama that we're separated," he stated.

She was a little disappointed by his request. "You didn't tell her?"

"I was going to, but she called about her surgery." He shrugged. "I thought the timing was bad."

Felicia understood. "I'll play the loving wife," she sang.

"Would that be acting?" he asked seriously. They were at a stoplight.

She remained silent.

"Well, ignore me then," he joked when the light turned green.

*Damn,* she snapped in her head. Sometimes she had wads of toilet paper for brains. When he had said, 'would that be acting,' she couldn't think of anything to say in response. She couldn't just blurt out that she wanted to return.

Why didn't she think to say, 'No, playing the loving wife would not be acting.' That truthful statement could have opened the door to a dialogue about them reconciling.

In her fantasy, Warren said—" *So playing the loving wife won't be acting?"*

Felicia, *"Not at all."*

Warren, *"So you do love me?"*

Felicia, *"With all my heart."*

Warren, *"Then baby, come back to me. I've missed you so terribly. I haven't slept a wink since you've been gone. Can't you see the dark circles under my eyes? I haven't had any appetite."*

Felicia, *"You do look tired, and about twenty five pounds lighter."*

Warren, "*Come back to me, Felicia. Please, please, please, please, come back. I'm so sorry I betrayed you. Oh, come back.*"

When Warren went over a railroad track, she was jolted out of her Walter Mittyish daydream, wishing that it turned out that way.

*** 

"Lordy! Look who's here," Miss Shirley exclaimed, using a walker and being assisted to her bed with the help of an orderly. She was coming out of the bathroom.

Warren and Felicia had just arrived and were standing by the old lady's bed. *How sad,* Felicia thought, looking at Miss Shirley with the orderly. The Miss Shirley she knew and loved was invincible, vital, and active. She gardened, drove her friends to the market, and to their doctor's appointments. She enjoyed matinees and played bingo every Friday afternoon.

Warren and Felicia took turns kissing his mother's coffee colored cheek.

The orderly helped Miss Shirley into her bed. "And flowers," the septuagenarian huffed, admiring the arrangement Warren had set on the bedside table. "You children going to spoil me."

"You deserve it," Warren said. "You're the best."

"Y'all take a load off, and have a seat," she said, being the gracious hostess. "I would offer refreshments, but this ain't my house," she joked in her throaty, authoritative voice.

Prompted by Felicia, Miss Shirley talked about her surgery. "So, you are doing okay?" Felicia asked, wanting reassurance.

"Oh, child, I'm fine. Just miss my house and my own cooking. I don't eat out often, but the food here can't compare to the buffet at Morrison's." Morrison's was Miss Shirley's favorite dining establishment.

For her birthday and Mother's Day, Warren and Felicia tried to talk her into going to an elegant restaurant. But she refused to go anywhere but Morrison's.

Looking at Felicia, she said, "This morning, they gave me a so-called cheese omelet." She shook her head.

Smiling curiously, Felicia said, "Why do you say so-called?"

"Well, the eggs were folded like an omelet," Miss Shirley explained. "But won't nothing in between them. And it had that Cheese Whiz mess squirted on top. Now, that's supposed to be a cheese omelet!" She smiled wryly.

"You're kidding, Miss Shirley," Felicia interjected.

"I wouldn't lie to you. Now, a hospital is supposed to be a place where folks go to get better, and how's that gonna happen if they feed the patients junk? That old Cheese Whiz ain't nothing but a box of salt. Child, if I ate that mess, my blood pressure would have soared to stroke territory. I told the nurse to get it outta my face."

"No, you didn't, Miss Shirley," Felicia exclaimed.

"Yes, ma'am, I did." She nodded emphatically.

Felicia thought of her and Warren's Sunday visits to his mother's.

The two Mrs. Wainwright's sat on the couch, with glasses of iced tea on the coffee table, chitchatting about grocery bargains, or what the characters on *The Bold and The Beautiful* were up to, or a scandalous tidbit about a church member.

Warren would be positioned across from them in the leather recliner, looking damn near comatose, clearly bored to tears.

When the visit drew to a close, he would perk up.

He adored his mother, Felicia knew, but he simply wasn't interested in her and Felicia's Sunday powwows.

But Felicia thoroughly enjoyed Miss Shirley. She would have appreciated having a mother like her.

Growing up, Felicia wished her mother had been like Della Reese, or Claire Huxtable, or Florida Evans from *Good Times*. Those women were strong and tenacious.

Before leaving the rehabilitation facility, Felicia offered Miss Shirley her assistance. "You're going to need someone to cook, and clean, and run errands. If you need me, I'm available."

"Thank you, my dear. That's so kind of you," said the old lady. "But Warren's sister, Carmen is coming up from Carolina to help me out."

Felicia and Warren gave Miss Shirley goodbye kisses on the cheek, and Felicia promised to call to check on her.

***

At a stoplight," Warren said, "Want to get something to eat?"

She hadn't had a bite that morning. "That would be great," she said cheerily.

"Chinese, burgers, something more posh? You pick."

"I could go for a burger."

"How did I know?" he teased. "You could eat burgers for breakfast, lunch and dinner."

"I'm a burger holic. What can I say?" she joked.

In the lobby of a Wendy's, they pigged out on doubles, French fries, and Coke. Felicia had hers with lettuce, tomato and pickle only. Warren had the same thing but with mustard.

She thought about the early days of their marriage when cash was as scarce as it was during the Great Depression, and eating at a fast-food joint was an extravagance.

They were so in love back then...So happy, and what they had was inviolate, indestructible.

But look at where they were now.

***

"You know, the applesauce/cinnamon cake that you like so much?" Felicia said when Warren pulled up to the curb facing Keith's house.

"You made one," he guessed, his face lighting up.

"Yesterday. If Keith and Robert haven't devoured the whole thing, why don't you come in and have a slice? It can be our dessert."

"Now, that's an invitation that I can't refuse," he said.

She was glad that was his response. She wasn't ready to let him go. A part of her desperately wanted to say, 'I'm ready to come home. Let's gather up the few belongings I have here and put them in the car.'

She was sure that he'd think that was a marvelous idea. She had seen the way he looked at her when he collected her at Keith's a few hours earlier. And at Wendy's he regarded her with love in his eyes. He seemed animated and upbeat in her presence.

Maybe, over cake, she'd muster the courage to tell him that she wanted to come home.

Keith had given her a key to the house, and it was empty when she and Warren entered and she was grateful for that. They could talk in private.

Over cake and tumblers of sparkling water, he gabbed about work, and asked if she had been doing any writing, and she told him that she had been working on a lengthy article about her sister's battle with the bulge.

"Universal subject," he said.

He praised a movie he saw the other night on cable.

And as she listened to him go on and on about what a great actor, Morgan Freeman was, she sipped her water and thought, *I can do this.*

"This cake is da bomb," he complimented.

"Glad you like it," she said. *Tell him you want to come back. Swallow your damn pride*, urged her inner voice. But he would think she was wishy-washy, wanting to come back after being away for such a short time.

*So what. Tell him.*

Okay, I can do this, she thought. She moved her lips to speak.

"Have you found an apartment to your liking?" he asked.

For him to ask her such a question, evidently, he wasn't eager for her to return to the house. "I haven't started looking yet," she said, feeling disappointed, but not letting it show.

He mentioned a new complex off Ridgeway Boulevard. "From the outside, they look nice."

"Well, I'll have to check them out," she chirped. "Thanks for the tip."

\*\*\*

"I feel like a fool," Felicia pouted to Keith. Warren had been gone for about an hour.

"Why?"

"I was all prepared to tell Warren that I wanted to come back and work out our problems, and right as I was about to say it, he asked me if I had found a new apartment."

Keith shrugged. "Why didn't you say, 'No, I haven't, and I have no desire to do so. I want to come home.'"

"Keith, I couldn't have done that," she said, shaking her head disapprovingly.

"And why the hell not?"

She sighed. "You just don't get it, do you?"

He frowned. "No, I don't."

"If Warren wanted me to come home, if he really, really wanted me back, he would not have asked me if I found an apartment." She released frustrated air. "That would have been the last thing he would have said to me."

"Aw, that's bullshit," Keith exploded. "Felicia, the guy was just making conversation. When you left, you told him that you were going to get your own apartment. And he simply asked about it." He sighed. "I don't know, Felicia."

"What?"

"The other day, you said that you aren't fickle. You said despite wanting to go home that you were going to stay away for a few months. Okay, fine. That's your call. But here it is less than seventy-two hours later and you considered telling Warren that you want to return. Guess what girlfriend, you sound fickle to me."

"I have a right to change my mind, you know," she said in defense of herself. "And," she sighed. "Today, I saw Warren's mama, and the visit was nice. And he and I had a good time at Wendy's and later, we enjoyed cake.

It was marvelous, made me feel all warm and fuzzy, you know. I felt better than I have in a long time, so I thought I'd swallow my pride and tell him I want to come back. But then he asked me if I had gone apartment shopping." She rolled her eyes.

"Well, I guess when you love somebody, and they hurt you, and you're torn between anger and love, the most resolute person can become a little wishy-washy," Keith conceded.

"Oh, believe me, you can," she said, thinking about her initial reaction to Warren's betrayal. One day she loved him and the next she hated his guts. But that was behind her now.

And she had grown to realize that during their separation, Warren could date other women. He'd be free to do whatever he damn well pleased.

*Well, he did that when he was with you,* said that troublemaking side of her personality.

*Oh, shut up,* Felicia replied, having no desire to revisit the past.

She had to look forward. Had to tell Warren that she wanted to come back. But why did she have to do the asking?

After all, she had been wronged, cheated on.

*Well, you were the one who left,* said her inner voice.

And Warren repeatedly apologized for what happened. He suggested a vacation. Evenings out. The boy groveled.

Now, it was her turn.

# Chapter 43

Felicia was in bed, and the house was dark, and the phone was ringing. She turned and squinted at the clock on the nightstand. It was 1:17 in the morning. Phone calls at that hour always spelled disaster.

For Keith and Robert's sakes, she hoped it was a wrong number.

They didn't need any trauma to deal with.

The pealing ceased, and a short while later, there was a tap on her door. Sitting up in the dark, she covered her boobs with the blanket and clicked on the lamp. "Come in," she said, squinting from the glare.

The door squeaked opened halfway, and Keith was standing under the frame, wearing his bathrobe. "It's for you," he whispered, sounding grave.

Frowning, Felicia said, "Me?"

"It's Warren."

She sighed. "Uh, let me put on my robe." Her insides became jittery.

He shut the door, and while belting her robe, she wondered why Warren was calling her at one something in the morning?

Did Miss Shirley have a relapse? A relapse from knee replacement surgery, she thought, scowling? But any kind of surgery could lead to complications. And Warren's mother was not twenty-two.

She sighed. *Oh, God.* She hoped the news wasn't awful, but for Warren to call at this hour, it had to be.

Miss Shirley seemed fine a few days ago, Felicia thought, going to the kitchen, where she found the receiver on the table. She picked it up. "Warren," she whispered.

"Hey, Fefe," he said soberly.

"Warren, what is it?" she asked in a panicked tone, looking at Keith, leaning against the kitchen sink.

"Oh, my God," Felicia replied, her voice rising. "Uh, when? I-I-I see. Um, I'll be right over. Thanks for calling." She hung up the phone.

"Felicia, what's going on?" Keith asked.

"Sandra has been taken to the hospital," she explained calmly. "I have to get dressed."

"Me too. I'm going with you."

\*\*\*

From the passenger's seat in Keith's car, Felicia said, "Warren said that the hospital called the house looking for me. Sandra was found in an alley, beaten pretty badly."

"Oh, wow, that's whacked," Keith said, driving down the boulevard. Traffic was sparse. Businesses were dark. As they waited at a red light, a police cruiser pulled in the lane next to them. "How did they know to call your house?"

Felicia sighed. "I guess Sandra told them. Or maybe she had one of those 'in case of emergency' cards in her purse."

Sandra and Felicia had not been on speaking terms, so Sandra did not know that Felicia was staying at Keith's.

"Who could have done such a horrible thing?" she said, on the verge of tears.

"There are a lot of nutty people walking the streets."

"I predicted that Sandra's stripping would lead to trouble. I just knew it," Felicia wailed.

"You think what happened is related to her dancing?"

"More than likely. I mean, she was found in an alley behind the club. I bet one of the customers jumped her and beat her up."

"Well, you won't know for sure what happened until you talk to Sandra," Keith said.

For several minutes, they rode in silence. And when they reached the entrance of Willow Oaks Regional Medical Center, Felicia sighed and turned to look at Keith. "Thanks for being here," she said in the dim car. "I really appreciate it."

He patted her hand.

# Chapter 44

"Good Lord," Felicia said in a shocked whisper when she saw Sandra lying in the hospital bed.

Sandra's lips were puffy, broken, and bloodied; her left eye was swollen shut. Light in the room was faint.

"Girl, you act like you're looking at a horror movie," Sandra kidded in a low, throaty voice.

"I can't believe that you're cracking jokes," Felicia said, hovering over Sandra.

"Ain't no use in crying about it. It happened."

"Sandra, who did this?" Felicia asked.

Sandra sighed. "Look, Felicia, my head feels like a high school band is practicing in it."

"Well, didn't they give you something for it?"

"Some pain pills, which ain't doing a lot of good right now. And I don't feel up to talking about what happened. Just know, that I'm okay. I got a tetanus shot, and they took X-rays. I've got some broken ribs, so this is going to be home sweet home for a few days."

Anticipating what was coming, Felicia asked, "And you want me to take care of Laquita?"

"If it's no trouble," Sandra said.

As usual, Sandra's telephone call was about needing a favor, doing something for Sandra. But this time, it didn't matter. "I love Laquita. I'll gladly take care of her," Felicia said. "Where've you been staying?" she asked, remembering that Sandra had moved.

"Been sharing an apartment with a girlfriend," Sandra revealed. "That's where Laquita is now. The girl's watching her for me." She rattled off the address to Felicia.

Felicia got a piece of paper from her handbag, and jotted it down. "I'll get her tonight."

"Thanks, Felicia. And, um, look…" She trailed off and paused.

"What?" Felicia said pleasantly.

"Well, uh, when I found out you couldn't have a baby, I, um, said some nasty stuff to you. And not too long ago, in the grocery store, I acted like a real bitch. I want you to know—"

Felicia guessed Sandra was trying to apologize. Felicia and her sisters had such a hard time humbling themselves, or admitting when they were wrong. Sandra was having difficulty saying that she was sorry to Felicia, and Felicia couldn't come out of her face and tell Warren that she wanted to come home.

Felicia shook her head. "Sandra, don't worry about it. Sisters quarrel. That argument is yesterday. Now, you get some rest." She tapped her shoulder. She wanted to kiss her cheek, but those repulsive cuts prevented her from doing so.

***

When Felicia emerged from Sandra's room, she spotted Warren, in the waiting area, sitting next to Keith. There were other people wearing distressed expressions, and sipping what she assumed was coffee from Styrofoam cups.

As soon as Warren made eye contact with her, he jumped off the seat and rushed to her.

"Hi, uh, what are you doing here?" she asked. Her tone was not hostile.

"That's a silly question," he said. "You should have known that I'd be with you at a time like this."

That was comforting to hear.

"Right after I got through talking to you, I drove over," he said. "How's Sandra?"

"Not in a partying mood," Felicia kidded.

"Who the hell did this?"

Felicia sighed. "I asked Sandra the same question, but she didn't feel up to discussing it. She asked me to take care of Laquita."

"Where is she?" he asked.

"At an apartment that Sandra shares with a friend. I have the address." She held up the piece of paper. "I'm going to go and get her now." She looked at him awkwardly. "Well, thanks for coming by. Um, I'll call you tomorrow, and let you know what's going on."

"Well, where are you going to take Laquita?" he asked.

"Well, with me," she said, thinking that was a dumb question.

"To Keith's?"

"Yeah."

"Felicia, don't you think that would be too much of an imposition?" Warren said bluntly. "I mean, Keith is showing you his hospitality, and now you expect him to take in your niece."

Yeah, he did have a point. "Well, where else can I take her? I suppose I could stay at Sandra's," she said, thinking out loud. But that idea did not appeal to her in the least. Sandra had a roommate, and Felicia had never met

207

the girl. She didn't want to share an apartment with someone she didn't even know.

"Why don't you bring her to the house?" Warren suggested. "Laquita likes the house, the backyard, and she has some toys there."

Yes, the child had spent many nights at Felicia and Warren's, using the guestroom. "Oh, okay," Felicia said brightly. Laquita wasn't the only one who liked the house.

"I'll bring the car around," Warren said.

Felicia nodded. "I'll meet you out front. I have to tell Keith what I'm going to do."

But instead of going right outside, Warren followed her to where Keith sat. He thanked Keith for all his help and support, gave him a good-natured slap on the back and exited the hospital, reminding Felicia that he was going to pull the car around.

She told Keith that Sandra needed her to watch Laquita, and that she was going to pick up the child and take her home with Warren.

"Well, that's good," Keith sang approvingly. "Crisis have been known to bring people closer.

\*\*\*

Felicia and Warren entered the living room. She clicked on the overhead light. He asked, "Where do you want me to put her?" He was referring to Laquita, who was asleep, clad in pajamas, with her head slumped on his chest.

They had collected the child from Sandra's roommate. "Well, I'm going to sleep with her," Felicia said. "I don't want her to wake up in a different environment and get upset. If I'm with her, she'll be okay."

"So then, I'll put her in our bed," he said. "It's bigger. I'll use the spare bedroom."

*Well, there won't be any kissing and making up tonight,* Felicia thought, disappointed. But the point was that she was back in the house and she'd get around to telling Warren that she wanted to stay put.

They went upstairs, and he lay Laquita down, and placed a kiss on her forehead. Felicia spread a blanket over her. It was Indian summer, and muggy out and the air conditioning cut on intermittently, making the house a little nippy.

Warren and Felicia practically tiptoed out of the room, and gingerly, Felicia closed the door. "You aren't going to lie down?" he asked in the hall. "You need to get some rest too."

Appreciating his concern for her, she smiled. "I'm too wound up to sleep. I'm going to sit up for a while."

He shrugged. "Why don't I make you a cup of tea? It'll help you to unwind."

"I'd like that. Thanks." And looking down at her jeans and blouse, she thought a change of clothes would also aid relaxation. "I'm going to get out of these clothes," she said while Warren was going off to make the tea. She returned to the bedroom and quietly swapped her outfit for a silk robe.

She yanked off the hair accessory that kept her ponytail in place, and raked her fingers through her hair. She knew it looked like hell, but she didn't care.

Downstairs, she found Warren on the sofa. Her steaming cup of tea and a snifter of brandy was on the coffee table.

And man, could she use a slug of brandy about now. She remembered how it used to unwind her. And it had been a most upsetting night, and a tranquilizing brandy would be nice.

And besides, she was at peace with the fact that she couldn't have children, and that her husband had gotten another woman pregnant.

So, considering all that, she had faith that she could resume having an occasional glass of wine with meals, or a glass of brandy to unwind, without worrying about becoming a lush and having to join Alcoholics Anonymous.

The halogen lamp next to the couch was on its lowest setting, giving the room a hypnotic, romantic feel, and making Warren look even more handsome.

Women weren't the only ones whose looks were enhanced by soft lighting, Felicia thought.

Warren spotted her, and for a moment, he simply gazed at her, making her feel a little self-conscious.

"Uh, why are you looking at me like that?" she giggled, going to the sofa.

"Because you're so beautiful."

She rolled her eyes. "Oh, man, please. It's after three a.m. and I don't have on a lick of makeup. And my hair looks like I just fought my way out of a tornado."

He chuckled. "You're one of those rare women who wake up in the morning looking lovely. You don't need rouge and all that stuff."

"You're sweet," she said, now sitting next to him. Looking at the steam swirling from the teacup, she added, "Thanks for making that. But I'd like to change my order to a brandy."

He frowned. "Brandy?"

"Yeah."

"But I thought, well, you know because of the wine."

"I can handle it. I no longer need crutches," she said.

So he poured her the alcoholic drink, and after taking a swig, she put the snifter down on the coffee table next to his, and threw back her head and sighed.

And because it had been hours since she had last had food, the spirit quickly made her feel warm and relaxed.

And boy, she appreciated the feeling. She sat up and took another sip of brandy. It felt wonderful to be off her feet, loosening up in familiar, cherished surroundings. Her thoughts drifted to Laquita. And that shabby neighborhood Sandra was living in, and that cramped apartment she shared with her roommate. When Felicia and Warren arrived to pick up Laquita, Miss Roommate was sitting in the dark, stretched out on the sofa, at two something in the morning, drinking beer and watching an old episode of *Gomer Pyle*. And the smell of pot was in the air.

And when she learned that Sandra was hospitalized, her first response was, "Well, I hope she found somebody to take care of her kid. I don't mind watching her at night sometimes, but I ain't taking care of Laqueenie round the clock." She didn't even ask what happened to Sandra, and if she was okay. Her only consideration was being inconvenienced. *Some friend.*

"What cha thinking about?" Warren asked, noticing her faraway expression.

"Kids," she stated simply. "How dependent they are. When we picked up Laquita, she was in dreamland."

He sipped his brandy. "Didn't have a care in the world."

"And you lifted her from the bed, and she didn't budge, not once. And on the drive over here, she slept undisturbed. If I didn't hear her breathing, I would have checked the child's pulse...Kids are so needy, and dependent. They need responsible people to take care of them, and Sandra isn't doing the best job of taking care of her daughter. Sure, Sandra makes sure the girl's fed, and clothed, but she needs a decent job and a decent place to stay. Sandra is not setting a good example for her daughter."

"Fefe, it's late, and you've had a dramatic night. Just put everything out of your mind, and let the brandy do its work... Turn around," he said.

She did as he asked, putting her back to him.

"Now don't think about anything," he told her, using a soothing voice. "Just know that Laquita is upstairs, safe and sleeping, and that Sandra is in the hospital. And you have zero concerns."

"Are you about to put me under hypnosis?" she joked, though she knew what he was about to do.

He began massaging her shoulders. "Oh, that feels great," she cooed, drawing out the word, with her eyes closed. She felt the kinks unknotting. It was like her muscles were braids, and with each rub, a braid loosened, making her feel relaxed and wonderful.

Eventually, he transferred his hands to her scalp and masterfully rubbed it, making it tingle…move…stretch, putting the pressures of the night off in the distance.

She felt separated from the troubled world that she had inhabited the past few weeks, like she was on holiday.

Some people thought sex was the ultimate pleasure, and good sex was magnificent, there was no denying that. But in Felicia's opinion, a first-rate scalp massage definitely ran a close second. "Ooh," she said in an orgasmic tone as Warren massaged her head.

# Chapter 45

The birds were singing and brilliant sunshine poured through Felicia's kitchen, where she was at the counter making breakfast.

According to the microwave clock, it was only a few minutes before eight, so she had only slept for a few hours. After the fabulous scalp massage, she had whispered goodnight to Warren, and joined Laquita in the king-size bed.

The brandy had helped her to sleep, and now she was making flapjacks and humming.

Warren appeared in the kitchen. "You're already up?"

"I've been up for a while," she said.

"I thought you'd sleep later."

"I don't know what time Laquita will wake up. Children are usually early-risers, and I wanted to be up and about when she opened her eyes."

"What you making?" he asked, looking at the bowl on the counter. He wore a blue tee shirt tucked into jeans, his weekend look. The short sleeved tee shirt displayed his muscular arms.

"Banana pancakes," she answered. "I wanted to do something special for Laquita. And I know how much she loves banana pancakes."

"Well, she and I have that in common," he said. "So, save a stack for me."

"You got it." Peeling a banana, she said, "She's bound to get upset when she learns that her mother is in the hospital."

Warren looked sympathetic. "Yeah, poor kid. But we'll do everything we can to make her happy. And you made coffee," he remarked, looking at the carafe of freshly brewed Colombian supremo on the burner of the electric coffeemaker.

"Want me to pour you a cup?" she asked.

"I'd appreciate it," he said.

After filling his favorite mug with some of the steaming, aromatic liquid, and adding some half-and-half, she handed the cup to him.

He thanked her, and took the coffee to the table, where that morning's edition of *The Willow Oaks Free Press* lay.

And while sunshine poured through the kitchen window, Warren read the paper and Felicia's attention was on the bacon and the pancakes cooking, and it was classic and old-fashioned and she loved it.

Flipping a pancake, she heard Warren greet Laquita. "Hey, little lady," he said.

"Hi," the child replied sheepishly, wiping her eyes. With her pigtails, she looked like a caramel colored Pippi Longstocking.

Looking bewildered, she asked, "Where's my mommy?"

"Warren, would you keep an eye on this," Felicia said, referring to the bacon and the pancakes cooking in the pan. "I want to talk to Laquita."

"Sure," he said and accepted the spatula from Felicia.

Felicia went to her niece. "Sweetie, sit down," she said, pulling out a chair and motioning for the little girl to sit.

But Laquita didn't budge. "Something happened," she stated.

*Perceptive little thing,* Felicia thought. "Your mother's in the hospital. She was in an accident."

"A car wreck?" Laquita asked, concern written all over her pudgy, cherubic face.

Felicia shook her head. "Not that kind of accident. I don't know the details. But she got hurt, and she has to stay in the hospital for a few days."

"Is she going to die?" Laquita asked, alarmed.

"Oh, no, honey. She's okay," Felicia said, stroking her niece's face. "I saw her last night and she's hurt, but she's okay."

Laquita looked relieved.

Felicia said, "And while she's getting better, you're going to stay here with me and Warren."

Turning to looking at Laquita, Warren asked, "How do you feel about that?"

Laquita nodded. "I like it here."

"And we like having you here," he said.

Laquita smiled.

"I'm making pancakes and bacon for breakfast," Felicia said, returning to the stove and relieving Warren of chef duties. He returned to his seat. "How does that sound?"

"Good," Laquita said.

"It'll be ready shortly. So, why don't you sit down and have some orange juice while I finish up?" Felicia suggested. A pitcher of juice was on the table.

"I drink Pepsi in the morning," Laquita revealed.

That sounded like something Sandra would allow, Felicia thought, lifting a disapproving eyebrow at Warren. But since the child's mama was in the hospital, she wouldn't make an issue of it. Laquita deserved a little indulging.

"Pepsi in the morning?" Warren said, incredulously.

Laquita nodded, now sitting at the table. "Yeah. I have it every morning with my cocoa puffs."

"Well, if you want it, you can have it," he said. "But you should give o.j. a try? It's good for you, loaded with vitamin C, which helps to prevent colds. Why don't you give orange juice a shot? You don't want to go around sneezing and coughing all the time," he joked. "We can have Pepsi with the hot dogs we're going to have for lunch?"

Laquita's eyes got big. "I like hot dogs. We're having them for lunch?"

Warren shrugged. "Sure, why not? It's a sunny Saturday morning, so we'll go to the park, have some fun, and when we get hungry, pig out on some frankfurters."

He was so good with her, Felicia thought.

***

That afternoon, Felicia and Laquita dropped by Sandra's apartment, and picked up some of Laquita's clothes, shoes and her toothbrush. And when they returned home, the two females and Warren went to the petting zoo, the park, and had hot dogs and Pepsi for lunch.

A few times during their outing, he had lifted Laquita from the pavement and bounced her in the air, making her giggle hysterically. Laquita was clearly enjoying the attention.

*Girlfriend loved being spoiled,* Felicia thought. *But what female didn't?*

Warren and the child hit the swings, leaving Felicia at a picnic table, eyeing them dreamily, and thinking that Warren would make a magnificent father.

*Why was life so damn unfair?* Warren wanted a child, and she couldn't give him one. And then there were irresponsible creeps getting women pregnant and not bothering to take responsibility for their kids.

***

"Lord have mercy," Denise said when Felicia told her what was going on with Sandra. "Well, who beat her up?"

"I don't know," Felicia answered. "It happened last night, and Sandra didn't feel up to talking about it. I'll get the details when I visit her this evening."

"I'll bet it was one of those perverts who hang out at strip joints," Denise said. "Probably got fresh with Sandra and she told him off, and he didn't like what she said, and fed her some fist."

"Yeah, it crossed my mind that one of the customers in the club attacked her."

"How's she doing?" Denise asked.

214

"Bruised. Scratched. She has some broken bones. The doctor is keeping her for a few days. I called this morning, and she said that she felt better."

"Well, that's good to hear. After I'm done talking to you, I'll call her and fill her ears with some nice words."

That made Felicia smile. She knew that Denise loved Sandra, but Denise firmly believed that people should take responsibility for themselves. And she simply refused to coddle Sandra. "I assume you're taking care of Laquita?"

"Yeah, actually, she's staying with me and Warren."

"You're at the house?" Denise asked, sounding surprised to hear that. "I thought you were staying with the gay dude."

"I was. But there was the drama with Sandra and I needed a place to take Laquita, so I brought her here...Warren suggested it."

"He wants you in that house. He loves himself some Felicia, or shall I say, Fefe?" Denise teased.

"And I love myself some Warren."

"So, have you two reconciled?" Denise asked.

"Well, not yet. But I'm going to tell Warren that I'm no longer interested in getting my own apartment, or a job."

"And I'm sure hearing that will put a smile on his face. It sure puts one on mine. You and Warren belong together."

"Yeah, I think so too."

# Chapter 46

Felicia entered Sandra's hospital room, carrying a box of chocolates and a helium balloon that said, *Stop fakin' and Go Back To Work.*

Sandra was lying on her side, gazing at the wall.

Her roommate, a thirty something blonde sat up in the next bed, giggling at *The Golden Girls*. Felicia caught a glimpse of Dorothy's son, Michael telling Dorothy that he wanted to marry an older black woman. Felicia had seen the episode a few times, and thought it was hilarious.

"Sandra," Felicia whispered.

Sandra turned. "Hi," she said quietly, obviously delighted to see Felicia. "I didn't see you come in."

"You were off in another world."

"Yeah, lying here, thinking."

And still looking battered, Felicia observed. The swelling had diminished a little, but the cuts were still fresh.

"I see you brought some goodies," Sandra said.

"Candy." Felicia held up the box. Before coming to the hospital, she had stopped at the supermarket and picked up the little gifts.

Felicia handed Sandra the chocolates and tied the blue string of the balloon around the bed rail.

"So, how's my baby?" Sandra asked, tearing the cellophane off the box of candy, and removing a lump of chocolate. Felicia shook her head when Sandra offered her a piece.

"She's fine, and she sends her love, and a big kiss."

Sandra's eyes filled with tears. "I miss that little girl."

"And she misses you too. But be assured that she's in good hands, being spoiled rotten by Warren."

So that she and Sandra could talk in private, Felicia drew the curtain to the adjacent bed, creating a partition. She sat in a chair to the side of the bed. "Now, tell me, who did this to you?" she asked Sandra.

"A transvestite," Sandra revealed.

Felicia was astonished. "A what?"

"This person…thing…whatever came to work at the club. She…he…it had breasts, long hair. Didn't have an Adam's apple. Voice sounded okay, but I suspected that she was a guy. And a few of the other dancers thought something was up too. And girl, if somebody is questioning somebody's gender, something is up."

Felicia nodded, hungry for more information. She was spellbound by this unusual tale.

"So I asked her straight up, if she was a woman," Sandra stated.

Felicia frowned. "You *asked?*"

"Show did."

That was rather brazen."

"Oh, she denied it," Sandra said. "But she was up on stage, dancing, teasing the men…rubbing her implanted titties in their faces. And they were tipping her and enjoying her performance…That shit pissed me off."

*Sounds jealous to me,* Felicia thought.

"I didn't think it was right for her to be deceiving those guys. They come to the club to see *women* dance. They liked getting turned on by *women.* So, I went on stage, grabbed the microphone, and told the audience what I thought."

Felicia was secretly aghast that Sandra did such a thing.

"Some of the guys shook their heads in disbelief. 'Nah, uh-uh,' they said. 'No, damn way.' Some looked like they wanted to throw up. Oh, she said it wasn't true. Accused me of being jealous and crazy, and strutted off the stage, claiming that she had never been so humiliated. But she was puttin' on, just trying to play it off. And then she quit and stormed out of the club." Sandra paused. "She did that because her gig was up. I had blown her cover."

Sandra was way out of line, Felicia thought. Her behavior was mean, malicious and inflammatory. But she kept her opinions private.

Sandra took a deep breath. "And later, after the club closed, I went to the car I had borrowed from my roommate. When I put the key in the driver's door, somebody tapped me on the shoulder. I turned around, and it was that freak. 'Hey, bitch,' she said…Before I could even think what to do, she punched me in the face. I scratched her a few times, grabbed her hair." Sandra's eyes filled with tears and she took a deep breath. "But she pounded me again and again. I fell to the pavement, and then she kicked me in the stomach."

Felicia scowled, when she considered just how diabolical some people could be.

Sandra said, "I ain't never had nobody treat me like that."

While plucking a few Kleenexes out of the box on the night table, Felicia thought that violence was abhorrent, that no one had a right to put their hands on another person, only in a matter of self-defense.

And she truly loved Sandra, and she certainly did not deserve to be beat up. But humiliating that person was *begging* for trouble. And Felicia felt disloyal for even thinking that. "Here, you are sweetheart," she said, handing her sister a wad of tissues. "Did you report this to the police?"

Wiping her eyes and nose, Sandra nodded.

"So, was this person arrested?" Felicia asked, noticing an itty-bitty piece of tissue lodged in one of the cuts on Sandra's cheek.

"She sure was, and I hope she rots in jail," Sandra snarled.

"I'm sure that she'll pull some serious time for committing such a vicious assault." Felicia took Sandra's hand. "Sandra, I've said this to you before, and I'll say it again, but you need to find a new line of work, and get into something with a future."

Sandra sighed. "I agree."

That was the last thing Felicia expected to hear. She thought Sandra would put on that broken record about how stripping was respectable, and that the money was spectacular.

"Felicia, I've been wanting to get out of stripping for a while. A lot of shit goes on in those clubs. In addition to stripping, some of the girls prostitute on the side. Guys see us dancing, and offer us money to go home with them. And some of the girls do it. Some men pick up girls for three way sex with their wives and girlfriends."

*Some people,* Felicia thought. Imagine your husband bringing home a lap dancer for a threesome.

"And some bisexual women come in the club with their husbands or boyfriends looking for a dancer to take home. I've been propositioned. But I always say n-fucking-o."

"Sandra, what in the world made you go into stripping?"

"Attention, mainly. Girl, you know how I looked when I was younger. I made Cinderella's wicked stepsisters looked like beauty pageant contestants." She chuckled. "But plastic surgery prettied me up, and then guys began noticing me." She sighed. "That had never happened before. I mean, I became center stage and I guess, I just went berserk." She paused. "But a long time ago, I realized that stripping wasn't entirely about getting attention. Oh, wanting to be in the spotlight played a major role. But another reason I became a dancer was because I was angry."

Felicia frowned. "Angry?"

"Yeah."

"With who?" Felicia asked.

"Our daddy. Or your daddy, but he was my father figure." She sighed. "That man treated Mama like shit."

"You don't need to tell me," Felicia replied matter-of-factly. "I remember."

"Cheating on her, leaving her. I think his treatment of her was what made her so cold, made her crack up."

"I'm sure it did," Felicia said. But in her opinion, their mother should have been stronger, and she shouldn't have loved so hard.

"And then there was Laquita's father," Sandra said. "What a toilet stool full of shit he was. Knocking me up when I was just seventeen and then dumping me." She exhaled angrily. "I made up my mind that no man would ever hurt or use me again, that it would cost them just to get aroused by me."

"So that's why you started prancing around half naked?" Felicia jested.

Sandra nodded. "But I want out." She sighed. "But I don't know where to start. You and Denise are lucky. You've been to college."

"You could go to college," Felicia said.

"High school dropouts can't go to college," Sandra said.

"Well, you'll have to get a GED."

"I know, but I don't know if I'd be interested in going to college. I was never much of a school person. But when I'm sprung from this place, I'll have to find a new line of work."

God, hearing that made Felicia want to leap out of her chair and dance around the hospital room.

"What excites you?" Felicia asked.

"I never thought about no career. I just knew that I needed to earn the rent money. One of the girls got out of dancing, and took a civil service test and became a mail carrier. That ain't for me. Dogs barking at me, working in the rain, snow and roasting heat." She made a face. "Another girl became a bank teller. When I was in Maryland, I worked at a Dairy Queen. I had a ball making hot dogs and barbecues, and filling cups with soda." She acted embarrassed to say that. "I know it's not the same as writing articles."

"Hey, there's nothing wrong with working at a Dairy Queen. It's honest work, and if it brings you joy, that's all that matters."

"But I can't support myself and my daughter working at no DQ."

In a bright tone, Felicia said, "Why not open up a Dairy Queen type restaurant?"

"That would be nice. But girl, you need bucks to do something like that."

"You can *save* for it. Find a decent paying job, and put those spare nickels in a piggy bank."

Her face looked thoughtful. "I could do that, I suppose."

"Sure, you could."

"I like this," Sandra said.

"What?"

"Me and you talking like this, acting like sisters."

Felicia said, "I like it too. We should do it more often."

"Felicia, I'm going to need help," she said earnestly. "Getting my life back on track. Sometimes it's hard trying to figure things out. I'm not dumb, but sometimes I need advice, a second opinion, some input."

"We all do, and I'm here for you, Sandra."

# Chapter 47

Wearing a silk robe, Felicia sat at the patio table, sipping from a tumbler of iced tea. It was night. Stars twinkled in the sky. Off in the distance, the sound of a dog barking could be heard.

Laquita was upstairs, bathed, in her pajamas, asleep, happy to know that her mother was okay, and would be released from the hospital day after tomorrow.

Earlier in the evening, Felicia called Sandra's hospital room and put Laquita on the phone, and mother and daughter chatted for a few minutes.

For dinner, Laquita had assisted Felicia in making tacos. She placed the child atop a stool and let her pour sauce into the skillet and take the shredded lettuce and cheese to the table.

After supper, she bathed and brushed her teeth, and she and Felicia sat up in bed and watched *Anastasia* on the big screen TV.

Warren had eaten with them, but begged off when Laquita had asked him if he was going to watch the movie with her and Felicia.

While the little girl was in the bathtub, playing in the bubbles, he whispered to Felicia—" Can't deal with *Anastasia.* Not my cup of chamomile," he joked and went to the den to work on some briefs.

"There you are," he called, coming out on the patio, breaking into Felicia's reverie.

"Here I am," she whispered, glancing back.

"I peeked in the bedroom, thinking that you had nodded off, but you weren't there."

"It's no where near eleven. You know, I can't go to sleep before midnight."

"Well, with all the running around that you've been doing the past few days, I thought you'd have conked out earlier than usual." He sat down at the table.

She sighed. "When Sandra is released from the hospital, I don't want to go back to Keith's," she revealed.

"You don't," he said.

"I want to scratch my plans to find my own apartment, and a job. I want us to reconcile. I want to come home. How do you feel about that?"

Warren gushed. "Baby, you know how much I want that."

"I'm going to bury what happened with Angie, and never exhume it. Adultery is wrong, but I've done a lot of thinking lately, and I bear some responsibility for what happened."

He sighed. "I shouldn't have broken the vows I made to you."

"Well, it's over with, but if it happens again, there will be a divorce." She paused to make sure that her announcement sank in. "There will be no negotiation, no heart-to-hearts. I don't care how much I love you and miss you…it will be over. If you want to be a playboy, I'll give you your freedom and you can go have a ball with as many women as you want. I won't put up with affairs." Her mother had tolerated that nonsense and became an angry, bitter woman because of it. Felicia would not stand for it.

"It'll never happen again," Warren said. "I promise you that."

For a moment, they were quiet. "You're so good with Laquita," she said.

"She's a sweet kid."

"And you'd make some sweet kid a great father," she complimented.

"At some point, we can adopt," he said.

"Or use a surrogate."

He chuckled. "*You're* suggesting that we use a surrogate? If I'm not mistaken, aren't you the lady who said it was unnatural and wrong?"

"As I said, I've been doing a lot of reflecting lately, and… I think I know why I opposed the idea of us using a surrogate."

He looked at her curiously.

"You were…are my husband, and I didn't like the idea of another woman carrying your child. And I realize now that I was being stupid and self-centered. I mean, *you* want a biological child, and I can't give you one. And you can get one by using a surrogate. So, I'm now agreeable to the idea of us using a surrogate."

His expression indicated that he was pleased to hear that. "We'll discuss it at some point down the road," he said. "For now, I think we should concentrate on getting to know each other again."

"I like that idea," she said, smiling warmly.

"We can take a trip."

"Sounds nice. It can be a second honeymoon," she said.

Warren went to Felicia, squatted on his haunches and put his lips on hers and they passionately kissed. And she luxuriated in the delightful sensation. It had been a long time that kissing her husband felt right and natural and that was because she had no qualms about whether she wanted to be with him.

When the kiss ended, he regarded her, and she saw incontestable love in his eyes. He even appeared younger, more relaxed. And she knew that was because he was overjoyed that she was coming back to him. And she was equally overjoyed about returning.

For a long time, they sat on the patio and talked, and he told her that his mother was home from the rehabilitation center, and that she was doing great, and that he visited his sister, who was helping his mom.

And when they decided to call it a night, he scooped Laquita from the bed that he shared with Felicia, and relocated the child to the guestroom.

He and Felicia slept in the same bed that night, but they didn't make love. They simply slumbered in each other's arms. Lovemaking would come in time…all that mattered was that they were together again.

# Chapter 48

Felicia picked up the kitchen phone. "I have some terrific news," Warren spluttered excitedly. "And I'm coming home immediately. So make sure you're there. Forget about grocery shopping, or going to the cleaners. Just be home. This can't wait until I come in at my usual time."

Looking chaotic, she chuckled. "Okay, I'll stay put. But what's going on?"

"I'll tell you when I see you. Bye. Love you."

"Love you too." What in the world was that about, she wondered, hanging up the phone, and returning to her laptop, which was on the table? She had been having a sprightly writing session.

She had sold the piece on Denise's weight loss. And the magazine had requested more articles. So, she was currently assembling one about a marriage surviving adultery. Hey, why not get stories from her backyard?

But after that cryptic call, she couldn't concentrate on that, so she put the lid down on the portable computer.

Why did Warren want to come home so early in the day? It was only ten 'til noon. Did he snag a big case that would bring him fame and notoriety? Was he going to work with Johnny Cochran?

*Yeah, right,* she thought.

Well, it could happen. Warren was certainly smart enough to work with the bigwigs.

They had investments. Did one of them bring in a tremendous windfall?

Oh, who knew what was going on? She'd find out when he walked through that door.

They had been reunited and joyful for two months, carrying on like newlyweds, making love, taking a two-week vacation to glorious Hawaii, and spending six days in Daytona Beach Florida. One of the advantages of being your own boss was taking off whenever the mood hit you.

They had been going out to dinner, dancing, and seeing friends.

Because of Angie's betrayal, Felicia grew to distrust women, and avoided her girlfriends. But eventually, she grew to realize that not all women were treacherous whores.

So, yes indeed, lately, life had been treating Felicia magnificently.

And Sandra was doing okay too. She had stopped stripping, and was working two jobs, checking groceries part-time, and putting in a forty-hour week at a Dairy-Queen type restaurant. And studying for her GED.

Go Sandra. At Warren's urging, she sued Laquita's father for child support.

The creep demanded a paternity test, which proved that he was the child's daddy, and a judge ordered him to pay support, and provide medical coverage for Laquita.

And Sandra's dream was to one day open a Dairy Queen type restaurant, so she was dropping twenty bucks a week into a savings account, more when she could. "I already have a name for it," she had gushed to Felicia.

"Oh, really?" Felicia asked, genuinely interested.

"I'm going to call it Bleachers." Sandra's face glowed with excitement. "What you think? Know how when people go to a baseball game, they eat a hot dog while sitting on the bleachers?"

"I like it," Felicia sang, happy that her sister had goals and was doing something positive with her life.

After getting her GED, Sandra said that she was going to take some small business courses at the community college, so she could run her business properly.

Felicia was so proud of her.

***

Warren rushed into the kitchen; his eyes were wild with happiness.

Felicia chuckled. "Man, you should take up fiction writing. You certainly know how to create suspense. I've been on the edge of my seat trying to figure out why you wanted to talk to me."

He took a deep breath. Usually, he was so calm and unruffled. *This must be big,* Felicia thought.

"You know, Carol Randolph?" he said.

Felicia nodded. "Tall, blonde woman."

"Yeah. Well, as you know, she's a lawyer, and she knows about our situation, that we can't get pregnant. And that we want a child. She handles a lot of private adoptions, and recently, a lady contacted her. She and her husband want to put their baby up for adoption."

Felicia frowned. "Why would a married couple want to give their child away?" She sat down at the table.

Getting a Pepsi from the fridge, Warren said, "They had adopted a little boy." He threw some ice cubes in a glass and covered them with soda. "And then they decided that they didn't want to be parents."

Scowling, Felicia said, "Hold up. Let me see if I got this straight. These people *adopted* a baby, and now they're putting the child up for adoption?"

Nodding, and coming to the table, he said, "It happens more often than you realize." He pulled out a chair.

"I don't see how anybody could do something like that. My goodness, we're talking about a baby, a human being, not a pair of boots that you buy from the store, decide that you don't want, so you take them back."

Warren shrugged. "Well, what they don't want can be our gift."

Felicia smiled warmly. "True. Tell me about the baby? You said he's a boy. How old?"

"Ten months."

"Oh, nice," she said, sounding like she just came out of the sweltering heat and entered an air-conditioned room. "And at such an age, he won't be traumatized by being uprooted."

"He's biracial," Warren said, "a product of a teenage romance. The teen's tried to raise the boy for eight months, but it was too much for them. And their parents thought it best to put the baby up for adoption. They say racism isn't their reason, but that the kids were too young to be parents."

Felicia sipped from Warren's glass. "So, there's a chance we can get a baby?"

He nodded.

A faraway expression appeared on her face.

"What you thinking about?" Warren asked.

"Formula, changing diapers, teething. I'd love every minute of it."

"I know you would. So, you want to adopt Michael?" he asked.

"Why ask pointless questions?" she joked. "And Michael's a nice name."

"I would have preferred Warren Jr."

"So would I, but let's not change the child's name. I mean—"

"He's been given up for adoption twice, and his name is Michael. And he doesn't need to be put through anymore changes."

"Exactly," she said.

"I know. I just would like a namesake."

"Well, maybe with our next child." They wanted four children, and they had decided to use a surrogate and adoption to get them.

He nodded. "Michael's current set of parents wants to meet us," Warren said. "They want a face-to-face with the people they're giving the baby to. I guess they want to size us up."

"Well, that's understandable," Felicia said, but her expression became worried.

What if they don't like her?

226

# Chapter 49

Four evenings later, around six, the sun was fading and nature had painted the sky salmon.

And Felicia and Warren were in their living room. A plate of cookies in three neat rows was on the coffee table and Folgers was percolating in the kitchen.

Earlier, Felicia had vacuumed, squirted Pledge and Windex. Everything was gleaming and welcoming, which was how she wanted her guest to feel. They'd see this house was a great place for a baby to be.

"Biscuits, as the French say," Warren quipped, looking at the plate of cookies. He grabbed one.

Felicia took a deep breath. "How can you joke around at a time like this?"

He tossed the cookie in his mouth. "What's there to be nervous about? They're just two people."

"True," Felicia said, taking a deep breath, and thinking that was a good way of looking at it. "This is no big deal."

*They're just two people. They're just two people.* But making that her mantra did not make the butterflies in her stomach flit elsewhere. She nervously chewed her lower lip. "I haven't felt this jumpy about meeting anybody since you introduced me to your mama all those years ago."

Warren chuckled from the sofa. "Just calm down." He patted the cushion. "Come. Take a load off."

Going to the couch, she said, "You know, Warren, on second thought, these aren't just any two people. They want to see if we have the right stuff to parent a child. What if they don't like us?" She released a nervous breath.

"Chill," he repeated, grabbing another cookie.

"And why don't you *chill* with the cookies?" she admonished. "I put them out for our guests. I want the plate to look full, and inviting, not picked over. You know, how when you go in a bakery, and if there's one doughnut left on the tray, you pass on it. Or in the ice cream store, if your favorite flavor is almost gone, you don't want the little bit that's there. People don't like stuff that looks picked over."

Warren chuckled. "You're babbling."

"I'm nervous."

"I can see."

"What if they don't like us?"

He said, "You already said that."

"Yeah, but it's a possibility," she said.

"Well, we better not mention my love affair with my crack pipe," he jested.

Since reconciling, the atmosphere in the house was lighter. They were joking and bantering. But now, Felicia was in no mood for it. She shot him an irritated expression.

And when there was a knock on the door, her heartbeat accelerated. "Oh, God, if I don't calm down, you're going to have to take me to see a cardiologist," she said, taking a deep breath.

Warren opened the door, admitting Leslie and Stuart Rogers. Leslie was a columnist for a newspaper in a neighboring city, and Stuart was an English professor. They were both 44.

Felicia had wondered about the appearance of a woman who would relinquish a child that she had adopted. That sounded so radical; so far removed from the norm. She expected Leslie to have nose rings and have esoteric interests.

So, the day after learning about Michael, Felicia went to a magazine and gift shop and bought a copy of the newspaper that Leslie worked on. And the head-shot showed a delicate looking black woman with a small nose, a line for a mouth, glasses, café au lait skin, and boy's length hair that was a bunch of curls.

In person, Leslie was about 5'1, and Stuart was tall, chocolate colored, bespectacled with a box shaped head.

There was nothing odd about their appearances, but what they were doing was peculiar, Felicia thought.

Warren told them to sit down.

"I made coffee," Felicia told her guests. "Would you like a cup? Or if you like, I have iced tea or soda?"

"I'd like coffee," Leslie said in a low voice.

"So would I," Stuart stated.

Warren went to the kitchen to get it, and while he was gone, Leslie complimented their home, and asked about a painting. Warren returned with a tray and four mugs and a container of half-and-half.

He poured coffee for everyone, and there were murmurs of appreciation.

"There are cookies," Felicia said, nodding to the plate on the coffee table.

Leslie took one and nibbled it. "I bought pictures of Michael," she said, unzipping her purse and removing a few snapshots. She handed them to Felicia.

"Oh, my," Felicia gushed, looking at the photos. Her eyes filled with tears at the sight of the precious baby. He was round, and grinned profusely; his skin was the color of a graham cracker and drool was on his fat chin.

Without thinking, Felicia kissed one of the pictures and handed them to Warren.

"Good looking, kid," he said.

There was silence. "I'm not judging you," Felicia said to Leslie. "But I don't see how you can give up that gorgeous baby."

"It isn't easy," Leslie said.

"Then, why are you doing it?" Felicia asked gently. "If you don't want to discuss it, you're not obligated to," she added rapidly, considering that Leslie and Stuart's reasons could be private and painful, and she didn't want to antagonize her benefactors by intruding in personal matters.

Leslie sighed. "I don't mind talking about it...I'm 44, so is my husband," she said, nodding at Stuart who sat across from the sofa, next to Warren in one of the Queen Ann chairs. "And when we married, we decided that we didn't want children. I write for the paper and I also write thrillers on the side."

"I write too," Felicia said. "We have that in common."

Leslie gave a little smile. "Stuart is a professor, and we decided that our careers were enough for us...I didn't come from a well-to-do family. There were six children. And my parents toiled long hours to pay the bills.

I was the oldest...so I had to help out. I prepared school lunches for my brothers and sisters, and helped them with their homework. I washed and ironed clothes. I was literally a little woman...And my younger brothers and sisters were so needy, so dependent, always wanting something. Every time, I turned around, it was 'Leslie, I need this. Leslie, I need that. Leslie, Leslie, Leslie.'" She paused. "I remember thinking that when I grew up that I didn't want children...I wanted breathing room, and the freedom to do as I pleased. So Stuart and I didn't have kids, and for many years, we were content. We worked, traveled, socialized. But then our neighbor Mrs. Browning made us reassess our decision about not having kids."

"How?" Felicia asked.

"She's in her seventies," Leslie explained. "And her husband had a stroke and is in a nursing home. She lives alone. And has no children. And she's so terribly lonely. She comes over to chat, bringing pound cake." She took a deep breath. "She's lonely, scared and old. She can't drive at night. She has no one. I help as much as I can, taking her to doctors' appointments, grocery shopping...Dealing with her made me think that the day would come when I'd be her age, old, gnarled, stooped...arthritic. And I wondered, 'who'll be there for me?' 'Who'll be there for Stuart?' I believe that adult children should watch out for their aging parents."

"I agree," Felicia said, thinking of Miss Shirley.

"Amen," Warren stated.

And some of what Leslie talked about had crossed Felicia's mind, about being old and alone.

"So Stuart and I discussed it and decided that at the ages of 44 to become parents. Some people thought we were nuts," Leslie said. "They pointed out that we wouldn't want to deal with a defiant teen when we were in our fifties, and that we'd be close to retirement age when the kid graduated from high school. But it didn't matter. We wanted a baby." She shrugged. "So, I tried to get pregnant. Tried and tried. But nothing happened. So we went to a fertility specialist."

Felicia looked at Warren and smiled wryly. "We can relate," she said wearily. She mentioned their ordeal.

"Physically everything was fine," Leslie stated. "The doctor wanted to give me fertility drugs." She made a face. "But I heard that those things can lead to multiple births. And we didn't want to take the chance of becoming the parents of quads. We wanted just one child." She took a deep breath. "Or so we thought. To shorten the saga, we adopted Michael, and the minute we took him home, we realized it was a mistake."

"Why?" Felicia asked.

"He craved nonstop attention."

"Babies do that," Felicia said, masking the irritation that Leslie's comment brought on.

Leslie said, "He needed diapers changed...needed to be fed...to be played with."

*That's a baby for you,* Felicia thought.

"Stuart and I could no longer come and go as we pleased," Leslie said.

*What a pity,* Felicia thought, sarcastically.

"So we decided to put Michael up for adoption."

There was lengthy silence.

"My sister was furious," Leslie said. "She thought our decision was heartless and cold-blooded."

*It is on the odd side,* Felicia thought.

"These days, she's cool towards me," Leslie said. "She considered taking Michael, but her children are now young adults—one's in high school, and the other's in college. And she and her husband want to enjoy their middle years." She sighed. "But I don't want to be Michael's mother, and Stuart doesn't want to be his father," Leslie said pleadingly.

To Felicia, Leslie's desperate tone suggested that she yearned for someone to see her point of view.

Leslie said, "And what kind of parents would we be to a child that we don't want? Our insecurities made us take on a responsibility that we didn't want. And isn't it best for Michael to be with a couple who wants to be his parents? People who'd take joy in raising him, and not look at him as an inconvenience?"

Felicia looked thoughtful. "Yes," she answered truthfully. "What you're doing is for the best. With a child, you have to make concessions and sacrifices, and a child's needs have to be put ahead of your own...You don't want Michael, and to give him up had to take considerable courage on your parts. I repeat, I don't see how you can do it, but I think your decision is best for you and the baby."

Leslie's eyes filled with tears. "I care about the boy. He was with us for seven weeks, so I want him to be happy. But I'm not the person to make him happy."

"He'll be happy with me and Warren," Felicia said. "Be assured of that."

Leslie sniffed back tears. "I'm sure he will be." She unzipped her purse and pulled out a white business size envelope and handed it to Felicia. "It's a savings bond for Michael. I'm a big believer in education and I hope when he's eighteen that he'll use the money for school. But it's his, so he can spend it anyway he wants."

Felicia removed the bond from the envelope, and it was for five thousand dollars and it had Michael's social security number on it.

Leslie told Felicia the baby's nap schedule and that he was nuts about applesauce mixed with mashed bananas. "You'll need a crib and a changing table," she said. "You can have mine. I think using the crib Michael usually sleeps in will make his transition easier...He's going to be restless in a new environment," she said in a tremulous whisper, "so if he's sleeping in his normal bed, that will make the switch easier." Her eyes brimmed with tears. She covered her face with trembling hands and cried into them. "I feel so guilty," she said. She broke down and sobbed like someone at her mama's funeral.

Felicia's throat caught. She squeezed Leslie's hand reassuringly. "Leslie, Michael is going to be all right. What you and Stuart have done is intelligent and brave and best for everyone."

The sight of Leslie sobbing made Warren look down in his lap. Stuart joined his wife on the couch and she wailed against his chest.

***

"That was some evening," Felicia said, sitting up in bed with Warren. The bedside lamp dimly illuminated the room. After the Rogers left, Warren went out and got almond and pineapple chicken, which they ate while watching an old Sidney Poitier movie. Sidney befriended a blind white girl whose vile mother was played by Shelley Winters. "I didn't know what to make of Leslie until I met her," Felicia said.

"What do you mean?" Warren asked.

"Frankly, I thought she'd be a cold, self-centered b-i-t-c-h, but after listening to her, I think what she and Stuart have done is brave and best for all."

"I wonder if they'd have given Michael up if he was their biological child," Warren said.

"That crossed my mind too. I think they would have adjusted to the boy if she had given birth to him."

Warren nodded. "But what they don't want, we do. And right now, I want some of your hot stuff." He kissed Felicia and maneuvered her onto her back. It was so good to be back with Warren, she thought, happy and joking and planning a future.

***

"I'm terribly sorry," Leslie said. "But I can't give you Michael."

"What do you mean?" Felicia shrieked. "You promised us that you'd let us become his parents."

"I changed my mind."

"You can't do this. This isn't fair."

"I have a right to change my mind. So get over yourself," Leslie said.

Angie appeared. "Felicia, you just weren't meant to be a mother. Warren just wasn't meant to be a father. I lost his child. His child died with me. You guys just weren't meant to be parents. Why don't you buy a doll baby?" Angie chuckled.

Like a doll coming to life in a horror story, Felicia's eyes popped open. The room was pitch black. She turned her head and found Warren lying next to her, asleep. She glanced at the clock. It was 2:37 in the morning.

Nightmare, she thought, just a nightmare. Or was it an omen? Would Leslie and Stuart renege on their agreement to allow her and Warren to adopt Michael?

# Chapter 50

Felicia looked around one of the spare bedrooms, which looked nothing like it had a few days ago. She and Warren had painted the off white walls blue and had taken down the bed and put it in the garage.

On the wall in an array of primary colors was M-I-C-H-A-E-L spelled out in foam-filled alphabets.

A rocking chair sat in the corner. And on the bedside table was a Mother Goose storyteller lamp.

Felicia also bought miniature, polyester filled animals, which she intended to hang above the baby's crib.

Tomorrow when they picked up Michael, the changing table and the crib, the room would be complete.

*That is if we pick up anything,* she thought. "Stop, stop," she muttered to herself.

She had nagging doubts about the adoption coming to pass. "Fefe, all the papers have been signed," Warren had said. "Stop worrying."

She couldn't help it. So what if the papers had been signed. Legal documents can and have been challenged.

And being so guilt-ridden, Leslie could very well have a change of heart. "She ain't gonna do that," Sandra said when Felicia fretted to her. "She gave you that bond, and she signed the papers. She doesn't want that boy."

# Chapter 51

It was a warm, sunny day and a plastic stork was on Felicia and Warren's lawn. In the living room, there were balloons, streamers and a banner that said, *Welcome Michael*.

On a table were cookies, fried chicken, punch, chips and dips. A party celebrating Michael's arrival was in full swing.

The beaming new parents were there, of course, as were neighbors, family and friends.

The previous night, Warren and Felicia had collected Denise from the airport.

And with all the weight loss, she was practically unrecognizable. In Felicia's opinion, she looked better heavier. Maybe, it was what Felicia was accustomed to.

But Denise liked the new her, and that was the important thing.

Michael received bib overalls, tee shirts, pajamas, jogging attire and cash.

Denise and Sandra had assembled the party.

The sight of the plump, adorable baby made everybody ooh and ah. And despite not knowing any of these people, he smiled up a storm, displaying his few teeth.

Warren's brother brought out a camera, and Denise took a picture with Michael. So did Sandra, as well as Miss Shirley and Keith, and Laquita. "This is my cousin," Laquita said proudly and gave the baby a kiss on the cheek.

They took so many pictures that Warren had to make a mad dash to the drug store to buy more film.

The final shot was of Felicia with Michael on her lap, and Warren standing behind them, with a hand on Felicia's shoulder.

They were the Wainwrights, and they were smiling.

# About the Author

Pamela Hayes loves reading, baking, watching old movies, and quenching her insatiable thirst for knowledge. Ms. Hayes is a transsexual who resides in the south with her cherished spouse, books, and tropical fish. She'd enjoy hearing from her readers. Drop her line at PamelaHayes70@hotmail.com